Still On Dwyer's Desk

Still On Dwyer's Desk

◆

SODD

Samuel A. Nathan

iUniverse, Inc.
New York Lincoln Shanghai

Still On Dwyer's Desk
SODD

iUniverse books may be ordered through booksellers or by contacting:

iUniverse
2021 Pine Lake Road, Suite 100
Lincoln, NE 68512
www.iuniverse.com
1-800-Authors (1-800-288-4677)

ISBN-13: 978-0-595-41482-6 (pbk)
ISBN-13: 978-0-595-85831-6 (ebk)
ISBN-10: 0-595-41482-6 (pbk)
ISBN-10: 0-595-85831-7 (ebk)

Printed in the United States of America

Contents

Foreword

In an environment of secrecy, where the people are fed snippets of information, which at any time, may or not be true; a great deal of speculation, guessing and interpreting circumstantial signs have to be used by concerned citizens. Otherwise there would be a certain degree of reality void as far as knowing what the state-of-affairs is at any time. Under such conditions, it then becomes the duty of any-interested resident to use whatever available wits to glean views of the existing dynamics, situation and processes that aids understanding of what is happening within society.

This book continues in the style of the first one, in that articles written by a local politician are reproduced in normal text and my comments are tied to various statements made by the writer of the articles. Only those ideas which are disagreed with are responded to by this author or in very exceptional instances, parallel thoughts may coincidentally occur but these are very few and far between. The articles considered, also continues from the first work in date sequence and the comments are somewhat bolder than first time around!

To assist the reader, the original articles have been reproduced in normal script, headed by the dates on which they first appeared in the Saturday's newspaper aligned with Astaphan's political persuasion. Immediately following each article is my list of comments, lettered from a)…onwards and these are written using italic characters. Readers are encouraged to read the article first, when reference to a comment is encountered, skip to the comment section immediately following the article, marked by the corresponding reference alphabetical letter and read my views regarding whatever point was made or 'attempted at' by Dwyer. Alternatively, the comments could be read first, quote could be traced to Dwyer's point. Whatever technique is applied, the reader will no doubt settle down into a style of using the work. Throughout the book, my words are written in italics and articles by G. A. Dwyer Astaphan are reproduced using normal script.

In the climate of the polarization that exists between the political divide in this land. For example, there is no possibility of answering the weekly comments in the parent newspaper where the articles appear, since that medium do not print anything critical of ministers or persons on its side of the politics; on the other hand it is judged that the paper supporting the party opposite would not be prepared to make the requisite unedited commitment to someone who is not known to be in their camp and even if the author was such a member, he would be of low rank and not merit such consideration. Thus a book of this caliber is a more inventive and concentrated method of responding to the literary abuse that readers, in search of information through newspapers, have to endure, week after recurring week. Really, just because one is a politician, elected representative and minister of Government, does not mean that he can run wild with writing all sorts of stuff. Sometime, somewhere, someone will invent a method of telling the man that there are those among us who don't think much of his outputs and I feel certain that mines are not the only thoughts along those lines.

History, will no doubt find this work interesting, since it not only exposes the thoughts from a particular politician of this day; his ideas at times provide the catalyst to widen areas and speak to some of the things our group of ruling politicians get up to. Thereby providing glimpses of group behaviour which look and is unattractive.

22 January 2005

Having had the privilege of being born and raised in this lovely land of ours fifty seven years ago come January 27th, I have, of course, made 'umpteen' visits to Brimstone Hill Fortress. And every visit has filled me with breath-taking awe. Even when, as a boy living in Middle Island (where I spent two of my formative years), I would go the Hill and its environs for reason or other, sometimes with Emile Laplace to shoot birds, (See comment 1a), my focus would be less on the purpose and more on the Fortress and the awesome beauty of the island from the vantage of the Fortress. Influenced by such compelling magnificence, it is no wonder I was such a miserable failure with my little Daisy Gun. And I have many a time thought of the contradiction between the motivation of conquest, annexation, occupation, exploitation, domination and violence that drove those who commanded the Fortress, and the palpable tranquility which I feel when I am there. (See comment 1b). I have often reflected on the almost eerie silence that envelopes the Fortress, contrasting with the anguished screaming and wailing, in subjugation, in battle and in debt, which would have echoed horrifically from the Hill up to the heavens back then in an early dispensation of the seemingly insatiable and perennial hunger of some people to dominate their fellow men and the world. I am amazed and horrified by the thought of how much labour—slave labour—must have gone in to building the Fortress and how much suffering and death were caused in the process. (See comment 1c). And there are numerous other perspectives from which I have observed, and reflected upon, Brimstone Hill Fortress. Indeed, I thought that I had exhausted all of the perspectives. Foolish me. It was only last Saturday, as I accompanied a visiting friend to the Fortress that it dawned on me that I had never taken time to observe, as a layman, the **workmanship.** Man, when I started to ponder upon the linear precision, the assembling of the stonework, and so on, my mouth opened in pure awe! Now, some people will say that the architecture and engineering were done by the boss men. Such an argument would fly in the face of the factual context in which people were taken into bondage from Africa. You see, it would not have only been labourers, because, whereas nowadays you will find employers throughout the world who would do all they can to seek and exploit cheap labour (whether nonskilled, skilled or even professional), (see comment 1d), employers back then (no different from now really, just different times) would no doubt have looked for slaves, who could do a variety of duties. (See comment 1e) And so, when they were buying their slaves they would sometimes look for these special skills. How could it be not so? The slaves would have played a significant role, therefore, not only as skilled tradesmen and labourers, but also in the areas of architecture, engineering and planning. True, they would have no real say in the way things went, but they certainly would have contributed immensely to the intellectual, as well as the physical, side of the work. And as I imbibed the awesome power of the Fortress, I had a sense that maybe those men in bondage who were involved in the construction of the Fortress had **chosen** to manifest their excellence through the centuries so that future generations would connect to, respect, and be proud of this legacy of brilliance in spite of bondage, and this championing of the human mind and spirit. (See comment 1f). They could easily have been discouraged and distracted from excellence by the inhumane and brutal conditions under which they existed. They could easily succumbed to frustration and anger, and to the effort by others to permanently emasculate them, thereby depriving themselves of a glorious opportunity to send their **message** through time. That **message** of hope, optimism, pride, dignity, talent, the use and engagement of that talent, is what they would have wanted to send to future generations. Accordingly, they chose to, and they did, overcome, mentally, spiritually and physically, every obstacle that would have prevented them from sending their **message** to the future. (See comment 1g). Their descendants, and all others who respect humanity, must heed that **message.** (See comment 1h). If those slaves had been permitted to place an inscription on the Hill, it might have said: **"We have built this edifice, not as a Fortress for England or France, but as a monument to our brainpower, our discipline and our will, and to the greatness of our heritage. You, who follow us, must carry on that heritage with determination, as men who love freedom, wisdom, and hard work. The debasing of humanity must end, and all mankind must be elevated. This is our message to you. This is our legacy. Take it and build on it"**. (See comment 1i) Yes, indeed, last Saturday's visit surely had a powerful impact on me. (See comment 1j) Once again, the old Brimstone Hill had yet another lesson for me. There is so much knowledge that is available to us right here in St. Kitts & Nevis. So much that can guide us to being comfortable and confident in who we are as a nation. So much to anchor us and make us proud. So much for us to protect, preserve and enhance. (See comment 1k) So much here that we can use to teach and uplift ourselves and others. As I addressed a retreat of teachers earlier this week, and I mentioned my

Brimstone Hill experience, I felt a 'vibe' that the teaching community was ready for a paradigm shift towards a more relevant and 'user-friendly' approach to educating our nation's children, and to answer the call of their new minister, Sam Condor. I felt that they were inspired to dig deep within themselves, and to reach out to their students, the parents and the guardians. (See comment 1l) I really had this feeling that they were willing to move outside the traditional box that catered to academics and passed over the others. Indeed, I felt that the old style of so readily classifying students as "others', would soon be discarded, and that a new energy directed at reaching and uplifting every mind was about to take hold in the schools of this Land. I sincerely felt a surge of passion for the cause of putting every child forward. As they say, **"a mind is a terrible thing to waste".** As I spoke to those teachers about Brimstone Hill, I also felt the builders of Brimstone Hill reaching out to them with the wording of the inscription. I truly felt that a connection was made that day. **Teachers, you are the architects of the monuments to our nation's brainpower, its discipline and will, and the carriers of our nation's heritage. Carry this heritage on to the next generation with determination, and in the spirit of freedom, wisdom and hard work. Elevate our children, elevate our nation, and venerate the memory of the men of those slaves of Brimstone hill.** (See comment 1m). Until next time, Plenty Peace.

Comments one:

a. *Your youthful training includes shooting God's creatures for sport or/and pleasure. Was it that you were hungry as a youngster and had to supplement your nourishment intake? Or was it the cruelty aspect that attracted you? With the relative privileges that you were born to, being hungry in those days would have been the least likely cause for you to shoot poor, defenseless birds, Circumstantial conditions certainly points to an early trait of sadistic behaviour!*

b. *How do you think the birds that you once tried to shoot in that tranquility felt? With the pellets from your daisy gun whistling past their bird-like little ears? Scaring or killing defenseless little creatures like that were monstrous! As a modern day leader of this country. How are those traits now used? If it is true that 'a leopard never loses its spots, I wonder who is feeling their effects?*

c. *Is there any relic from antiquity, left behind by past civilizations which were not done at a cost? While, in the history of Brimstone Hill, there must have been some input from and exploitation of my ancestors; it is more likely that yours would have suffered more. That 'perennial hunger' you speak of is in my language called greed now-a-days; there is still plenty of it about. You and your colleagues should know that very well!*

d.   *In much the same way that politicians exploit the people they are supposed to represent.*

e.   *If only persons who run governments, especially in a small country like St. Kitts, employed the same approach as those managers from once upon a time, instead of using so called specialists for obscure areas of life; perhaps there might be a more equitable society here.*

f.   *Once more into the realms of fantasy you have slipped: Anyone of reasonable disposition who inhabits the real world would realize that persons working under the kind of duress that slaves of that era did is not going to have the kind of luxury to which you allude. They would be more occupied with the hostile and oppressive conditions under which they were forced to work. Not the aesthetic 'clap trap' that your imagination has led your head into. When life is harsh, the nice cozy poetic qualities of your dream are difficult to conjure, especially since the requisite skills for that kind of work did not exist in the regions from which the slaves were captured at that time. Further, the amenities' features included in the fort's design, would have been out of the capability range of slaves. When these and other factors are considered, it looks highly improbable that slaves would have been involved in the technical aspect of the fort's construction. Also, the building of the fort, would have coincided with the infancy of slavery here, a time when they were costly commodities and intensively used in the Sugar Industry; meaning that they were costly and plantation managers would not allow their chattels to go build forts, while they were needed on the estates. If you analyze your historical data, you will find that it is more probable that Brimstone Hill was more likely to be constructed by soldiers, whose groupings would have included a contingent of engineers. It is also possible that the resident Irish in St. Kitts at the time had 'stone working skills' and could have contributed to the building of the monument. Why, your fantasizing is equivalent to saying that the slaves who worked on the pyramids of Egypt used to enjoy themselves doing it! That has got to be nonsensical! Also, during slavery times here, skills of the stone laying kind were reserved for you whites and half whites. Don't think there were any half-white; half-Lebanese around then.*

g.   *You are saying that if slaves were involved in the aesthetic creativity of Brimstone Hill; their enjoyment of the work would have been of such a magnitude that had the opportunity to escape from bondage been available; that opportunity would have not been taken, since it was more important for them to finish the job. In the sense of the Colonel who had to finish the 'Bridge over the River Kwai', even though he was really helping the enemy. You also alluded that our forefathers did all of what you said because they wanted us of today to appreciate their artistic effort. One simple question is: how did they know that their descendants were going to be around until now so that persons like yourself could lead them with such twaddle? How could you speak for their mental, physical and spiritual conditions when you are caught up in a fantasy? Those slaves were not even permitted into churches then and what did they know about your concept of spirituality? Sometimes your imagination takes you too far!*

h.   *Looks like you are inventing a message from our African-slave ancestors which says that it is more satisfying to work under bondage than to escape from it. Clearly, your fantasy has to have been designed to be applicable to stupid people.*

i.   *The bold 'type' is the inscription, according to your logic, meant to be an edifice left behind by those slaves who were forced to work on the construction of Brimstone Hill? If they had the ability to write. Scribbling that contain sentiments such as: that work, was a monument to their brainpower, their discipline and their will would take priority over 'why was I born to this'? They would advise us who followed, to carry on the message and heritage. Which from their vantage point would have been: work with determination and carry on that heritage. Which means that they had no thoughts about freedom for themselves but saw life as bondage in perpetuity, for ever and forever. For that, they would want to elevate all mankind! If I had such an ancestor, he would be disowned for his utter stupidity.*

j.   *That was a powerful impact all right. It was more than that; it was out of this world, if what you wrote is anything to go by. In terms of lessons, that was not worth the time.*

k.   *Where did this come from? Where is the connection between this conclusion and the fantasy meanderings from the previous part of your article? There you go again with the 'we' and the 'us' things! Where do you fit into the club whose membership requires ancestry among slaves that helped to construct Brimstone Hill? It is hard to see how our ancestors, being forced to labour in the construc-*

tion of the fortress should instill those pride factors in later generations. If any-thing, it should serve to instill caution, where the likes of you are concerned!

l.   *This is beyond belief! You are telling sensible people that the pitch you worked yourself up to was fed to a group of teachers and to your satisfaction, they swal-lowed the dreamed up or imagined story after or during your visit to Brimstone Hill. Those teachers made you feel that they were going to regurgitate that drivel to their classes and you are 'up-beat' about that! God help our education system and the effect it is going to have on future generations. Iif the children of today have for their source of information: a) a man who confuses himself and others, foolish enough to take on the things he says, with illogical fantasies that no right thinking person would swallow; b) a set of teachers who cannot distinguish facts from fiction; c) teachers who are so overawed by being in the presence of a minis-ter, a whiteish one at that, thereby allowing themselves to be fed such drivel. There should be a warning sign pinned onto you bearing the words: young teach-ers keep away from this dreamer!*

m.   *You do not know that those who built the fortress were slaves. You invented that at the start of your article and there you are using it as historical fact, which can-not be substantiated. That is misleading and bad form. You felt a lot of things, none of which is logically 'bona-fide'. How can it be putting children forward, when the information they are fed is guesswork and how can your 'nancy' story be anything to do with uplifting? Sounds more like sowing the seeds for your own idol building, based on fictional meanderings. It really is a serious problem for this country, when someone with your influence cannot differentiate between facts and the outcome of inventions. The worst part however, is that unwitting school children have to absorb your drivel as historical fact! That ought to be an outrageous act!*

29 January 2005

I received a couple interesting phone calls this past week, both from persons for whom I have a great deal of respect. The first caller congratulated me for the content, and for the absence of politics, in last Saturday's article. I thanked him. He was being genuine, as he expressed his pleasure with a politician manifesting some dimension beyond the confines of the political realm, and engaging in public discussion of other important, interesting and perhaps more edifying matters. The other caller was equally supportive. He, however, scolded me for sitting back and allowing the foolishness and distortions in relation to my Ministry and myself to continue in the media without me firing back and setting things and certain people straight. I also thanked him, and advised him that I would not allow the devil to dictate my agenda, or to lower me to his levels. In time, all truth comes out, and in every single case, the **'fooler'** becomes the **fool.** Speaking of cases and fools, some time ago I received a Court judgment against the Democrat in the sum of $50,000.00 plus costs. (See comment 2a) This judgment debt has been owed to me by them for some time. Last month, the Court appointed a receiver for the Democrat in relation to the judgment debt. The receiver is working diligently, I am sure. That is between her and the Court. To date, through no fault of the receiver's, I have not yet received my money. (See comment 2b) Meanwhile, I am told that people involved in The Democrat are telling their trade debtors to write cheques for The Democrat, not to the Democrat Printing Company (DPC) but to another company called PAM Publishing Company (PAMPUBCO). PAMPUBCO has been in existence for a long time. It was set up to be the publisher of the Democrat, While DPC would own the printing press and the other assets, and collect all revenue from advertisements, and so on. The intention there was to use PAMPUBCO pretty much as a 'paper' company with essentially no assets. Although it would be the newspaper's publisher, the arrangement would be to save all of the revenues paid to DPC. In addition, PAMPUBCO would pay fees to DPC for a range of services. The net result of all of that is that PAMPUBCO would, for all practical purposes, always be on the edge of insolvency and always indebted to DPC for the services of the latter in relation to printing, use of its personnel, etc. So if you wanted to sue PAM-

PUBCO, you would find little or nothing there to satisfy you, in the event that a Court were to award you damages. And if you decided to go after the DPC, they would tell you that all they do is provide printing and related services to the publisher (PAMPUBCO) of the newspaper. This is a scheme which the PAM bigger bosses cooked up many years ago in order to evade judgment creditors and to subvert justice. A question which might need to be answered is whether both DPC and PAMPUBCO, and, for that matter, whoever else may be involved in the ownership, printing and publication of The Democrat have delivered to the Registrar of The Supreme Court a declaration in accordance with the Newspapers Act, or are listed in such declaration. It would also be instructive to know whether DPC, PAMPUBCO or anyone else involved in the ownership, printing or publication of The Democrat has breached the said Act. This is the kind of thing PAM has done with their God-given brains over the years: **rob justice.** (See comment 2c) Problem is, Willy Liburd, who was back then the editor of The Democrat, did not carry out the scheme as per the instructions of the bigger bosses. And so for a long time, the DPC was collecting the revenue. No doubt, this was one of the reasons they wanted to dump Willy, but they chose to take their time with him. But as the law suits and the court judgments began to pile up on the back of the DPC, Consie, Grant, and the rest decided that the ancient scheme would now have to be implemented, but with a variation. What they set out to do this time, in their never ending quest to rob justice, (see comment 2d) is to set up the following arrangement: DPC and a company in St. Maarten print, and **nobody is the publisher.** The January 15th—21st issue of the Democrat states that it is published "**at the office of The Democrat Printing Company Ltd.**" Nowhere in the paper is there any indication as to the **identity of the publisher.** Helpful as the little piece of information about **where** the newspaper is published may be, it is nowhere near sufficient. Because every newspaper **must** notify its readers and public as to the **identity** of its publisher. What good is knowledge of the location of the facility where the newspaper is published when you don't tell us who the publisher is? (See comment 2d) Suppose we want to write to the publisher. Suppose we want to sue the publisher. If you look at any copy of The Labour Spokesman you will see broadly and boldly that its "**published by the St. Kitts & Nevis Trades & Labour Union.**" **And look at any other Self-respecting. It all tell you the identities of its publisher.** That is what is required by the law and by decency, accountability and transparency. But the Democrat does not appear to subscribe to laws, rules, or any other tenet of decency, accountability or transparency. They want to set the rules for us, but they do not want to abide by rules. (See comment 2f) And that is a fundamental, characteristic of The Democrat and PAM. Remember, it took PAM over 30 years before they had a constitution to govern their affairs. They sat in the government of this country for 15 years, and it was only towards the end of their tenure in office that they chose to establish a constitution for their own Party. The self-answering question must be asked: How could they be expected to govern the country with respect to our Constitution and our laws when, for nearly 30 years, half of which were spent with them **in** Government, they willfully and stubbornly refused to adopt a constitution for their own Party? (See comment 2g) **What could be more disgracefully autobiographical than that?** And that sacrilege was only part of their serial assault on propriety, accountability, transparency and respect for law and order. Remember they tried to overthrow the Labour Government in 1967, after contesting and losing their first election in 1966. They were not prepared to accept the decision of the people, so they chose to take up arms in a dastardly act that would have caused thousands of Kittitians to be slaughtered, as New Town, a great deal of Basseterre, Fry's village, Greenlands, LaGuerite and other places would have been destroyed by fire and explosives. (See comment 2h) And just as the Jewish people will not allow the world to forget the Holocaust, so must Kittitians and Nevisians never allow the 10th of June, 1967, attempted coup d'etat by PAM to be forgotten. Because that **act** was the defining moment for PAM, then, and over the past forty years of its existence. But they have consistently over that time acted in blatant and wanton disregard for propriety and respect for the law. Remember who introduced the gun, drug and thug culture here in the early 1980's when cocaine-laden small planes used to land here in the dark of night to drop off stuff and to refuel on their way to North America? If not, learn about that. (See comment 2i) Remember that those small planes had owners and that the owners had arrangements with powerful people here in St. Kitts? If not, learn about that too. Remember a book to which I have previously referred: **"The Big Sting"**? It is about the biggest sting operation in Royal Canadian Mounted Police history (up to that time). And it is filled with references to certain citizens of this country, all of them PAM bigwigs. Remember the International Bank which operated in The Circus, with its financial fraudsters, and remember who were the local people behind and connected to it? All PAM bigwigs. Remember the international scandal that erupted when the Globe & Mail newspaper of Toronto picked up the story? Remember the worldwide publication of the news that the most powerful, man in PAM was also the biggest money launderer in the Caribbean, and that he was connected to the Cali Cocaine Cartel in Columbia, and to the selling of guns to the IRA in Ireland (which assassinated Lord Mountbatten, the uncle of Queen Elizabeth)? Who can forget that the US Government said that if the former Prime Minister were to insist on retaining Billy Herbert as his ambassador plenipotentiary, Herbert, when visiting the USA, would be restricted to a 50-mile radius of the United Nations? (See comment 2j) And do you remember Dr. Simmonds taking away Bill's ambassadorship to the USA, but keeping him on as plenipotentiary? What do you think all of that was about? Similarly, who can forget the stinking scandal that erupted with the US $26 million deal which those guys signed? Do you know that the Italian Government is still asking for its money? Who can forget the notorious Drug Gang in Cayon and the enormous damage they have done to the people of this country? The youth that exists in St. Kitts and Nevis have their genesis in the children of former PAM leaders. Do you know that? And there are scores and scores of other incidents of shame that punctuate the pages of our country's history over these past forty years of PAM, which have brought disgrace to the people of St. Kitts & Nevis. All revolving around a central theme of PAM's abiding disrespect and disregard for the law. They may want the people of this country to forget, or to be distracted from, the truth as to who PAM are, what PAM have done and what PAM continue to do. But it will not happen. Like the Jews and the Holocaust, the people of this country will never forget. (See comment 2l) Look at PAM's leaders of today. Grant published an untruthful declaration of personal net worth last year. Which sensible person in this country believed him? Whatever little credibility he may have had before that evaporated into air right then and there. Just as an aside, and to demonstrate his wishy-washyness as a leader, when he published his farcical declaration he also declared that he would have everyone of his candidates do likewise. Not surprisingly, not one of them has followed suit, and a year has already passed. But let's not get diverted from the embedded PAM disrespect for the law and rules. Grant has had marches and meetings, in flagrant disregard for the law. Leading up to, and on, Election Day, he went to extremes to test the faith and fabric of the law and the peace keepers of this country. (See comment 2l) High-level friends (or are they members?) of his Party have been involved in smuggling certain things into St. Kitts. They think that people don't know, but they couldn't be more wrong. (See comment 2m) One of them has been trying to pry sensitive information in relation to Camp Springfield and the St. Kitts & Nevis Defence Force. Might this be in relation to the notion of a 2005 effort to repeat 1967? (See comment 2n) A few of them have been trying to subvert, undermine and destabilize (through friends) certain segments of our peace-keeping forces in order to create disruption and tension there, and in the country generally. Some of them were planning a number of heinous activities leading up to the last elections. Grant went on a public platform in Market Street after the election and said that the mistake they made was that they didn't buss dem Labour people heads early election morning down in Constituency Four. And so it goes. It would therefore surprise no one to see what PAM are trying to do with The Democrat in order to frustrate creditors and subvert justice. Nevertheless, one must ask why Lorna Callender, the managing editor of The Democrat, would want to tell her readers **where** her paper is published, yet she does not want to tell them **by whom** it is published. Why is it that they must operate in that 'wutless' way, and still expect people to respect them? Well, I have some news for them. For as 'wutless' as they think they are, I will put my tenacity against their 'wutlessness' any day. (See comment 2o) They must have forgotten the tribulations, the death threats, the abuse and the vilification that they poured on me without relent when I had the audacity to run against their leader, and, worse, yet, **knock him out!** So if they think they will win this war, they wrong! I am going to get my money that they owe me, and the longer they fight me, the more blows they will get, in the Court and on the road. (See comment 2p) For sure, **I will get me money wut!** Until next time, Plenty Peace.

Comments Two:

a. *Wow, no wonder such a bullish, even cocky attitude emanates!*

b. *And no doubt, you really need it?*

c. *Why is it that when you are involved and stand to gain. Your high morale tone is flashed around that way? Robbing justice indeed. How can anyone rob justice, when that state has nothing material to lose? What you mean is that they are frustrating you from getting your hands on their money, awarded to you. It ought to be admitted that accepting a directive like that is not easy to accept and if it can be avoided, then it would be foolish not to attempt same. It's not as if that sum was earned in exchange for any kind of service. It cannot be easy!*

d. *It is somewhat extreme, accusing your nemesis of robbing justice and not for the first time. That twist on your definition seems intended to include, a form of dramatic effect and perhaps, in there somewhere, is a feeling of being righteously correct because the award was in your favour. However, it is a bit much for you to be awarded such a bonanza for being done to, what has been done to others all the time. Makes one wonder about what justice is and the morality of the need to escape it.*

e. *Sounds as if some form of indirect trumpet own-blowing is at work here. Some frustration is detected because the entity has not set itself up so that some 'fortune-hunter', of political persuasion can pick it off whenever 'pocket-change' gets to be the object of the game.*

f. *It is just possible that the purpose of the writing here reflects some frustration of the writer with the cunning from the opposite political entity. Looks as if they of the opposite party have realized that the writer is on a 'gold digging' expedition. They have probably calculated that the judiciary is slanted towards serving ministers of government and has a tendency to find in their favour. Because of the 'knock-on' effect of such realizations, it is completely reasonable for any entity, disadvantaged in such a manner to protect itself against an establishment of that flavour. What other option is there, when ministers of government make laws to suit their personal interests first, then see to the remainder of the community afterwards? Looks like a jungle where ministers see for themselves and God looks after the rest of us. No one can really blame the Democrat for trying to protect their instrument of survival, when the writer appears to be: hell bent on financially destroying it.*

g. *There is another problem here with meandering logic. If as you say, PAM had no constitution during the period stated, it does not necessarily follow that they could not work within one that existed outside of their organization. If they had no rules, it could have been that a period of evolution was being courted to discover and allow practices and routines to develop. There is absolutely nothing wrong with experimentation. Is that not how the Labour Movement was developed in this country? Many starts and stops; experimentation; clandestine operations were necessary to bypass the oppressive rules of that time. So how could PAM be blamed for coursing a path that suited their organization?*

h. *This is the ump-teenth time you have made that claim-cum-accusation. Each time, the same response is offered: those persons accused of the crime according to you were taken before the court and were found not guilty. In the earlier part of this article much emphasis were placed upon observing and obeying the law; yet here and in earlier articles, we see this perpetual, regurgitation of the 'overthrow' attempt, even though the court dismissed the case against those so accused. Looks to me as if you are implying that the same law you are advising those you are not in favour of to obey; is being ignored by you. In other words, the laws you subscribe to only works when they are in your favour or approval not when they are applicable to persons other than yourself!*

i. *Guns were in policemen' holsters here, on the streets of Basseterre, during the early to mid 1970's. I remember remarking to a friend at the time that "once the police are armed (carry guns), it would be just a matter of time before the public follow suit. With regards to that guns comment of yours, your date of commencement is years after the actual event. Who knows? Maybe that is true of the other items associated with the 'guns' accusation?*

j. *Remember when New Labour took office in 1995. The initial minister of Foreign Affairs did not last for very long. Before the first term was out there had to be a cabinet re-shuffle resulting in switching of persons around that post. Why was that? Was it due to disfavour by officials in the US? If the answer to that last question is yes; then let whoever is without sin, cast the first stone.*

k. *Never is a long word. It is usually somewhat risky for anyone to use 'never' in that kind of context. Just for the record. The people of this country did forget how your party wasted and squandered our resources on two commissions of inquiries during your first term of office. Those who had experiences of ministers feathering their own nests must have forgotten. Looks like the people are about to forget the socially retrograde shenanigans against the masses currently being perpetrated. The people will also soon forget how fast so called Labour ministers became aristocrats, whilst at the same time retarding the masses to retrograde social conditions. For someone like you sounding up-beat about 'the people will never forget' is really flying in God's face, when current performances are taken into consideration.*

l. *Talk about testing the law! There is one which requires electioneering posters be removed from lamp posts. I think all posters of that type should be removed on the eve of any election date and that requirement is legally binding; yet members of your government still have mounted advertisement bearing their election campaign promises, some are weather worn by now and pollutes the environment. Indeed, campaign posters from the 2000 electioneering campaign could still be seen in places. True, posters from all three parties can be seen in various places. Point is though that you are going on about who has what respect for the law; you are a member of government and you are just as guilty of disrespecting the law, much the same as what Grant is being accused of by you.*

m. *If you know that persons are breaking the law; surely as a minister of Government, you are obliged to do something about persons smuggling or whatever illegal activity is taking place. Indeed, as Minister of National Security, it is even* more diabolical that you know of crimes taking place and instead of taking action, you use your newspaper medium to deliver slurs to Grant's friends.

n. *Shame on you! Being alarmist without offering any evidence in this oblique claim. Maybe it is just as well that this particular article has not got many fickle readers; otherwise the place would have been in uproar when that kind of slanted question is posed.*

o. *There is a need for clarification here. You said that you will match their wutlessness with your tenacity. Is there some common measure by which the two qualities can be graded or compared? Will the application of your tenacity be applied via the common quality of 'wutlessness'? One has to be tenacious at something, since it usually means the persistent or unrelenting repetition of some action. Therefore, when you are going to match your tenacity against their wutlessness, it must be done via some form of disturbing force. Since your implied boast suggests some flexibility, the common tool of 'wutlessness' is not ruled out and could easily be adopted or something else will be used. What will it be? Perhaps in more subtle forms, eh?*

p. *Looks like your greed is re-awakened here. There was hardly much doubt that it existed. "…I am going to get my money…" would give the impression that they owe money once owned by you. When in reality, the money you appear so desperate to get your hands on, never was owned by you. There are those who believe that had the Democrat more 'spunk' and appealed, a different tune would have been sung. "…the more blows they will get, in the Court and on the road." What exactly is meant by giving them blows on the road? Does that imply a physical threat? It could be easily interpreted as such. Does such a remark not contradict the intent of the 'Peace Movement'? How does the lines of your song: "Its peace we want and its peace we gone get", measure up to that threat? Should the Minister in charge of Law Enforcement be using the newspaper to threaten members of the public with physicalities? Tut, tut and more tuts.*

NOTE: in the article below, the reader is invited to suggest a meaning for the term: 'bling bling' or even a single bling will do?

12 February 2005

It ain't now that bling bling killing people, you know. From as far back as 5,000 B.C. (hey, that's 7,000 years ago) and onwards in Central and Eastern Europe, Africa, Ancient Babylon, the Americas and Asia, bling bling has definitely played a vital, and indeed a deadly role in the affairs of mankind, used and enjoyed, for the most part, by the rich and famous, whether for status, ornamental, ceremonial or other purposes. I am told that in the 15th century B.C., the Nubians of Egypt started using gold as the medium of exchange for international trading transactions. This was followed by the Chinese some four centuries later. This formalization of gold, added to the already existing lust for it amongst the rich and famous, contributed significantly to the global rush for it among the stronger nations of the world, as it became, not just a status symbol, and a valuable item in and of itself, but also an essential medium for trading. (See comment 3a) This global rush for gold was yet another manifestation of imperial adventurism into the resources and the patrimonies of the world's poorer societies and nations. As a result, gold, silver and diamond mines, as well as palaces, tombs, places of worship and other shrines, museums, art galleries, and everything else in sight became fair game for the rampaging crusaders from the North. I know that when I write like this, some people try to categorize me in one or other negative way. For those who do, I would ask that they objectively and diligently research the content of my writing, check out their history, and come to their own conclusions. (See comment 3b) And I do not bring up these insights into the hurtful past to maliciously open up old sores. Instead, I do so in the hope that the lessons of the past will not be lost on us, and that a better understanding of it will lead to enlightenment in thought, action and lifestyle on our parts as individuals and as nations, today and tomorrow. (See comment 3c) I want for a moment to refer to Angola, an African nation blessed (or some might say cursed) with some of the finest diamond and oil resources on the planet (see comment 3d) Portugal colonized her form 1576 to 1975. And all she got for her four hundred years of troubles was **more troubles,** becoming a hotspot in Africa where the powerful nations of the world fomented and maintained instability in order to get their hands, and the hands of their corporate constituents, on her diamonds and oil.

The country has been ripped apart by civil war and all manner of tribulation, mostly because of those diamonds and that oil. Companies like De Beers (formed, I believe, by the Englishman Cecil Rhodes who went down to Africa in the name of crown and country, and ended up getting a whole country, Rhodesia, now Zimbabwe, named after him) have for years had Angola in a hammerlock, exploiting diamonds from arrangements made not only with the Government, but also with the rebels who controlled much of the land where diamond deposits sat. Playing both sides against the middle, dividing and ruling, and running amok with the nation's bounty and its patrimony. De Beers have been involved in 'legal' and illegal mining, sometimes deriving great benefits from the toils of workers, standing waist deep in water, clinging to stones, and clad only in underwear and trying to eke out meager existences. (See comment 3f) And out of these dens of inequity and pseudo-slave labour situations, De Beers would show a glistening face to the world, as its products would reach the fancy shops of Cape town, London, Amsterdam, Paris, Brussels, Zurich, Rome, Tel Aviv, etc. "Diamonds are a girl's best friend", they say. The net result of that has been a ravaged Angola, classically, brutally and savagely pillaged and debilitated by the old 'divide and conquer' maxim that has been so well mastered by the imperial adventurers of the North. (See comment 3f) And while Angolans agonized, others prospered. All of that from **Angola's** bounty, placed in her land by the work of the Almighty. A classic example of the **deadly** impact that the bling bling has had on poor peoples and poor countries. True, we have all heard of the saying: what is fun to the butcher is death to the **pig.** But, Lord have mercy! If one party this heinous scenario is indeed a butcher, the other is certainly no pig! We are talking about **people** here! (See comment 3g) What we need to pay some attention to is the haunting fact that, with the depletion of the natural resources of a country (we use Angola as an example) by the imperial adventurers, we have always seen an attending erosion of that country's cultural footings, (See comment 3h) of its moral and other traditions, of its standards of health, of its people's confidence, and, inevitably, of its public sector. All of this leads to, the record will show, economic, social and political ruin, causing the hue and cry for the World Bank and the IMF, themselves creations of the said imperial adventurers, to step in to have a very close look, maybe even to "adjust" that country. (See comment 3i) So the 'sufferation that the bling bling has brought throughout history to those poor peoples in the lands where God put the bling bling, has been deadly. Of course, it did not have to be like that. Conscience, decency, and respect for a people and their land could have played a more important role in the activities of the imperial adventurers. But, I suppose, that would have made them mere adventurers, and not imperial ones. And that was not, and is not, the way barley grows. And so conscience and decency have not, traditionally, been the hallmarks of entrepreneurship. (See comment 3j) And colonialism has never been the yardstick by which good governance, democracy and respect for human rights are measured. (See comment 3k) So, tough luck for the Angolans, the South Africans, etc. So here we see the process by which the blling bling is extracted from its sources, and how it gets to market throughout the world. One would think it sad and bad enough that the poor people of the countries where it is found would be the only ones to suffer. And that it would end there. But no. As would be expected, a proven and successful way to wealth is for the entrepreneur to sell products and services to as wide a market as possible. The idea is to create an appetite for things people do not necessarily need, but to fool them into thinking that they need them. And as economic development takes place, more people 'down the food chain' (as some people like to say) look to get their hands on everything that other more financially able people have. Get a chance to buy things. So the entrepreneur goes into every level of the food chain. Because he wants to make sure that he too **get the money wut. Humanity is sacrificed on the alter of greed.** The entrepreneur, with his maniacal focus on making money, often loses sight of the fact that where the human fabric is damaged or destroyed his chances of making money sustainably are reduced. For him, it is now for now. (See comment 3l) He doesn't realize that once he creates the appetite, the poor man is going to do every thing he can, rob, steal, kill or otherwise to get his piece of the action and to show that he too can get his hands on things. And so big man chases after everybody's dollars. Now the poor, the ghetto people throughout the world, the brothers and sisters of those sufferers in Angola, South Africa, Latin America and every where, are being targeted for their **two pence ha'penny.** What he strives for is to get the poor people to feel that they **have to** get the bling bling, and the more, the bigger, the better. He has to convince the ghetto people that they must show their bling bling, big and broad to everybody, because bling bling is their passport to status. It is what validates them. Smart man that he is, the entrepreneur knows that the best road to the wallet of poor people, and young people generally, is through the entertainment and sport industries. He also knows that the majority of popular entertainers and athletes come from poor backgrounds. And we all know that fads and fashions start in the ghetto and work their way up the social ladder. So he gets some of these folks, the right ones and the right blend, to buy into his scheme. He has them advertise his stuff. He has them produce lyrics or dress in such a way as to promote his blling bling. The music videos are used as a major medium by which to send this message. And bingo! Or should I say bling blingo?! The ghetto youth are captured. Everybody wants the biggest, thickest chain, the most rings on the fingers, nose rings, belly jewelry, and so on. Of course, the tattoos are a big part of the foolishness too. The music, the attitude, the talk, the dress and the bling bling create 'gangsta' characters who become the models for the youth. And so we see the birth of the 'gangsta' culture, with the bling bling right in the centre of it. (See comment 3m) And what do gangstas do? They shun education. They shun solid values and behaviours. They think and act like criminals. They smoke a bunch of dope and drink the drink that they push, as puppets of their boss entrepreneur. They develop a turf mentality. They seek to defend their turf. Turf that probably belongs to some rich landlord anyway. Feuds develop. Revenge and recrimination follow. They continue, and they worsen. The guns, the knives, the cutlasses come into play. They use each other as role models: the blind leading the blind. The desperate leading the desperate. Pain and destruction. A game plan for failure and physical and spiritual, death. (See comment 3n) If you take away a man's bling bling, he'l cut your throat or 'buss a cap in you'. His bling bling becomes his brain, his heart, his soul! His status symbol, desperately holding on to **something** that will validate him. A false God. No, a devil. Next thing you know, there is a procession of ambulances to the hospitals, and funerals to the cemeteries, causing deep, deep anguish for the families and for the poor people generally, depriving them of the opportunity to fulfill their God-given talents, and depriving mankind of the benefits of these same talents. (See comment 3o) And just like their brothers and sisters in Angola, South Africa, West Africa, Latin America and Asia, they receive far more pain than joy from the bling bling. What a mighty and terrible tragedy! Jesus Christ!! Wake up, People. (See comment 3p) Bling bling a kill people in Africa, and it al kill people in a America and the West Indies. Third World people find more suffering and humiliation that anything else from the bling bling. Time to reprioritize. **Until Next Time, Plenty Peace.**

Comments Three:

a. *Using gold as the 'Nubians' of Egypt did, for trading; using the same metal for international trading; but also an essential medium for trading. Do they not all mean the same thing? Get into the point and stop wasting space with repetitions!*

b. *Regardless of the accuracy concerning your historical brief reproductions. It is not really necessary for much deliberation before pronouncing that what was done then by rampaging crusaders, slave abductors, slave auctioneers, slave-owners, colonialists, adventurers or so called pioneers. It was all in the past and must help us to recognize that your cabal in Cabinet has most definitely taken over from those exploiters here in this Federation. You are therefore, well advised that when writing stuff like this; look in a mirror and you will see one of the modern day version of those you are about to condemn.*

c.   *Not necessarily thanks to you, some of us are already way ahead and that is why, those who think, can clearly see through what you and your fellow, successful politicians are doing to the masses. One day, believe it or not, the rest of this country will, its history will indeed achieve that enlightenment and see you for what you now are.*

d.   *I would question the oil component that you ascribe to Angola!*

e.   *There, but for the 'grace of God', go we black people in this country! Slave owners and plantation owners, ably abetted and supported by your ancestors, had the same designs as described about the Angolans, on us. God only knows what your attitude would have been, if such an atmosphere prevailed today? The mind boggles! However, we are made of more rugged stuff than them. Check Toussaint of Haiti, who gave Napoleon's army a hard time and even here in little St. Kitts: our riots of 1896 and again in 1935, loosened up the shackles so that we would eventually shake the white man's burden. Alas, we have got rid of one exploiter, only to be replaced by another and guess who that is?*

f.   *The lessons of those adventurers are certainly well learnt. Who is in the chair now and doing very nicely thank you? Pillaging and ravaging is not even necessary! It is done by lying, cheating, fooling the masses and through the ballot box.*

g.   *Would it not be nice, if it could be remembered that we are talking about people when names like Grant, Consie, the Herberts and 'others who belong to PAM' or even UNEP are spoken about.*

h.   *To this day, that cultural erosion is galloping along nicely, under your watch and the imperial adventurers have long departed. Our cultural importance appears to matter to you, only when it useful for political or argumentative mileage when it suits.*

i.   *Your reasoning is a possibility. Of course, there are others. One other can be due to a situation that is closer to home: where greed and possibly corruption by those elected to lead, drains a small country's resources so badly, pushing that country to the brink of economic precipice, putting its people under dire financial stress. For-*

tunately for those apparent heartless politicians; the masses have no idea what is happening to them because they are fed regular 'hype' about who the real villains are, by villains in disguise.

j.   *Neither have conscience and decency been hallmarks for political opportunism. It is as wide as it is broad and could be equally applicable to your trade.*

k.   *Colonialism and democracy cannot be in the same political set. However, it is theoretically possible to have good governance in both!*

l.   *Is it coincidental that the negative critiques so far of entrepreneurs; apply equally to persons in your trade? How easy it is to cast stones when one forgets that he also lives in a glass house!*

m.   *A lot of efforts have been invested in the development of your theme, based on that stupid, double word phrase. Although you like to give the impression that your ideas are beyond doubt; I have to tell you that there are alternative theories to that you painted. Here is mine: people, old and young see you political aristocrats, dashing around, taking more than your fair share of everything: resources, women, power, privileges, etc, etc… Consequently, you become examples of laziness and reasons for not taking life and what it has to offer seriously. In the same manner that the police got to carry guns first, so they were copied. You lot are getting away with a lot of stuff and the youth are trying it also. When perhaps, honesty and integrity get to be examples by persons of high rank, a start might be made in straightening out our youth. Alas, the 'rot' has set in so deeply; that determined, disciplined and unswerving remedial action has to be applied to give the desired directional development to tomorrow's people!*

n.   *If you think that the signs so clearly indicate those Agamemnon type outcomes. Instead of bleeping about it all the time; do something to stop it! Save those young people from themselves. Is that not what is done to the mentally insane? Instead of squandering so much effort and resources on yourselves; use some for the under-responsible members of society, to help them progress in socially responsible areas, whether or not they want to. After all would it not be for their good?*

o.   *God knows, we do not need your so called gangsters for depriving mankind of their God-given talents. You already do a reasonable job at that, using your vindictive and venomous talents. Therefore, between you guys and these young gangsters, God help us in this country!*

p. *Yes indeed, wake up people! It may be that here in St. Kitts more people are being killed by your so called stupid named bling bling. It has got to be debatable as to who is doing more damage to this country and its people. If partly for failing to adequately tackle the problem by writing about it instead of acting, among other things! Do the job you so lucratively pay yourselves to do!*

19 February 2005

I saw a picture in a local newspaper last week that brought a chuckle. It showed Consie Mitcham, Greta Foreman, Chesley and Eugene Hamilton, and Glenroy Blanchette outside the Court House, beaming with glee and giving 'V' signs, as if they were celebrating some major victory. Simply by looking at the picture you could have thought that they had just won the biggest lottery in the history of the world. What was the source of their overflowing mirth? The High Court had just decided that **it had jurisdiction** to hear and adjudicate upon the election challenges which Blanchette, Grant and Eugene Hamilton brought challenges in Constituencies Numbers 1, 4 and 8 respectively. Interestingly, they had no challenges for Constituency Number 5. But time will deal with that. Hold tight. **That's all the hearing was about: whether the Court had jurisdiction to adjudicate on the substantive matter.** What happened was that the Attorney General had raised the question as to the Court's jurisdictional competence to deal with the election cases brought by the three PAM loser candidates, and the Court answered the question in the affirmative. Yes, said Mr. Justice Davidson Baptiste, the High Court does indeed have the authority to hear the substantive matter. For that Consie, the Hamiltons and Blanchette held their great celebration outside the Court House, **'posing for photo'** (as they say in Trinidad). Man, talk about desperate people grabbing at straws. Now, the substantive matter is to be heard by the Court. We must all wait the process and the result. I want to say this with absolute, pellucid certainty. Anyone who thinks that he or she is going to bamboozle anybody and try to introduce kangaroo justice in this matter, or at all, had better think again. (See comment 4a) I say this because I know how tricky some people think they can be. You see, a number of persons have been approached on certain matters. It looks as if some persons are looking to make some devil deals. It won't work. I want also to say that oftentimes you see people asking for something and when they get it they are sorry they asked for it. You know what I mean? There is a certain information out there and I am sure it will be revealed if and when necessary. It is information relating, inter alia, to non-citizens and non-residents who were brought in here from other countries to impersonate and vote in the names of duly registered voters in this country. That is plenty trouble, and no amount of hush money can lock down this one, because the cat is already out of the bag. This bomb will be 'bussed' if it has to be. It's just a matter of marking time and marking a man. (See comment 4b) I am sick and fed up with these charlatans and hypocrites trying to fool and bamboozle people into thinking how decent and upright they are, when **nobody more wutless and bad than them!** (See comment 4c) Let's move on to other matters now. I was in Jamaica last week attending a meeting on regional security (which incidentally, is a matter of paramount concern, even anxiety, amongst all sane, sensitive and informed persons and organizations in the region, all whom agree that on an individual and regional basis, we are vulnerable and have much work to do). Of course, I had visited Jamaica on a number of previous occasions. And I have always found it to be an amazing enigma. What a country! Such breath-taking, natural and human beauty, yet so much man made ugliness. So much wealth and beauty, yet such unbelievable poverty, wretchedness and squalor. I saw people from all levels of society. I saw some of the intellectual, entrepreneurial and cultural dynamism and panache of the Jamaican people. I also saw some of the hubris and dismissive disdain of the rich of the powerful, and the equally palpable, seething anger of despair of the poor and the dispossessed. (See comment 4d) I sensed in a wide cross-section of the society a feeling of cynicism and distrust towards the political process and politicians. (See comment 4e) I heard people say that much of the violence in Trivoli Gardens, Garrison and other difficult areas has been fomented by political interests, including the provisioning of weapons and ammunition, passed on during political seasons, then irretrievably lost, and used for robberies and murders. In Jamaica, they murder at least one a day, sometimes three, four and five. It's like their daily dose of vitamins, except for the fact that **VITA** means life, while the guns mean death. I felt that I was in paradise and hell at the same time. A paradise given by God, turned into a hell by mortal greed, corruption, neglect and callous deprivation. (See comment 4f) I heard the desperation of wealthy and influential individuals who expressed reluctance to speak out because of fear of recrimination towards their business interests and even their very lives. They felt that they had too much to lose. I saw men and women, mostly young ones, who had nothing to lose, indeed, nothing at all but life in its wretchedness, scavenging the streets, clinging on to any passing chance for survival, even amidst the elegant and modern areas of New Kingston. I saw slums that would cause people living in St. Kitts & Nevis to cry 'long water' for their downtrodden brothers and sisters in Jamaica, while at the same time thanking God for being able to call St. Kitts and Nevis home. (See comment 4h) I saw areas where it is said that police simply do not enter. I saw a society, one microstep away from the monstrous and ongoing tragedy that is Haiti which, in the minds of the metropolitan manipulators, was never to be forgiven, or given a chance to thrive, because it had the gall two hundred years ago to take its own independence. And as I saw and felt Jamaica last week. I couldn't help but wonder how much 'distance' there is between Jamaica and Haiti in this desperation and instability, and what crime Jamaica may have committed to be such an enduring paradise and hell at the same time. (See comment 4h) Yet while all of that sobering and stirring reflection was taking place. I saw youngsters with eyes wide open, happy and hopeful in their fleeting moments of innocence, which only set me more deeply into thought as to what would become of them in the Jamaica of today and tomorrow, and how long it would take for their enthusiasm and vigour to evaporate and be replaced by bitterness and despair. I had interesting conversations with the Jamaica Police Commissioner and with other regional National Security officers. I was very impressed with the will and commitment to the monumental task which they face, and indeed which we all face, considering our awesome national and regional challenges. There was one particular dinner gathering to which I was invited, attended by persons representing about one billion U.S. dollars in wealth. And all of them were Jamaican people. Good-hearted, and, as we say, God-blessed people. People willing to use their wealth to promote and stabilize Jamaica. I found in them a deep desire to help right things in Jamaica, (See comment 4i) but also a sense of despair about what they describe as **"the dangerous politics and the politics of Jamaica"**. I made my pitch, inviting them to consider putting some eggs in our basket here in St. Kitts & Nevis. And if you all know me well, and you do, you will be assured that I will keep applying the full-court press on them. I also had the distinct pleasure and privilege to spend some time with Philip 'Fatis' Burrell, a promoter of artistes, and the famous Miguel 'Sizzla' Collins. They both expressed a keen desire to work with us in our effort to build and spread our Circle of Peace, and I am hoping that Sizzla will keep to his promise and send me a little jingle to help spread the message. (See comment 4j) He had me at his home where I met his kids. Likewise for Fatis. Fatis kept playing my little CD, "A Message of Peace" in his Dodge Ram truck and when we reached Sizzla's house and he heard the little tune he hugged me and said: **"Yes, Dada, it's peace we want"**. They were truly wonderful and giving of their love and solidarity with the Circle of Peace. They even asked me to return to Jamaica to go into the ghettos there to help spread the word to show Jamaican politicians how to relate to ordinary folks. (See comment 4l) Lord poor me! Boy, me fraid! A number of them told me that they need a good man like to be a minister in Jamaica. People in other places say that to me too. Boy, it looks like Jamaica wants me. Antigua want me. Dominica want me, and the rest. (See comment 4l) It seems that its only PAM who don't want me. I wonder what I do them debble dool dool people. Boy! Fatis, Sizzla and others asked me to tell the young men in St. Kitts and Nevis to open their **hearts,** their **minds** and their **books,** and to stop following somebody else's rule that says that they must hate and fight down each other. They told me to tell the young men to be true, loving and genuine fathers. (See comment 4m) Fatis said to me: "Mister Minister, somebody put hate inna we and we a use it feh fight down and kill one another and ah keep we self poor! It's is only love, respect and understanding that can change that!" Isn't that Farrakhan's message? And isn't it the right message? Of course it is. Fatis also said to me that **people have to take responsibility for themselves,** to ensure that they receive their education and prepare themselves for successful lives, because the world owes no man a living. God has given us life. The rest is up to us. Yes, some of us need more help than others, but in the final analysis, once we are of sound mind and body **we cannot go vexed with and blaming the world.** We got to do out thing. Fatis is wise man, indeed. I also had the opportunity to have a chat with Junior Kelly who traveled on the same flight with me back down. He was going to do a fund raiser for Grenada. He also expressed an interest in our Circle of Peace, and I asked him to work with Fatis and Sizzla on it when he got back to Jamaica. He said that he would. (See comment 4n) It seems therefore, that there is broad, consensus that what we are trying to do here in St. Kitts & Nevis is right and timely. Indeed, one person in Jamaica pleaded with me to make sure that St. Kitts acts now so that it won't deteriorate like Jamaica, cautioning that unless firm and consistent attention was brought to the matter, we would inevitably fall into the abyss in which poor Jamaica now finds itself. (See comment 4o) Two of the causes of the crisis in Jamaica is a failed education system, and a failed social development system. This has opened the door to drug dealing as a way of life for ghetto people. And like any other business, drug people are territorial, and they firth to protect their territory. And they have their own concept of 'free enterprise' and 'capitalism'. In addition, they have their own system of 'justice', which is ruthless and pretty much indifferent as to whatever collateral damage they may cause, whether to innocent individuals or the nation, in executing their 'justice'. Extra large sums of money and guns in the hands of poor, under-educated, deprived, disregarded, dispossessed, angry and 'dissed' young men are seen by them as mighty attractive levers of empowerment, dangers notwithstanding. Yes, Dear Reader. Jamaica is a paradise and a hell. Whither goest St. Kitts & Nevis? What are **WE** going to do about it? (See comment 4p) On Monday morning of this week. I listened to my dear brother Sam Condor address a group of students at a workshop. He told them about his own life. His poverty, going to Irish Town School without shoes, drinking a little swank sometimes for lunch because there was no food, working for the Union as a messenger boy for a dollar a week, and generally painting a picture of abject poverty and material deprivation. He related his story not to seek pity but to make a powerful point. He never felt sorry for himself. He never felt that the world owed him and that he had to get even. And he always felt, indeed, he always **knew,** that once he applied himself to the task of his own educational and other development, he could achieve everything in life. (See comment 4q) H said he always felt so, because his mother had told him that he had the ability to go far, and he believed her, and **he believed in her.** Just as **she believed in him.** For as poor as he was materially, he was enormously wealthy in spirit, decency, discipline, ambition and 'broughtupsy'. He chose the guidance of a solid, caring, responsible mother, rather than the pressure of his peers, all of whom were themselves in need of guidance (what the heck do you expect at that age?) but some not as fortunate as he was to have a parent like his mother. (See comment 4r) He had no paternal presence, so his mother was mother, father, toot, mun and baggai! Sam attended University, gained his degree, and advanced to the point where he is the Deputy Prime Minister of a nation. (See comment 4s) No self pity, no complaining, no blaming the world for his woes, but thanking God and his mother for life and guidance, and **doing the rest for himself.** Sam Condor did what Fatis said poor youths should be doing. And as Sam addressed those young people on Monday morning, I saw positive energy, hope and youthful exhilaration in their eyes, as if they were listening to their own futures unfolding right then and there. (See comment 4t) I pray that we adults will make it our business to ensure that the message of Sam Condor will sink into the heads and hearts of these youths. I hope that we will stop telling them how stupid and hard-headed they are. I hope that we will give them the hope, the love and the guidance that they so vitally need as their foundations for the future. I pray to God that we will appreciate the urgency or our task and that we will stop the decadence and degradation which we have too long been taking for granted, even encouraging as adults. I pray that we will rise up with our standards and restore the moral, spiritual, cultural and intellectual foundation upon which our great achievements have been built, so that we can reach higher heights. (See comment 4v) The Circle of Peace has to be extended, not only to the length and breadth of S. Kitts & Nevis, but it must reach Jamaica and Trinidad, St. Vincent and the Bahamas, Cayman and Grenada. It is our only hope. It is critical, and its solutions will have to be a dramatic, innovative and even unorthodox. (See comment 4v) We cry for

Haiti, and we are crying for Jamaica. We are crying too much. We must turn those tears to joy and laughter. That takes work and resolute commitment. (See comment 4w) Until Next Time, Plenty Peace

Comments Four:

a.   *Are you saying that you are so sure of yourselves? Regardless of whatever (if anything) went down during the dark hours of Election Day, 2004, right up to the morning after. Is this a 'bullish' attitude on display here?*

b.   *It is over one year since this article was written. To date, nothing representing the 'bomb' you refer to being 'bussed' and with regards to some 'cat being out of the bag'. Until this time there is no idea what you are talking about. There is a sense of some kind of threat, implied at by this article. However, while the writing is at the current level of vagueness, one is at a loss about the sense of the text.*

c.   *Wow! 'More wutless and bad than them!' It is remembered that a few months before this article, a certain letter hit the rounds. That letter was addressed to your cabinet colleagues, written by yourself about a number of persons, which included ardent supporters of your clan and those subjects were not written about in exactly glowing terms. Indeed some references were really offensive to the subjects. If that was not, in your words, "Wutless and bad"; I don't know what was! The point is: if there is anything to your claim about those fictitious persons you are in the process of pulling apart; then guess who is tarred with the same brush as them?*

d.   *Surely you could see much the same thing here at home: instead of "the dismissive disdain of the rich the powerful" read 'the dismissive disdain of the rich and politically powerful'; instead of "seething anger and despair of the poor and dispossessed" read 'seething anger and despair of the usefully ignored and socially discarded'.*

e.   *Guess what? You did not have to go all the way to Jamaica for that. If you sniff the air here, you could smell the same thing. Rotten aroma filled with all kinds of bad vibes, based on that, the crop we have are no good also.*

f.   *It should be wondered: how long will the same sense of rot here, be evident to a casual visitor? A number of the ingredients mentioned in your narrative are already here. The question is: when will that slippery slope lead to the kind of social milieu you describe. From the way things are going, it does not seem long!*

g.   *Don't kid yourself too much. There are people here living out of garbage cans also. Last time I saw Conaree dump there were scavengers there also. Indeed, in your constituency, individuals live on the streets and sleep in the most surprising places. Check it out some time. There is a saying: pick the beam out of your own eye before.........*

h.   *St. Kitts could also be placed in that equation of comparison and wonder. Perhaps with fewer variables. However, given time, you politicians will undoubtedly produce the missing dimensions to drag us down to that level of despair. Already you are leading the way as measured by the greed criteria.*

i.   *It is a pity that some of those traits you sensed did not rub off on you. Perhaps some of the embedded greed would have given way to a desire to put things right here. Instead of just 'lip service' to what you say for the benefit of the public audience.*

j.   *Over one year later and still no sign of those promises made to you materializing. Are you sure that this report on your sojourn in Jamaica was accurately reported upon? Let's face it, your track record in terms of inventing stories or dreaming up desired outcomes is widely suspect and since there appears no sign of the promises reportedly made to you. The whole escapade could well have been a relaxing jaunt at the expense of the already overburdened tax payers here.*

k.   *They are welcome to you and permanently as far as I am concerned. To see you as a typical example of a politician who can relate to ordinary folk has to be a testament to your ability as a 'papaguyer'. They do not know you very well do they? Do me a favour? Go live with them for a couple of years and if they still feel the same about you, I will apologize.*

l.   *They, all of them can have you. Go man go! Why are you still here when you are in such demand elsewhere? Especially when you really are not needed here. If there is anything in your list of countries that want you; it might be something to do with your colour. As you well know, Caribbean people of colour still have this thing about idolizing those of the lighter skin and the lighter, the better. That perhaps, might be the appeal to those misguided foreigners who do not know you. Personally, they would be welcome to you!*

m.   *Are you sure that you are not making all of that up to suit your design and expectation back home? Who else beside you heard all that have been written by you? It would not be the first time that imagination got the better of you. It is too bad for someone who has designs on manipulating the masses to regularly write stuff which is fanciful and without foundation. Further, it is just as well that not many who reside within this country reads the articles that are invented or at best: suspect. Otherwise, God only knows what they might think of us!*

n. *It has to be an item of curiosity to find out what the prelude was to Junior Kelly expressing an interest in your Circle of Peace? Did he capitulate after listening to what possibly was a boring narrative about some project that would turn out to lead nowhere? It is easy to conclude that even an angel would succumb to torture of a milder form.*

o. *I like the advice to act now in order to avoid deteriorating to the state of Jamaica presently is. As already stated, we really are not that far away from them. Sad, however that you did not take the proffered advice for since then, we most certainly have slipped further down that slippery slope because what your Jamaican advisors did not or could not realize is the fickleness of you and your colleagues with your collective heads up your individual plots of fantasies, without the necessary backbones to do what needs to be done. Each stuck into your own time warp. That is why over a year later, the Jamaican advice is still on the shelf.*

p. *Is that not your job to lead the way in redirecting the culture back to a nice orderly society? However, suspicion is that you and your crew have not got a clue how to go about reclaiming the order which once was taken for granted. That is until your team demonstrated disregard for the same harmonious existence that you now so desperately crave!*

q. *No doubt Sam said those things in your report. However, you and he failed to mention one important ingredient. You see, all of you politicians, especially your particular crop, now that you have achieved a certain amount of notoriety. You fail to recognize those whose shoulders you climbed up to where you are. You are also disrespectful to the amount of luck and good fortune which 'kismet' bestowed upon you when it did. For example, if Sam was not at that certain place that night when the late, great, Fitzroy Bryant uttered those magic three words: "look Sam here", he might be just like me now: A used tool to further the ambitions of ungrateful users like you! So much for drive and ability!*

r. *Once again, you are way off track. You are not properly interpreting the story that you heard. You are off into another wonder-world of your own. Of course, what do you know about the sort of poor society that Sam was talking about?*

You, from your 'well-to-do', comfortable existence of those times could not even imagine what life was like for the poor of Irish Town or the streets Of Mc. Knight. Of course there were peers, especially for we who had to use street lit areas for our living rooms. The point is that our peers were not were like the rest of us: not greedy, hungry yes but not greedy. We sat in cane fields and filled our empty bellies but we did not 'mug' old or young women from what they had. Yes we begged for the odd penny or half-penny; we did not steal them. That was when any grown up was a disciplinarian without being an abuser. We had fun grow-ing up because our pastimes were adventurous and exploratory without being criminal and destructive. Thus there was nothing wrong with the peer group in those days!

s.   *Stop, stop, stop! You are moving too fast. Taking too many giant steps! A lot of us starting from the same disadvantaged take off point, did that! Not all of us had the same degree of luck. Much as I like my namesake, Sam. The implied uphill picture of struggle as you describe it is typical of your puncheon for glossing over reality. I would not presume to simplify Sam's achievements. However, the leap from academic dexterity to Deputy Prime Minister-ship cannot be allowed to pass like that. Such status and position were due purely to the man's good luck. Labour in Constituency three is massive and at the moment, unbeatable. Anyone, even you Dwyer, could not fail but to win that seat. No struggle involved, no hard work, just a gift from days of old and a tribute to all those ancients who built the Labour movement. Certainly not as you made it out to be!*

t.   *You are always seeing things! There can be no message because the times are dif-ferent. Gone are the days when self confidence aimed at preservation was within range of poor youngsters with ambition. Ambition which was motivated from watching men of stature then. Today, the men of stature in the eyes of youngsters do not reside in this Federation. Mass media in this country 'bigs up' politicians of dubious character and it is doubtful if our young people are looking at them. Our youths can hardly be categorized as poor youngsters! They are pampered, do not know how to explore the countryside, like we did, do not know what hunger or hardship is. To say that they were listening to their own futures is once again, a stupid implied, commonality with an age long gone. You have to find solutions within the context of today's dynamics! Not with conditions from the past!*

u.   *Going backwards is not an option! That is impossible. Life goes on with every new day. We have a social situation which is not very attractive, here and now. Perpetually harping on about recapturing what used to be is not going to solve or move us out of what we are in. evolutionary leadership, compassionate but firm discipline are needed to steer society towards the plan for life which you persons who begged to be voted into office should spare no effort to draw up; instead of spending so much effort and energies in feathering your own nests!*

v. *Looks like you see yourself as the saviour of the English speaking Caribbean basin. Is there no limit to your dreams? It won't work as too large a proportion of your ideas are balmy. Groaning to a tune with the words: "It's peace we want an its peace we gun get, yeah." Has not exactly got magnetic or even attractive qualities. Look at us quite a lot of months later and in spite of that stupid jingle, the situation has actually got worse. Which, really and truly, does not surprise many persons who think for themselves. I mean one of the first thing you did was to place at the head of the Police Force a man who does not command a lot of respect, inside or out of the Police Force, a man who has suspicious operational integrity. How on earth can anyone of character treat as serious your stated desire to steer society on the right track when you do daft things like what has been done so far? You certainly have been unorthodox, even if not innovative.*

w. *People are laughing but not for the reason implied by you. They are laughing at the spectacle of your ineptitude or inability to do the job for which you are so handsomely paid. Society wants to see meaningful action to make it feel safer and freer from fears of all dimensions. In addition to hard work and resolute commitment, required from you; we also need meaningful leadership, instead of fairy dreams, hallucinations and a load of empty words, buried in your biased political newspaper.*

26 February 2005

The Government's budget for 2005 has now been delivered and debated. The Prime Minister brought smiles to thousands of faces, while he disappointed the doomsayers amongst us who were predicting the re-introduction of personal income tax and a host of other oppressive fiscal measures, cynically hoping that such measures would destabilize the Government and the country, and prepared the way for them to regain control of the country. (See comment 5a) Those doomsayers should now be man and woman enough to publicly repeat and critique their own comments, and repent. But I'm not holding my breath for that to happen. However, fool that I am, I was hoping to hear Shawn Richards, in his presentation to the Parliament, make an effort to provide PAM"s remedies and alternatives. Unfortunately, Shawn helped nobody, least of all himself and PAM. I thought he made a miserable mess of yet another opportunity to represent the people of Sandy Point with the aplomb, intellectual quickness and dimension, wit, personality, confidence and dexterity that would be expected from a representative of that great community. Yet, as he spoke, I could not avoid wondering how many voters in Sandy Point might be wincing and gnashing their teeth with regret at this fellow being their Parliamentary Representative. Worse so those who voted for him. (See comment 5b) What made his parliamentary and political suicide attempt all the more tragic were the accompanying nodding and gesturing of support which he was receiving from two blind mice sitting in the gallery, Lindsay Grant and Chesley Hamilton, which served only to further encourage him in his folly. (See comment 5c) And for a while I questioned myself as to whether they were in fact as hopeless as he by his own admission, was, or whether, because of malice and jealousy over his success and their failures at the polls, they might be trying to dig out poor Shawn's eyes and hasten his political demise. (See comment 5d) You can never tell with those fellows, you know. They often behave 'funny'. But in the end, I concluded that this was a classic case of a political corpse being accompanied in his funeral procession to his political grave by two already politically dead cronies. What was needed was a political exorcist. And guess what! One appeared. For as soon as Shawn concluded his presentation, an exorcist named **Timothy** stood up in Parliament and began to speak. I had never seen three men leave a room so fast in my life. And again an interesting thought came to me. Ask them to join up with Kim Collins, and we would have a world class 4x100 meter relay team. But to make sure that they **all** run fast, just after the starter gun goes off, you get somebody with a roaringly loud voice to shout out: **TIMOTHY COMING!** Watch 'pon speed all you would see. Nothing less than a bronze medal for SKN. Now later on in the evening, while I was absent but well informed, he returned to Parliament. I don't think that the Exorcist was there, so the way seemed clear. And guess what. He entered the Chamber in a jacket but wearing no tie, improperly and impertinently attired. And he was asked to leave and get a **tie.** So, like a chastened offender, he stepped outside and donned a tie that was loaned to him by the clerk of the Parliament. At the end of the session he was reminded to return it, just in case he might have forgotten. Seriously though, and no disrespect intended to any of the individuals mentioned, to their organization or to anyone else, I could not avoid the hopelessly catastrophic thought of PAM winning a general election in this country with Lindsay Grant being Prime Minister, Shawn Richards being Deputy Prime Minister and Hamilton being Minister of anything at all. What a calamity that would be! (See comment 5e) Yet there are individuals and organizations in this land who (and which) are so hateful towards Labour that they would support and encourage, and **finance with big dollars,** just about anybody who ran against Labour. (See comment 5f) There are also a small number of individuals in this community who seem to have a very special hatred towards me personally. From the moment I declared my candidacy back in 1992 to contest the Central Basseterre seat against their man of business, Dr. Kennedy Simmonds, they declared war against me. (See comment 5g) They had their friends say and write all manner of nasty and false things about me. Some of them even took personally to the columns of The Democrat and later the internet. They encouraged and personally engaged in all manner of cruelty towards me. They spoke in the most pejorative of terms about me while engaged in their day-time routines or while knocking cocktail glasses at their homes. In their arrogance and indiscretion, they would not have noticed, perhaps not even cared, about the fact that their helpers and servers were listening and watching, and bringing the information. Notwithstanding their fury and hatred, I managed to win the seat in 1995. (See comment 5h) Poor me, because that only deepened their hatred towards me. They came up with all kinds of reasons why I should not have been appointed as Minister of Tourism. They said that I was hostile to them. Then after the 2000 general elections, when I was allowed to continue with Tourism and received Commerce and Consumer affairs, and Telecommunications additionally, they became even more furious. One of my earlier statements with regard to Telecoms was that in the new dispensation of a liberalized telecoms environment, it would only be right and proper to try our vest to assist small, local people in the OECS in getting involved in ownership of new enterprises, so that empowerment could be ushered to the small man in the new economy. They said that I was a socialist, and they said all manner of nefarious and accusatory things when Clecton 'Quash' Phillip, a bright, ambitious, and, might I add, deserving, young man from New Town, was awarded a telecoms license. All you remember that? They heard me repeatedly saying that they needed to pay their workers better and to reduce prices of basic goods so that poor people can have better spending power, to spend their little extra money with-who else but **them?** (See comment 5i) One of them responded publicly, again accusing me of being a socialist and saying that I was using this rhetoric to attract people to a Labour Day march which would follow a few weeks later. They said that I was not business-friendly. (See comment 5j) I told them at a meeting at RLB that if they continued to stand by and not invest at Port Zante, I would go to St. Maarten and bring in those high-powered businessmen to set up shop here and to help establish St. Kitts as a top shopping destination for tourists, so as to attract more ships and to encourage the spending of more money at home by our residents. (See comment 5k) That got them vexed too. And when succeeded in bringing people like Boolchand's, Kay's Jewellery and others here, and Port Zante finally started to get into swing, the handful of Dwyer haters said that I was engineering concessions for the foreigners that were not being made available to the local business, when nothing could be further from the truth. Incidentally, this is the same Port Zante which, because of haste and political desperation on the part of Dr. Simmonds, would have turned into a white elephant, regularly referred to by some of his members and friends as "Port Panty", were it not for the intervention of the present labour Government which was able to rescue the project after having to expend over 100 million dollars. (See comment 5l) For the record, everything I had said about Port Zante prior to the 1995 general elections proved correct. You may recall that I had said that it was being built in haste and desperation, that its location was not a problem, but there had not been sufficient thought, planning and consultation, that the threat of the Simmonds Government to double the head tax from US$5 to US$10 immediately the pier was ready would be suicidal, and that it was a potential white elephant which could and would only be rescued by Labour. (See comment 5m) What happened there between 1995 and even today represents efforts involving my own stewardship as Minister of Tourism. (See comment 5n) A number of them went to great lengths to destabilize relationships between myself and other ministers, including the Prime Minister, and leading members of Labour, in an effort to create a wedge and have my ministries taken away from me. (See comment 5o) They tried with their lies to get me fired several times. They also heard me repeatedly call upon hoteliers to make a greater commitment towards destination marketing and airlift support. Most of my calls were in vain, as they complained as to how difficult things were with them and how unable they were to provide the counterpart commitments which I was asking of them. Thanks to the initiatives of the Marriott and the St. Kitts Scenic Railway, both brought to St. Kitts during my time as Minister of Tourism, new levels of private sector proactiveness were reached here in St. Kitts. (See comment 5p) Enterprises that came here under my stewardship helped to substantially increase these fellows' revenues and bottom lines, and all they could do was accuse me of being anti-business. I wondered why. But not for long. Because I soon found out that they did not really believe that I was anti-business. Their problem was that **they** were, and are, anti-Dwyer. And for personal and political reasons. On the other hand, while they accused me of being anti-business, the foreign businessmen, international businessmen, men of great honour and international repute had nothing but praise and support for me. (See comment 5q) I kept telling the Dwyer Haters that Government was continuing to take the lead in capital development programs and in wealth generation, and that it was necessary for them as a private sector to take a more proactive role generally. I say "generally" because some enterprises have in fact been proactive and progressive from time to time. The result of these comments by me? More abuse in The Democrat and more accusations from certain private sector voices that I was anti-business and a socialist. I called upon them to pay their taxes, and I used my occasional refrain about 'small tief and big tief', which some people hate to hear. I remember once saying at a formal meeting that if certain major players paid their collective taxes properly on an annual basis, that Government's deficit on current account would be effectively addressed. They laughed at me. (See comment 5r) And they continued their campaign of hatred and marginalization. They told me to make sure that the taxi drivers, the craftspeople, the barbecue people, the braiders and people like them pay taxes on their earnings too. They told me to tax the "informal sector", who, they said, were getting away with murder. I told them that the "informal sector" was paying their duty just lie everyone else, and perhaps were getting away with less than the bigger people. They laughed at me and called me socialist. (See comment 5s) I told them that the "informal sector" was made up of people who wanted work, many of whom could not get work in the businesses in St. Kitts and therefore took it upon themselves to be creative and to become entre-

preneurs. (See comment 5t) I applauded the spirit of confidence and true enterprise of the "informal sector". The Dwyer Haters kept tagging me as a socialist
and as being anti-business. They said I was looking for votes. When I kept calling
for the private sector to get involved in the construction of homes for low income
earners, thereby establishing long-term, mutually beneficial relationships between
home builder and home owner, with home builder also being mortgagee, finan-
cier, insurer, credit sales provider in terms of furniture, appliances, cars, etc, while
at the same time taking some pressure off the Government and also helping to
depoliticize what the see as a politicized process of home delivery by Government, they ignored and rebuked. Not even the attraction of them getting the
lands at pittances and being granted duty free concessions in relation to the construction and delivery of these homes for the poor people who would clearly
develop strong sense of loyalty to them. (See comment 5u) Not even in the
present climate in which we see 'corporate' politics in the extreme I certain quarters, an din which they can gain friends fir their friends, will they see the light of
doing the thing commercially and otherwise. That is how badly blinded and self–
destructive people can become because of hatred. (See comment 5v) When I
achieved some success with placement of micro-businesses from the streets to All
Kinda Ting and Amina Markets and the Ferry Terminal, the Dwyer haters,
declared that it was their **"victory"**. Such is the level of their arrogance and dishonesty. (See comment 5w) So when, after the elections of October 25, 2004, I
was appointed to my present ministerial post, I expected the campaign of hatred,
I expected the campaign of hatred, if not to end, certainly to abate somewhat.
But it seems to have gotten worse. I suppose my being appointed as Minister of
Labour may have something to do with it, to add to the already solid foundation
of hatred that lies within the vaults of those few hearts. And I suppose that the
fact that the hatred will not have diminished one iota from the fact that I had
declared, supported and guided by the Prime Minister himself, that all employers
must pay their workers the recently established minimum wage, failing which
vigorous action will be taken against all offenders. Similarly, I don't suppose I
would have earned a reprieve after my statement in Parliament on/Thursday to
the effect that employers who had reduced their employee's work from 40houra
to 39, 38, 37 hours and thereabouts, simply to save themselves from paying their
workers the extra $6.25 for the one hour, $12.50for the two hours, $18,75 for
the three hours, or $25.00 for the four hours over the period of one week were
unreasonable, disrespectful and contemptuous. (See comment 5x) I wonder if
they will vocalize their hatred similarly for the PM, as his comments were even
stronger than mine on this matter. I am not looking for enemies. Particularly

considering that I am committed to a sacred trust and mandate to serve all interests with honour and equity. I also do not pretend for a moment to be perfect and to have all of the answers. (See comment 5y) But it seems that every time I open my mouth and call for equity between employers and employees, or for greater effort for social equity, or when I call upon certain commercial interests to play a more proactive role in the economic and social development of our people, I become the target for invective and ridicule from those certain quarters. It almost seems as if they feel themselves sacrosanct and untouchable and beyond reproach. It seems that they believe that it is only they who have the right and the responsibility to speak about transparency, corruption and all of that good stuff, and the moment somebody else opens up his or her mouth to demonstrate a different perspective, it is abuse, vilification and character assassination. (See comment 5z)But all of that comes as no surprise to me, because that is the same approach that their minions and messengers who run PAM for them use and have used from day one: OUR WAY OR THE HIGHWAY. They speak about free enterprise and competition, but they don't really mean it. They speak about tolerance, but they are intolerant to the point of being ruthlessly dictatorial. They speak about transparency and nobody can hide and cover up like them. Earlier in life, I was always someone respectfully incline to express my opinions, and to be the first to admit being wrong. Nothing has changed when it comes to that. I have served **all** interests in this country during my almost ten years as a minister and parliamentarian. My efforts, small as they may have been in the greater scheme of things, have visibly contributed to the creation of economic and social wealth in the nation. I have established an exemplary reputation regionally and internationally. If I may say so myself. (See comment 5aa) Here I am now, trying to guide young men and women away from the gun and gang lifestyle, and this oaf, who has more dollars than sense, and who perhaps thinks that he can manipulate me out of Government with his scheming, is saying that I am trying to set up my own army against the Prime Minister. Against my own Prime Minister. To overthrow him. (See comment 5ab) Can you imagine that?! Can you imagine how deep these people's hatred is for me that it would lead them to such extremes of dishonesty and wickedness in an effort to have me removed as a minister?! I will not bore you with the list of Dwyer Haters right now, but I will tell you of a special and recent report. I will outline the information as I received it. A few weeks ago a certain so-called intelligent, influential gentleman told someone that I, Dwyer Astaphan, along with a couple others in Cabinet, was chasing people out of St. Kitts (mind you, the same Dwyer Astaphan who **invited** these businesses and investors to St. Kitts in order to join our community, to help grow our economy and provide jobs for our people), that I am setting up vagabonds and young gangsters into an army, and that I am inclined to create insurgency in an effort to overthrow my own leader ad party from Government, as Bernard Coard and others did to their leader, Prime Minister, Maurice Bishop in Grenada in 1983. (See comment 5ac) The person to whom this statement was allegedly made told me, and told another person. Both of them told me, at separate times and places. I consider this to be a serious matter. If I am encouraging youths to live stable, productive lives, is that not a good thing for all of us? Do business people not stand a better chance of sustainability in an environment of stability? Does the Dwyer Hater who is purveying this horrible lie have a solution to assist with guidance of the youth? Does he have a social stabilization plan? What is his position on corporate fraud, income shifting and tax evasion? Does he think that a scholarship or two and a sponsorship or three will do the trick for him? And at the same time, while he conducts himself in this cowardly, hateful, and dishonest manner towards me, his business is becoming increasingly tainted with PAM politics and becoming a haven and a tool for PAM. I need to let them know that I am a man of peace. An imperfect man of peace. I am also an honest and straightforward man. (See comment 5ad) I am not sure he can lay claim to that. I stand for something and I stand up to say so. I don't know if he can do that. I can also assure him that he could never be more patriotic and for stability in this country than me. (See comment 5ae) He may have put his money on the line, but I have many times put my life on the line for this country, and I still do so every day. I am prepared to let this go, as wild indiscretion on his part, in the hope that the will be more responsible and respectful in the future. (See comment 5af). Until Next Time, Plenty Peace.

Comments Five:

a. *Cynically, what you said in that first paragraph is your way of ensuring that during the remaining life of your Government, personal income tax and other host of oppressive fiscal measures would not be re-introduced.*

b. *Let us face it. No matter what Shawn was like, some form of critique would have been jumping off your desk! The guy would not have been able to meet with your approval at all! Just goes to illustrate how varied standards are: The Democrat was very glowing in its praises for the same guy. Who is nearer the real mark? Perhaps we will never know. Not as long as you politicians play those stupid games of fooling the public.*

c.   *The sight of those two PAM giants, sitting in your stomping ground must have driven you wild! No wonder there is so much venomous signs of poison-pen-arthritis.*

d.   *There goes that weird logic again. Seems to me that motives in others, where ever it is detected, has to be treated to comparison by your standards. It is possible for some politicians to include loyalty among their qualities of friendship, even among colleagues. Not all colleagues have to look over their shoulders at or wonder when they will be 'back-stabbed' by anyone close to them. Some have a high degree of trust embedded in their relationships.*

e.   *If PAM was to win an election, at the outset they would be no better or worse than you and your six colleagues were at July 1995. Everyone has to begin at the start, grow in confidence and eventually to some level of competence, just like you guys. Question is: competence at what? If the fear that 'the party waiting in the wings to form the next government will be a mere rubber-stamp of the present one' did not exist; you lot would have been gone and may be next time. The country needs persons of better integrity, honesty and ability in many dimensions. Rather than spending that much effort on ridiculing a new member on the opposite bench; you should be focusing on how you can grow to perform to the standard from which the country could benefit!*

f.   *You are doing it again: thinking that you are Labour and that Labour belongs to the Cabinet. That is not so! Labour is supposed to be about those who stand for certain ideals which historically and internationally support those ideals. However, since your collection of elite politicians hijacked the party, the masses are hood winked into believing that being Labour is what you say it is. Individuals are not really against Labour. What happens is that those who know what Labour should be, find it difficult to recognize it here. When you shanghaied the party, the biggest mistake was that you jettisoned those who knew how Labour is supposed to work. So, what you did was to throw away the baby with the bath water. That you have lost support, after such actions, was inevitable!*

g.   *It is not even necessary to go that far back. It is possible that you have collected more 'dislikers since becoming a minister of government, even most who helped you gain your seat in Government and to become their representative. I can sympathize how difficult it is to accept dislike when one perceives oneself to so fantastically great! It is a real pain! But as the people say: that's life*

h.   *Surely, what you mean is: the team who worked to get you elected won the seat for you. The statement "I managed to win the seat in 1995" has to be indicative of conceit and ingracious attitudes, among others. It is those attitudes that make you feel complete ownership and control of the mechanism and dynamics that got you where you are. That adds to your conceit and empowerment that you can do as you like, dispose of those you don't like when the whim takes effect on you, regardless of the potential for the country.*

i.   *As it turned out, there was no extra money, for it soon got swallowed up with competition phone cards and extra electricity charges. Turns out that most who follow the new telecommunications fad, would rather spend money on phone cards and related gadgets than buy food properly. Also, you guys saw what was going on, recognized an opportunity to get the masses to pay off you massive debt and consequently, almost doubled the price of electricity. That in turn caused almost every other consumer item to increase. Now, tell us again about that better spending power?*

j.   *If they said that you were not business-friendly, they were right; if they said that you were a socialist, they were wrong. True that traditionally, socialist principles were associated with Labour administrations but since you and your colleagues never did know what it was to be Labour, it would be a contradiction to expect you to know what it is like to be socialist. The first part is evident, since you are perpetually bashing the Chamber of Commerce and Industry!*

k.   *Let me get this straight? You are going to bring in high powered businessmen from St. Maarten, in order to the encourage our people to spend more money here? For that to happen, Porte Zante must become a duty free zone! To attract that group of business-people. Otherwise, them coming here does not make a lot of sense. If it is that the attracted business-persons got duty free concessions; why did you not just give it to our business individuals? once again the logic escaped me on this one!*

l.   *There you go again, off into your imaginary world. You do not know what or how Port Zante would have evolved under a PAM administration, after those hurricanes that almost erased the Port. It is sheer vain speculation to indulge yourself in those claims of yours. For all we know, there might have been more rapid progress; the place might have been more scenic and the cost of the rescue operation could well have been much less than your figure! You still have not given a definitive response to the claim that those swanky companies tempted to operate on Porte Zante, did so with corporate bribes that were not available to our people. Your dismissive attitude is not an answer one way or another*

m. *I do not remember you having said anything like that claimed in the early section of the paragraph. It is too easy to make claims of the 'I said this or I said that' variety. Especially when over one decade has elapsed. Nor do I believe that you said anything of the sort! However, in keeping with the bigging-up yourself side of you; that kind of claim must be beyond resistance. Plus, of course, there are those creeps out there who will slap you on the back and congratulate you about that. With regards to the 'double head tax' accusation. I recall that at that time, the entire region were considering a proposal along those lines. Could this be another bogus utterance? Capitalizing on people's long-term memories, having long jettisoned such matters. Especially since that matter has been closed for so long. Under those circumstances, clearly any kind of assertion that is fanciful could be reproduced with all sorts of claims attached to them!*

n. *I do remember that you failed to harmonize tourism in the region. Which is really what the industry needs in these waters. Something as strong as what the cruise lines have in their federation. You failed in that vital area and as a result the Tourism Federation picks off these islands at their whim. They say to us jump and we ask: how high? They make us invest in capital projects which they then proceed to take the best portions of. Then when its time to increase their shareholders' dividends, they call the development shots, repeating the cycle whenever the fancy takes them.*

o. *Do you expect readers to believe that you have always been squeaky clean? That it has always been the fault of others? That your actions have no bearing on the feedback attracted? Did you never keep the Prime Minister and others of the public waiting for a meeting with you? Did you not write a letter which got to be a public example of what could be contrived as the real you? In which some of your own Labour persons were tarred in bad 'lights'? It certainly could be reasonably deduced from certain past actions that some, if not all of the 'flack' that came your way, were deserved.*

p. *Is that the reason why you allow that hotel to take liberties at their whim, with the citizens of this country? Especially the black ones, who for the past two yuletide seasons have been barred from certain of their services. At least one of which had your understanding. You are remembered for making excusable remarks that sounded defensive of their insulting act. In any event, you attended the Prime*

Minister's gala during a period when blacks, local or otherwise, were not welcomed there.

q. *Ha! Here we go again! Taking unto yourself credit, supposedly passed to you by others. Were there witnesses? Someone of your years, should by now realize that praising oneself, even by proxy, is very immodest and when delivered by yourself, is very difficult to believe!*

r. *It would also be true to say that if you lot, who are Government were more considerate of the country's dilemma and showed more understanding, the deficit would not be as severe as it is and probably would not exist, especially if you were serious about the national motto: Country above self!*

s. *There is nothing to be ashamed of in being a socialist. Problem is that you do not appear to know what it is to be a socialist. If it was that anyone called you a socialist, then whoever that was, most certainly do not know what being a socialist is! I can most categorically tell anybody that Dwyer Astaphan is NOT a socialist! You see, a socialist cares about the global country!*

t. *Not just the businesses but also Government. With regards to working with or for the Government, one has to have credentials that are covered with the stamp labeled "party approval".*

u. *I really don't believe that you had the unmitigated gall to write such drivel! Social housing is the domain of Social Services, which is a government body. No wonder they laugh at you. Private enterprise is in the business of making returns for their owners and shareholders. If private companies started doing the government's work for it, then they will forfeit the title private and their shareholders would be entitled to demand their heads. On the other hand, government would be a pitiful excuse. Government must and ought to perform its roles rather than try to bully the private sector into doing its work. Socialism is to do with government looking after the people and not just those who elected them; not government looking after, first and foremost, its members, then try and get others to look after the people! It is quite clear that you lot forgot why you were elected!*

v. *A comment like that from you has to be self revealing! Your vibes radiate exactly what the subject of your comment is warning against. It has to be very confusing when warning is being given by someone who do not appear to be capable of practicing what he preaches.*

w. *You apparently are claiming some form of trophy by using the law to coral those who once vended on street places into your ancestors burnt out property. A place that is hardly on the main thoroughfare. However, as law abiding persons, trying to eke out a living, they had to move or fall foul of the law. By any standards, that really cannot be claimed as any kind of victory when bullying tactics were used to achieve the end result. It was more like do it or else! What kind of victory was that?*

x. *Looks and sounds like you are lashing out at businesses at a whim! Managers and owners of private enterprises must be allowed to take decisions in order t keep their companies afloat and vibrant. Rather than lay off employees; if they decide that cutting hours all round, thereby sharing the burden; surely that is much better and humane than sacking any one individual! Surely that makes better sense!*

y. *That committedness to serve all interests with honour and equity sounds like a badge of courage that is whipped out when the occasion demands. It is certainly well hidden and would not have remained unrecognized had mention not been made thereof! It never ceases to amaze how these glib phrases pop up in times of 'need to impress' but you and the rest of those who know Dwyer Astaphan will recognize the emptiness of the glib statements. There remain those of us who find it harder to be impressed by them.*

z. *I do not really see much evidence of what you are writing about, certainly not in the papers which I read. Admittedly, there is some oblique critique of some you say and do. However, as a politician, that has to be expected; since politicians are public figures and especially here, where democratic practices are laughable, one of the only means of getting to you guys is through the 'grapevine' which is not accessible most of the time. Therefore, this self-pity that is now oozing off your pages does not fool anyone because sensitivity of that type just does not seem compatible with the character!*

aa. *You may also say that 'self-praise' is no recommendation. In any event, that regional and international reputation so glibly mentioned has many sides to it! Is it good or bad? All reports heard were generated by you. So what is there to that? In any event that is your function and many of us are not particularly impressed. Thus when you write these fantastic reports about yourself, impression cannot go anywhere but down.*

ab. *Are you intimating that there never was a time when your behaviour, impression thereof, your actions or suggestions thereof, could have been interpreted by onlookers that you were defiant or in that kind of mood with your Prime Minister? If your answer to the posed question is: no. I would have to remind you of that letter written to your colleagues, in which a number of persons close to the party and Prime Minister were mentioned. What was that, if it was not a form of treachery? Even though you guys have this cabinet secrecy pact, word still leaks out about your behaviour and it does not paint a perpetual flattering picture!*

ac. *Seem to recall that shortly after being re-elected, there was, what looked like a campaign to remove Bachuss from his post at Radio WINN-FM and as a consequence from this country. Suppose that could be viewed as an attempt to chase that particular out of the country. On the other hand, it could have been sheer vindictiveness, dating back to before the election, when there was a strong impression that you were not best pleased with the outputs from that radio station. No idea about any inclination towards a propensity to overthrow your leader but I would not put that beyond your capability. Past experience certainly suggests that you are capable of anything your mind is put to.*

ad. *Disagree about the honest part. Using government employees to collect your son from school during working hours were not honest to the taxpayers. Misrepresenting others before Cabinet is not honest. Inventing tales without foundation and passing them off as factual is certainly not honest. Defending fraudulent practice is definitely not honest and failing to declare to the public about the diabolical misuse of resources by the in crowd is darn-right dishonest! That claim most certainly does not ring true!*

ae. *Perhaps your idea of patriotism is synonymous with greed. That greed plays a big role in your performance has clearly been demonstrated, which does not fit into the motto of 'country above self'! You appear to be talking the talk but most people knows better.*

af. *You started off building up to the point where it was felt that there was something to reveal and ended up saying nothing about what was said about you or by whom! That you see is one of the negative aspects about your performance and why it is difficult to attach any credibility to your claims.*

5 March 2005

Let's imagine this 14-year old school girl. She is on the street walking, by herself, at 10:30 on a Saturday night. She is dressed skimpily, exposing the shape and body of a voluptuous woman, but she's only a schoolgirl, remember. Some people say that it's all that fast food, riddled with hormones, that is causing young girls to pop out of their clothes so early, and also causing so much aggressiveness among youths. This girl is aggressive. She has a tattoo on her arm, and at least three body piercings, all not necessarily in her ears. Jewelry all over and don't forget the obligatory cell phone. She got herself a $250 outfit for her school's sports day last week. She needs to be in fashion. A car approaches her. It is sleek, well prettied up, with a crude message painted on its bonnet, and something passing for music bellowing our of it as if the driver can be that hungry for attention, or what we refer to as 'noticement'. Before anyone jumps up and says that I am speaking from the wrong side of the generation gap when it comes to this music thing, be assured that in my case there is no generation gap. I follow all kinds of music, and I know the difference between music and noise pollution. And the noise that some people make, go into studios and record, discuss in the media with the seriousness as if they are true artistes and creators, sell, and do very well selling, **ain't** music. (See comment 6a) It **ain't** art either. It's foolishness, with some people doing the fooling and others being fooled. And there is big money in it. So you dun know how dat go! With it go the clothing lines, the jewelry, the footwear, and so on. In America they call it '**bidness**'! Big 'Bidness'. And in it there is a lot of big Badness. It carries a 'lifestyle' message which many young people, and even their parents, are swallowing like crazy. So the driver, who is a 30-year old male with a beer in his hand and his eyes are red like fire, pulls over to where this 14-year old girl-forcing-woman is taking her leisurely walk. After a brief conversation, she steps into his 'chic–mobile' and off they go. They go to his place, where he gives her a drink, gets her to relax, turns up the sound system in the house, turns on his well-placed video camera, and the sex begins. How outrageous does that sound? It's only a 'nancy story', ain't it? (See comment 6b) Okay. But let's continue. When the sex is over, he gives the girl two hundred dollars and a chain. He promises her some clothes soon, and a season ticket for the upcoming music festival. He also promise help her with the money for her passport, because he wants to take her to St. Maarten for the big show down there with some artistes from the States. He then drops her off on the street where he picked her up, and she makes her way home at about 1 o'clock in the morning. When she gets home her mother isn't there. Or if she is, she is with **her** man, and she either doesn't know or perhaps doesn't care when her daughter gets back home, once she gets home in one piece. Now, I have to remind you that I am not claiming here to be making a statement of general fact. Nor am I referring to a specific situation. I am simply creating a hypothetical situation. If you know of a **real** situation that fits some of what you are reading here, that is entirely a matter for you. (See comment 6c) If you do, I hope that it would be important enough for you to raise it in every conceivable public forum for discussion and community and parental action. Yes, the mother of our imaginary 14-year old girl-woman might ask a question or two in the morning, but she won't cross examine the daughter with the passion and zeal of someone who really wants to or feels that she can do anything about her daughter's nocturnal activities. After all, the daughter brings in money that helps with the Cable bill, the lights bill, and Courts, so mother is, at best 'watered down' in her attempt at disciplining daughter. And even if mother was totally committed, she would probably run into a problem, because when everybody is in the same game, when adolescent girls are going with men, women with boys, and parents engaging in extremely negative activities in the presence of children, sometimes even actively encouraging their children to do likewise, (See comment 6d) the line between adult and child, between leader and follower, between authority and subordinate disappears, and discipline collapses. (See comment 6e) Are we seeing any of this happening in our society? And if we are, it's not because the mother is necessarily bad. She might be desperate **and** despairing. She may very well have started her sexual activities early, may have mothered several other children for different men, and may even be pregnant while she is '**trying**' to discipline her own 14-year old. Maybe she only sees the fathers when it comes time to collect child support, or to deal with a police or court matter involving one of the children. Momma has problems, to put it mildly. And she has regrets. If only she were able to persevere with school and hold off to the hormonal harassment, she might become a nurse, a teacher, an accountant, a secretary, or some such thing. (See comment 6f) But that didn't happen and she is angry, frustrated, severely limited, indecently dependent, and most vulnerable. (See comment 6g) And acting with consistent rationality in that situation is a challenge of gigantic proportions. Probably too great for her. Is it any wonder that the girl's teachers are unable to exercise authority over our girl-woman? Would we, therefore, be surprised to learn that she is not doing well in her schoolwork, that her attitude is poor, and that her very presence in school undermines the authority of the teachers over **other** children? (See comment 6h) Do we really appreciate the importance of **the home** in moulding the character and personality of an individual? (See comment 6i) Do we understand that often-times the greatest challenge faced by teachers is the home. True, the home is not the be all and the end all of everything, because the home exists in a community. And there is and must be a mutual dependency and a 'connect' between the home and the community, so that what comes out of the home goes into the community, and similarly, what comes out of the community goes into the home. Therefore, there needs to be a balance and a watchfulness between home and community, in the ongoing effort to maintain, even improve, standards that govern and sustains us as a society, and as home units which are the component parts of a society. (See comment 6j) Persons who occupy the same household must live like an **internal community** in relation to that place, or, if you will, like a family. Not just like a number of individuals 'looking shelter' under the same roof, with each and everyone going his or her own separate way, observing his or her own rules, or non-rules, as the case may be. That would be chaos in the house, spilling over into the streets and everywhere else. So the home is the key! (See comment 6k) And who is the boss at home? Look, I'm all, for democracy. But democracy **cannot** work in the absence of **leadership. Guidance is needed.** (See comment 6l) And the home is no exception. Indeed, and at the expense of being repetitive, it is in the home **more than any place else** that our personal foundations are to be laid, and so we must ensure that the principles of democracy, responsibility, leadership and discipline are first imparted and embedded there. And, God knows, as I write these words, I am driven to examine **my** many imperfections as well as the need to pull up my own socks as a parent. (See comment 6m) But in the scenario before us, we can see that the leadership required by our mom simply does **not** exist. So foundations for personal and characterological development probably cannot be properly laid. So Baby Girl is in trouble. But let's get back to the 'nancy story'. The sexual involvement with the man constitutes rape, because under sixteen, Baby Girl does not have the legal capacity to give sexual consent to **anybody**. (See comment 6n) Why did she give in to the man? Was she attracted to him? Was there a need for a father figure in her life? Is there a dangerous emotional characteristic amongst children for whom one or other parent has essentially abandoned his or her parental responsibility in terms of emotional support, quality time, solidarity with the other parent in the child's upbringing, etc. Did our girl make a conscious decision to hook up with this adult male who could provide her with her perceived needs, rather than with a boy in her age group who had neither chick, chick or come, come? Could it have been part of a plan to trap the man, giving him what he wanted, then extorting money from him in order to protect him from a rape charge and a long jail sentence, or simply to pull as much as she could from him, for as long as possible? (See comment 6o) Does she know what the man plans to do with the sex video? Does he plan to put it on the internet? Will he make money from it? Is she part of that deal? Will her reputation be forever tarnished? Does my story really sound outrageously unrealistic? God forbid she gets pregnant or, worse yet, contacts AIDS from connection with the man. Or both! Maybe she had AIDS and gave it to him. If any of that happens, then the burdens which that girl and her family, and the man will now have placed on the rest of society will be quite substantial, multiplying those that had existed before. Is that fair? No, it isn't. (See comment 6p) Who would be to blame? She? Yes. Her mother? Yes. The man? Yes. But what about the rest of us? Aren't we also blameworthy? Of course we are, because we are the community. We are the society. We are an integral part of that symbiotic relationship that must exist between home and community in order to ensure and enhance social development, stability and sustainability. (See comment 6q) And the scenario which I have outlined here indicates a breakdown in that symbiotic relationship. So we are all to blame. It is bad. But it gets worse. The adolescent males who, after all, are our Baby Girl's peers and schoolmates, perceive themselves to be at a competitive disadvantage in relation to the adult male who now has her attention and enjoys her favours. Remember these adolescent males have hormones raging through their bodies twenty four/seven, telling them to have sex, and to pursue it aggressively. The hormones and the competition drive them to extremes whereby they try to steel themselves with alcohol and other drugs, and they develop criminal behaviours to support a lifestyle that would enhance their confidence, status and competitiveness. (See comment 6r) They become part of the drug and robbing trade. They are 'allotted' territory by their suppliers, sometimes the same supplier overseeing a number of different territories. He reinforces in their minds the need to secure and protect their own territory, failing which they would lose it and lose whatever it is they have from it. He says that separately to all of the groups of young men who sell his stuff and steal and rob for him, or do that on the side. He manages them well, keeping them on edge with each other, just to ensure steadiness for himself. It's the old divide and rule principle that some of us seem to have mastered, having learned over the centuries from the masters themselves. All of a sudden these young men have money and spending power. Much more than their teachers. (See comment

6s) Much more than their parents. They rent cars on the weekends, travel to St. Maarten and Tortola, even sometimes to Antigua and St. Vincent. Why the hell would they want to work their tails off for a pittance, like regular folks do? The 'romance' of the gangsta life, the status, and the new and plentiful, accessibility of the object of their hormonal cravings make them feel that they have arrived. Of course, the lyrics in the songs, the crap on the TV and the videos, and the almost continuous intake of certain substances only serve to drive them deeper into that mindset. So boys seek to become men real fast, just in a desperate effort to be competitive, but they do so at the expense of their education, and with extreme frequency, their freedom and their lives. (See comment 6t) But boys do not become men, and girls women, in that way. They become human collateral damage. Growth of an individual can only take place if intellectual, spiritual and social nourishment occur. None of this can happen if we ignore that most precious of organs in the body. I'm talking about our **brain, it** is not being exercised sufficiently. It is the only organ in our bodies which ca allow us to understand ourselves and our potential, and enable us to contribute significantly to our families and our nations. (See comment 6u) It is our major instrument of personal and national liberation and growth. It is our repository for our education, which according to Malcolm X, is our passport to the future. So those who have no education will not have much of a future. (See comment 6v) What Malcolm might have said were he alive in today's world is that those who do not have an education don't have much of a present! (See comment 6w) Our baby girl was never encouraged o develop her brain and her intellectual skills. The emphasis during formative years was on other areas, physical and notional, of herself. She was, therefore, robbed of her chance to discover herself and her true potential as a person. (See comment 6x) Told that she was pretty, and sexy and stupid and stuff like that, she adopted other people's definition of her. She accepted an image of herself as a fridge, to be opened and closed at the convenience of others, albeit at an 'entry' fee which she would be sure to collect, so that she might keep that fridge stocked for as long as possible. (See comment 6y) Although for her, there is no perception of "long term". Ask her next time you see her what she wants to be doing 15 or 20 years from now. You might draw the biggest blank or the most unrealistic response imaginable. And ask her mother what she thinks of what her daughter is doing with her life. She is likely to tell you: "Me can't go wid she, Buddy!" Ask her teacher, and you are likely to hear that try as he/she might, the child and her mother are impossible to deal with, and the mother never believes the terrible accusations leveled at her daughter. Ask the young boys about their future and you might shiver. In many cases, their mothers are even more despairing than in the case of the mothers of the girls. They are definitely more frightened. But as in the case of the girls, the parents have dropped the ball with the boys. If you follow my story, you might wonder what on earth this country, this region, this planet will be like in 15, 20, 30 years from now, if we don't get on top of this mess now. (See comment 6z) That is, if my 'nancy story' has any truth at all to it. (See comment 6aa) If not, let's just roll merrily along. However, take a little time and have a look at what's going on. And after watching, discuss and act accordingly. (See comment 6) Until next time, Plenty Peace.

Comments Six:

a. *This may come as a surprise to you: the market in any commodity is determined by what people, of their freewill, want to buy. The buoyancy of any commodity market is directed by those operating in it. Not Dwyer Astaphan! So you do not agree with the popular taste. That is your prerogative but you cannot control it and thank God, it looks like the players in it do not give any kind of monkey's-fart about your opinion!*

b. *Yeah! You are full of those fantasy type of tales, which can serve to indicate the state of your mind. Some may find those tales of yours entertaining; others may pronounce them as manifestations of something more sinister. However, I see them as dangerous because you have this way of starting out with a dream and ending up passing those dream based notions as factual.*

c. *It is about time that reminders resembling such character are built into your wonderings. Too often some of your stories begin in similar vein and end up with the appearance of being factual. I hope this note is remembered for the remainder of this article.*

d. *Me thinks that you are getting carried away with this fantasy of yours: going over-board. It is unbelievable, in reality that many if any parents would behave to the level that your imagination has sunk. Even in the most remotest event that anything approaching your description is detectable, the odds would be so small, that it would not be significant for this country.*

e. *What discipline? The collective you, does not much, if anything to encourage discipline. In cases where conscientious individuals, in their line of duty, try to instill discipline in their area of influence. When such activity is brought to your attention, instead of giving your support; you pull the 'ground' from beneath the one who dared to stand up for good discipline. However, you probably had your tongue in cheek when that word was used.*

f. *If the poor woman's situation is as bad as you paint it, where is she going to find the inspiration, the time or the capability to reflect at the level imposed by you. There will be too many distractions both of the physical and mental variety. Once more, your logic does not ring true!*

g. *Hold on one minute there! One does not have to be socially disadvantaged as your imaginary person; nor has one got to be a woman, in order to experience indecent dependence or to be most vulnerable. Others with those experiences abound in the shapes of persons who disagreed or had differing views that did not coincide with those of the ruling elite and most of those had educational experiences beyond and above the required standards. This time, it's your blinkered logic which makes the nonsense here!*

h. *Hold on there! It does not follow that because your mythical girl-woman is a trollop, means that she is disruptive, violent or even disobedient. It is quite feasible that because of the extra curricular life-style, when she is in school, she will be resting, perhaps nodding off in her chair; since her energies would be reserved for her nocturnal activities. The other point is that if she has such autonomy at home; chances are that she won't be bothered to attend school.*

i. *If as the sentence suggests: the home is the most important influence in personality moulding. Why aren't you and your siblings carbon copies of each other? Since your early experiences, in your home were similar? The fact that you all turned out differently contradicts that assertion. The truth of what makes a person what they turn out to be is not scientifically proven. I will not deny that in some cases a good home leads to acceptable personality types. However, it does not always work that way. On the other hand, your earlier example of Sam Condor illustrates that the reverse is also true at times.*

j. *Most definitely wrong again! Just because you say so, does not mean that the idea of trading home values with those existing outside or can be balanced and traded as equitably. There exists a host of influence and dynamics, some of which can not even be identified, much less quantified. Such mental socialistic principles are not necessarily practical.*

k. *Seems to me like you are not sure of anything, or put another way, just fishing around looking for differing reasons why the home should be used as a pin cush-*

ion for your hypothetical 'responsibility corner'. A number of families, usually live in that style but they cannot be blamed for the ills of society. Yes, they have their personal and family problems but not to the extent suggested by you. More to the point, it is the greed detected from you and those of your colleagues who boast that they will never be poor again. They are the images that other greedy people see and attempt to emulate.

l.   *It is questionable weather or not true democracy exists here, under the perpetual cloud of vindictiveness and greed. That though, is no wonder since the quality of our leadership would be amongst the worst possible. Reasons for that analysis have been mentioned in various places so far and would no doubt surface again elsewhere. But when Labour leaders, who began in offices from humble roots. Eleven years later some are millionaires and the others, not much further behind and these are LABOUR MINISTERS! Some thing has to be wrong with that picture!*

m. *Don't forget as a person, representative and minister!*

n.   *Young people begin to feel their sexuality, well before the legal age of consent. Young people also do not know too much about the legal age of consent and those who heard about it, if not properly constrained or tutored in that regard will be have a hard time resisting the temptation. People do not walk around thinking: 'my gosh, the legal age of consent is set at eighteen, therefore I must not break the law'. To think that is how life works is to be 'out of this world'. Why in ancient times, the position of 'chaperon' was in place in most homes of quality. Why do you think that was?*

o.   *Hey! It is your fantasy. You can make it mean anything at all you want it to, just so long as you keep it fictional. I know how you like to turn these dreams into realities!*

p.   *Of course your imaginary situation, if it were real, would not be fair; so is a number of consequences from innocent actions which take place every day. Some as results of accidents; others innocently and more from deliberate schemes. Of which it is felt that actions of elected officials fall in the latter category. So before you work yourself up into some kind of frenzy, some reflection might reveal a greater source of unfairness to the citizens of this country.*

q.   *You can speak for your self in accepting blame for some fictitious action by some imaginary 'girl-woman'. Even if she was real, none of that blame would have anything to do with me or innocent by-standers. Apart from those immediately involved, the main blame has to lie firmly at the gate of those elected to direct the way normal folks behave. Part of the problem though, is that you ministers are so distracted with issues other than what is good for society, putting self above country, thereby allowing damaging effects to slip through to the people you were elected to defend and protect. Afterwards, as failure in any dimension shows itself, illogical officials like you, attempts to rope in society with ideas, suggesting your failures are all our faults.*

r. *You are doing it again: slipped over from your imaginary world, into the real one. As per usual you are getting carried away with a situation that you have not established, but have dreamed. Therefore, you're writing without any proper basis and is in danger confusing people or sowing wrong conclusions and that is dangerously irresponsible.*

s. *That is due to the fact that you ministers help yourselves to the giant share of resources. Thus, when it boils down to paying those who provide worthwhile service to the community, teachers being at the top of that group; there is hardly a fair proportion shared out to them. Therefore, is it any wonder that your derived 'brat' will have more money than his teachers. All you are saying is that your administration, pay teachers less than the pocket change of bad young men!*

t. *Perhaps they conclude also that because you and your cabinet colleagues victimize educated persons of 'good and honest' character, to the extent of denying such individuals from contributing to the development of the country by using the hard and costly acquired education. They see education gone to waste when one with internationally recognized degrees, put to work under others without equivalent or very inferior qualifications! What do you think that kind of example does to encourage young persons to take education seriously?*

u. *By all means exercise the brain. Not though, ignoring the other parts of the body. All of it needs to be exercised, so that those other parts, muscles and sub systems do not seize-up; that obesity does not overtake those parts which are not popular during normal usage, gets the proper work-out needed to keep them lubricated and in good order. Indeed, without the remainder of the body parts functioning properly; the brain in its turn will fail to function efficiently!*

v. *These grandiose announcements are issued by your standards, which does not necessarily be anywhere near what is accurate. Every individual's future is at his or her behest, not by your grand scheme of things. There are uneducated persons right here on this island who has done wonderful things with their lives. It is even the case that once turned off from the education system for whatever reason, individuals decide to settle for whatever their horizons contain; rather than what others decide should be the case. To my way of thinking a person's future is for that individual to decide, within the parameters that exists; not some pontificator!*

w. *He already said it! In the quote made above! Means the same thing! Don't quite see the point of the repetition?*

x. *Because you defined her like that! It could be that in reality, no such specimen exists. Therefore that kind of analysis to a fictional individual by you is what's known as: self fulfilling, which really is a waste of everybody's time.*

y. *Are you not confusing yourself somewhat? Mixing your metaphors certainly confuses the point you are trying to make and in so doing is bound to confuse a lot of people!*

z. *Now that your dreaming is near its end, let me tell you something: like everything else, life moves on in a direction that is beyond the control of any one individual, group or even President Bush—type alike. Each of us, 'ministers of governments' and all, contributes towards the building blocks in our own unique way. Each day that dawns brings with it newness for every person alive, some nice and others not-so-nice. You cannot turn back the clock! Where we are now is the sum of historical experiences which led us to this spot. All the belly-aching in the world is not going to change it. Like it or not, that is the way life is. It is not every person that is going to achieve the excellence that you feel the need to impose. Just like a classic 'Probability Spread': There will be a few at the top, more in the first quartile, peaking in the centre and then falling away to a few at the tail end. That is the rule which Napierian theory prescribes to all natural entities and life, communities, even countries are natural entities.*

aa. *Methinks 'truth' is not the word. Perhaps the word you were looking for would have been 'realism' and the answer has to be a big fat NO! It was all in your imagination.*

ab. *The area of action belongs to you. As the minister, that is your job, it is what you are being overpaid to do. Stop belly-aching, stop day-dreaming and get on with the job. Oh! I forgot, you haven't got a clue have you? Don't know where to start. So the next best thing is to rope everyone else in with your nonsensical articles based on hypothetical stories or by being abusive to those who do not share your views. Stop press!! It has just occurred to me that before you can get on with fixing the problem, it is necessary to identify what that problem is and you have not really done that? You do not even know what it is you have to fix! All these idiotic articles are really stabs in the dark; casting a wide net to see what is caught; fishing exercises to discover what can be hooked up on?*

12 March 2005

Inspired and God-blessed as he was, Abraham probably did not have the slightest clue as to the full consequences of his migration, thousands of years ago, from a little village named Ur, in ancient Babylon, now part of Iraq, to the land of Canaan, now part of Israel. Judaism, Christianity and Islam all lay claim to old Abe. Indeed, they are often referred to as "the Abrahamic religions". And all three observe and revere holy ground in separate areas of the city of Jerusalem in modern day Israel. Of course, from their separate starting perspectives, and with the passing of time and circumstance, the three developed different practices and traditions. And more often than not, the differences, which have come to define **each** of them, have outweighed their underlying common denominator (we are all children of the same One God) which defines them **all.** In the process, different, indeed sometimes vastly different, political and other philosophies and lifestyles have evolved among these three religions, reflecting the different directions that they have taken through the ages. Sometimes it is these very differences in religious tradition and outlook that have been used to create and worsen strife among different communities, societies and nations, filling the pages of history with wars, tears and destruction. Indeed, more men and civilizations have been tormented, dehumanized, decimated and destroyed in the name of Abraham and God than in any other name or cause. (See comment 7a) This has been caused by two things: (1) the inherent need for human beings to be **'of faith',** and (2) the diabolical and calculating manipulation of this need for individuals who, throughout history, have had a great lust for earthly conquest, dominance and glory. (See comment 7b) Such a mix has exposed 'the faithful' to pain and anguish in these deadly games of human puppetry and theocratic blasphemy. Poor Abraham, nestled as he may be in the eternal safety and comfort of heaven, loses his smile every time he looks down on the carnage and pillage mankind has so often caused throughout the ages in his (Abraham's) name, and the sacrileges which we have committed in the name of our Heavenly Father. (See comment 7c) Yes, indeed, many of the world's political crises **today** are connected to extremism and fanaticism among those same three Abrhamic religions. Now, in the geographical area where these three religions are said to have originated (I'm talking about the Middle East), the politics is particularly charged with religion. So much so that over the centuries following Abraham's migration there, (See comment 7d) the area has endured perhaps more volatility and political instability than anywhere else in the world, although colonial and post-colonial Africa is right up there on the 'sufferation' scale. (See comment 7e) (By the way, why is it that the birthplace of the Judaism, Christianity and Islam (the Middle East) and the cradle of human civilization (Africa) have been so relentlessly and ruthlessly ripped apart by strife and stress throughout history?). But, as I have said, the extreme influence of religion upon politics is not unique to the Middle East. Yes, most states refer to themselves as "secular". And they are correct, because the Church organization itself is not in actual or even virtual control of the **apparatus** of those states. Nor would it necessarily want to be. Nevertheless, the religious community and people's religious faith are powerful forces in any political scenario. That is true for Kittitians and Nevisians as it is for the Israelis, Palestinians, Egyptians, Iraqis, Iranians, Saudis, Afghans and everybody else. (See comment 7f) But it is far worse in the Middle East which is a religious **and** political fireball. And their 'fire' is not fuelled by religion only. It is also fuelled by that black hydrocarbon liquid called **oil.** That part of the world has been blessed (or is it cursed) with an abundance of **oil,** which happens to be the substance **which drives the world economy.** Imagine all the cars, the planes, the generators, the lighting systems, etc. I am sure that most people recognize that the typical business model in any area of commercial enterprise calls for consumption, consumption and more consumption, in order to create growth on the top line and the bottom line. And politicians throughout the world, who like to report ongoing economic growth, depend heavily on business people to help drive their economies, creating jobs, and all that good stuff. (See comment 7g) So the businessmen need to grow the economies, the economies need the oil, the politicians need both the businessmen and the oil, and the Muslims have the oil (or at least the biggest chunk of it). So the businessmen and the politicians have to work together in a symbiotic relationship (basically, referred to as 'hand-go-hand come') to make sure that the oil keeps flowing. (See comment 7h) This, to a significant extent, explains the corporatization of economic and foreign policy among the major nations of the world. A 'corporatization' which tends also to heavily influence, even dominate, national development programs of the world's less resourceful nations. It is frightening to know that the part of the world on which we are **most** dependant to drive the world economy, is also the most volatile and dangerous. (See comment 7i) Religion and oil, and politics and economics. Calamitous!!! You will therefore appreciate, not only the interest which the world's more powerful nations have in the Middle East, but also the critical impact on every single nation in the world by what happens in the Middle East. For example, let's look at oil prices. Prior to 1973, oil producing Muslim states never really took a strong stand as a group to protect their collective interests as oil producers. However, a series of hostile events between Israel and neighbouring Syria, Lebanon and Egypt in the late 1960's and early 1970's caused the oil producers to form an organization called the Oil Producing and Exporting Countries (OPEC), to take a stand in 1973 in order to demonstrate their displeasure at what they saw as a pro-Israel bias by the west in the long-standing hostilities between Israel and its neighbouring Arab nations. The price of oil went up, big time. If that increase were to have occurred today, we would see a price of US$90.00 per barrel, I'm told. (See comment 7j) So, not surprisingly, great panic ensued, as production costs of **everything** skyrocketed, which meant substantial **inflation,** and corporate survival and national and international stability came under serious threat. The American economy, 'driven' in no small measure by the automobile industry, felt major shocks, as consumers began to cut back, as US automakers began scratching their heads in search of smaller vehicles that were more fuel-efficient. But that would take time. Meanwhile, there was also born a new awareness of the need to conserve and to seek alternative sources of energy. Indeed, a new outlook on the earth and its physical and other resources was created. And that was good. (See comment 7k) But for the moment action was needed. And the ever-alert Japanese car manufacturers, with resources and aggression, moved in and capitalized on the unreadiness of their US counterparts, and the rest is history, because since then Japanese automobiles have secured a dominant share of the global market. Indeed, this masterstroke of common sense and opportunism by Japanese providers of goods and services, engendering exponential growth in business for them throughout the length and breadth of the planet. Not by any stretch of the imagination being a Japan, we in St. Kitts & Nevis were not equipped to capitalize on anything, so, apart from the many lessons which were to be learned from the experience, we, like nearly every other nation, took some serious knockabout. (See comment 7l) But, as I have said, lessons were to be learned. Nations, on an individual and collective basis, introduced programs in the ensuing years, some significant, others not, to buffer the impact of such a thing recurring. Some efforts included exploration for additional oil resources, development of alternative and renewable energy supplies, conservation, improved energy efficiency in engine and systems designs, improved awareness of limited global resources and of the need to protect them, and so on. I am disappointed that greater efforts have not been made to secure alternative and renewable energy supplies. (See comment 7m) Some nations introduced pricing mechanisms to protect their consumers. St. Kitts & Nevis was one of those nations. The idea behind it was to provide a buffer to cover the volatility in external pricing, rather than exposing the consume to price increases at local pump every time the external price increased. (See comment 7n) The Government would benefit from a small portion of the price as long as prices stayed low, but if prices rose, then the Government's margin would decrease, and perhaps even disappear. Government could even go into the 'red', which is exactly what happened as a result of rising oil prices in the global markets over the years. Therefore, the Government has been going into its pocket (that's yours and my pockets) to help keep the price of gas LPG steady. This major financial sacrifice on the part of the Government has contributed to the increase in the national debt. (See comment 7o) But with prices exceeding US$30, then US$40, then US$50 per barrel, Government simply could not hold to the old price of EC$ 6.60 per gallon, which had been introduced in July 2000, when the price of crude oil on the world market was **US$ 32 per barrel.** As I write this article, on Tuesday 8 March, 2005, the price is **US$ 55 per barrel.** Let me put it this way. The barrel price today represents a **72% increase** on the price of July 2000. A similar increase in price at the retail level, that is, at the pump, would have taken us to EC$ **11.35 per gallon.** You will therefore appreciate how stoutly Government would have resisted the urges of the economics theorists who may have advised that the price at the pump should always directly reflect the world price. In other words, the consumer must always bear the full burden. This is the practice most countries, where Governments have simply stepped aside and left market forces to operate essentially on their own. (See comment 7p) Not EC$ 11.35 a gallon, man! The matter has been discussed widely in the public, so I don't have to tell you that our pricing here is still lower than in several of our OECS sister countries. (See comment 7q) Does that give us any comfort? No. But we are comfortable in the fact the we tackled this problem with altruism, reason and compassion, and in a democratic and consultative manner. (See comment 7r) What we would hope for is altruism, reason and compassion among providers of goods and services. I am bothered by people who expect this altruism, reason and compassion to come from Government **only.** And I am bothered when scavenging and unscrupulous sellers of goods and services take advantage of consumers in situations like this, instead of being decent and try to maintain the support, confidence and respect of their customers. (See comment 7s) They must never forget what the Japanese did to American automakers after the 1973 world oil crisis. And if they keep their wits and their consciences, they might avoid the inevitable rush of bright, opportunistic entrepreneurs who will inevitably come through from this crisis with better offerings for consumers. This is a great time for optimists and conscionable opportunists. It is they who will gain from the present situation. It is they who will **adjust, reprioritize and capitalize.** And they will succeed because they will carry the benefit of their creativity to consumers throughout the world. Here in St. Kitts and Nevis. I pray that our suppliers and providers will be among the enlightened of the world. (See comment 7t) In this process of global adjusting, reprioritizing and capitalizing, the Middle East must begin to settle down, as the world's major nations and nation groups redesign economic and foreign policies, in an effort to achieve greater equity and balance. And all of that terrible wasting of humanity and the earth's precious resources might he halted, even reversed. In that case, old Papa Abraham might get his chance to keep his smile, at long last. Hey, I am an optimist. In the name of Abraham and God our father, this is my prayer. (See comment 7u) Until next Time. Plenty Peace.

Comments Seven:

a. *Would disagree with your comparative statistic. Claiming other people's space have been more widely used as reasons for war than religion. Sometimes they overlap, but if you analyze the various skirmishes-cum-outright-war. Example, the Second World War was not about religion in the main and more people suffered during that period than any other before or after.*

b. *It must run in the genes! You could well be talking about yourself! It must be a real pain to have so few numbers of people, like the Federation's population to play with? If only the numbers were in the millions, with you occupying a similar lofty position! WOW! You would have had a field day! Thank God for small mercies!*

c. *What about the psychological sacrilege and other ills, perpetrated by officials elected to serve, then turns around victimizes and bullies those who should be served. Takes much more than the fair share from resources of the land elected in, then bores the country stinking with unceasing idiotic lectures. Wonder what our Heavenly Father is thinking about all that? How much longer will he suffer his children to bear such philosophical carnage?*

d. *You probably know that Abraham existed long before Christianity or put another way, Christianity was not around when Abraham migrated. It might have been less confusing to readers if that distinction was made in your wonderings.*

e.   *If a 'sufferation' scale is being compiled; the black forefathers of us Kittitians and other Negro descendants across the Caribbean and the Americas has to be quite high up on it. Those cross Atlantic journeys were no joking matter you know? Of course you don't know! After all, your ancestry is not the same as ours! They came to exploit our forefathers. Some would say that the exploitation continues; only in a different, more subtle manifestation!*

f.   *That is why you politicians are always dragging 'God' into your meanderings, where ever you think fit. Whether genuine belief in what the word symbolizes is there, as far as you guys are concerned, is left to those on the receiving end of what you write or say to interpret. To the skeptics of your utterances, deitary mentions are really difficult to accept, since your actions imply against any kind of belief of a superior being. The impression is to convey to the masses that your system of belief is the same as theirs and all because you know that people's religious faith are powerful forces!*

g.   *Included in the phrase"all that good stuff' has to be entries like: create opportunities for our leaders to take more than their fair share of the country's resources; tempt elected officials to adopt personal get-rich-quick schemes and implement them for the world to see that one time, hand-to-mouth individuals are now local 'lords of all they purview', thumbing their noses at those who elected or helped them onto their ladders of notoriety. However, it is to be noted that: all good things come to an end.*

h.   *Next time you 'set about' any prominent business or the Chamber, it might be important to remember your so called 'symbiotic relationship'. It would be handy also if it is borne in mind when attempts are made to bully local organizations to finance some of your schemes. It is suspected though, that when writing these articles, 'grandiose ideas' invade your cranium and those thoughts encourage the forgetting of past idiocies. That is until the next time.*

i.   *Everything works according to scale. The world power implied works on a large scale, moving nations to actions or whatever their will may be. In essence though, you guys do the same sort of thing on a smaller scale to us; those who elected you! Thus in addition to volatile and dangerous, as far as we are concerned you could add a few more definitions like: vicious, vindictive, personally greedy and the time is approaching when the nerve would be summoned to use that 'C' word.*

j. *When that happened, no special effects were singled out for the benefit of indirect consumers here. Of course, the knock-on petrol costs were reflected at pumps. Nothing like what you lot did to the citizens of this country. As I write, the cost per barrel is US$75.00 and even while it was below US$60.00; you saddled the residents, with a 'Fuel Surcharge', whose effect was to raise the cost of electricity by some 80%. Even when the price of oil leapt upwards as you described, the residents did not get penalized in the manner like today. Thanks to the lack of sensitivity and concern for those who live here.*

k. *You assumed power as part of a government over ten years ago, knowing what you have just written and in that time, there has been no leadership in that direction by your regime! That is truly scandalous! All this time, you knew of the need to be energy conscious and instead of guiding the citizenry in a conservational direction; you have sought to get fatter on channeling resources in personal directions instead of getting the nation better organized to be more self reliant, energy-wise. History will not forgive you for that!*

l. *Of course that would happen and the same thing would occur again. Indeed, we are on the precipice of history repeating itself. It is not because the resources are lacking, especially, the human variety; it is because your government do not trust its citizens to deliver what they are capable of, they are not supported when the 'going gets tough'. You prefer to bring in foreigners, especially if they are light of skin and those outsiders tend to make the situation worse. Generally, the advisors of your choosing tend to be no brighter than you lot and so we plunge from bad to worse. Then on top of that, there is the political tribalism factor. There are perfectly professionally qualified persons with experience to solve most of our problems. Plus, with so much expertise that can offer or formulate solutions to avoid future related problems. However, as soon as you assume office, these highly skilled persons are shunted to the professional 'scrap heap', never to be resuscitated, even though the expertise are desperately needed. All because, their political affiliation is different from your party. There has got to be a lot wrong with the embedded logic behind that mentality!*

m. *Especially here in the tropics where we have more than our fair share of sunshine and wind energies. There could have been incentive for nationals or any investor for that matter, to research and develop natural driven energies generation systems. Therefore, your disappointment should really be self-directed.*

n. *Balderdash! Then like now, whenever oil prices for whatever reasons move upwards and the trend is generally upwards. What you political types do is to penalize the population, so that your margin of comfort does not have to deteriorate, even if it is only incremental. Politicians in government are especially prone to cover themselves when things begin to look bleak and that cover usually tend towards protecting whatever 'perks' the rest of the community do know about.*

o. *The theory sounds alright but the actuality of what the government you belong to has been up to. The frequent increases in utilities and price at the pumps suggest that not for a moment, have Government approached anything resembling a loss, never mind digging into its pockets. Would appear that there is some kind of margin, below which when the price falls; the cost to the public goes up. Thus, in spite of what ever frame such mechanism is dressed in, it is the public who always picks up the tab. Lately, of course, Government have devised an automatic method of screwing the masses by tying increases of oil on the world market directly to the public and that's as sensitive as it is possible to get. They call it 'Fuel Surcharge.' That stroke covers a multitude of sins!*

p. *It could be argued that the consumers were exploited before prices increased. In that Government overcharged them until the rising prices erased profit margins. From that perspective, it would have been kinder to follow advice given by the economic theorists, since increases would reflect only those on the world market. What we now have is a basic price which includes the cost of oil from when it was pegged and on top of that, there is the 'Fuel Surcharge' reflecting oil at market prices, in essence the electricity user is paying for the same commodity twice! How long that will be got away with has to be left to be seen!*

q. *That is a stupid comparison! Our sister-islanders work for more money than we do; their politicians are paid less; they are not as heavily taxed as we are and a host of other advantages they enjoy compared to us. To pick that one dimension, if at all there is any truth in it, does not say anything worthwhile at all!*

r. *I am not sure that it is true that any of your compassionate, democratic or consultative references were or is true. I certainly do not remember being consulted individually, as part of the community or if there was any national consultation process invoked. An announcement was made and that was it! In fact it is fairly certain that none of the claims made at this juncture, ever took place!*

s.   *You think that you are the only one who is bothered. The whole of the thinking fraternity of this Federation also has reason to be bothered! We are bothered by this New Labour who initially refused to pay the outgoing prime minister from the last regime his self imposed pension and then in short order legislated for themselves to receive, after serving one term, a pension which is tagged to 100% percent of their salary, for life; to allocate for themselves a pension that is over ten times the percentage rate awarded to pensioners; whose allowances are of such magnitude that it is estimated that they do not need to touch their salaries for existential purposes, persons who applied to be elected as labourites are now aristocrats in the style of pre-colonial masters. The fed-up-ness is firmly in the camp of the masses I'll have you know!*

t.   *Is that why you have brought to these shores so many merchants of eastern origin? Because they are optimists and opportunists? Is that an effort to force the pace? So that you can boast that your ideas were worth the chance taking? Dwyer, you are a short sighted and blinkered fool. Those foreign people who pepper Porte Zante, have no interest in the development of this country. Like the Jews, they will suck whatever juice they can find here and squeeze it out in their countries of origin, just like your ancestors intended to do when they first came here and fooled the masses into thinking that they were on our side. You have flooded this country with eastern types, offering them all kinds of incentives, which really could have gone to our people, who we know has commitment to this Federation; instead you litter the place with speculators of your own 'gene' type. Perhaps that is your latent purpose to swamp us with those of your genetic kind and in time, we would approach the ethnic stew that prevails in Trinidad and Guyana?*

u.   *Papa Abraham's smile would be even more meaningful to us here if those who we chose to represent, protect and defend us were honest with themselves and us. He would be well pleased if they would only honour the national motto: "Country above self" rather than their version of: "Self above Country" as they have paraphrased it. And an appropriate prayer would be: Dear God, help them to realize that no matter how much greed they could muster, in the race as to who will be the richest politician before Labour is dethroned, that in time they, like the rest of us are going to die and leave all of our ill gotten gains behind anyway. In much the same way that Papa Bradshaw's accumulated wealth has withered, like blood in the sand!*

19 March 2005

I have been receiving much feedback on my article of two weeks ago in which I addressed some of the sexual and social problems facing our youth. (See comment 8a) I'll share some with you. An 18-year old female had been told of the article and had read it. She came to talk with me. She said that she had been adopted, and that between the ages of 12 and 14 she had been having sexual intercourse with her 'father'. "Why did you allow him to do that?" I asked. She answered that she was afraid that he might put her out of the home, or otherwise victimize her. She said that she had been so cowed by him that she had not even told her 'mother'. She revealed the man's identity to me in strictest confidence. I was disgusted. We had a good conversation. As we spoke, her mood swung between cheerfulness and gloom. Her self esteem and confidence levels were quite low. But somehow I felt that she was going to try her best to develop a positive outlook and make something of her life. (See comment 8b) Yet, she was clearly still quite fragile. For example, out of the blue she asked me: "You think I'm fat?" Now this is a young woman about 5'3" with a figure of perhaps 33-23-35 and weighing, I would guess, about 110lbs. I said to her: "Why do you ask that question?" She replied that her last boyfriend had told her that she was fat. I said to her: "Girl you aren't anywhere close to being fat!" I said: "Who is he anyway?" She did not reveal his name, but she told me that he is a policeman, age 28. I asked: "When did the two of you become boyfriend and girlfriend?" She said: "When I was 16. I was still in school". "And why did you all fall our?" I asked. She said that he was too bossy and possessive. She told me about other relationships, how they started, and so on. She was 'easy' because she not only felt cheap, but she also found a sense of acceptability for herself in giving her sexual virtues to these men. She had a problem saying no to men who were flattering her and sweet-talking her, as against her 'father's forceful, bullying approach. And while all of this emotional havoc was being wrought on the poor child, her education suffered. To her credit, she seems to have garnered sufficient inner strength to begin turning her life around, assisted in no small measure by a solid and compassionate lady who is nurturing and guiding her. Thank God for that. But, as I said, she is quite fragile. Then there is this other young woman. She is 19. She tells me that when she was 15 and in high school, a male teacher kept **'putting question'** to her and promising her the world. Eventually, she gave in to him, flattered by the attention of a big man. However, and not surprisingly, the relationship was fraught with stress and grief, causing her severe emotional distress, and a break-down of discipline and the chain of command in the classroom. To make matters worse, there was a lot of tongue wagging in and around the school. You know school children already! (See comment 8c) She did not reveal the identity of her paramour. And, like the young lady referred to above, she too came out of the experience quite messed up emotionally. Then there is this 16-year old girl, who went through Forms 1 and 2 in high school at the A-1 level: **1A-1** and **2A-1.** A bright child. But a 22-year old man took a liking to her when she was in Form 2. She is now in **4 G-4** (I think that is the designation of her class), and is a regular offender against class and school discipline. In addition, her poor mother, already saddled with having to raise five other children, all younger, has virtually no con-trol over her. The mother tells me that she has made all types and financial and other sacrifices in order to satisfy the child's demands, yet nothing seems to have worked since the 'love affair' with the old man began. (See comment 8d) the girl is now itching to move out of her mother's home to go and live with the man. He is a pretty charismatic fellow. He works as a labourer. It doesn't look like he plans to further his education. So unless he is consistently industrious or he wins the lottery or hits some other jackpot, and can keep out of trouble, his future might not be all that bright. (See comment 8e) So here is how this story is likely to unfold. If the girl has her way, she probably can kiss education and the good life goodbye. She will soon become a mother, totally unprepared financially and emotionally, and the cycle of misery will continue for her, for her kids, and for the whole society which will be faced with the burden of taking care of her and her children. (See comment 8f) We may even have to pay a greater price to pro-tect ourselves from them. We are also seeing the emergence of girl gangs in the schools and communities. So girls such as those to whom I referred above would find 'guidance' and support among their peers. I wish I could say something right now to lift your depression, Dear Reader, but I can't. (See comment 8g) How-ever, instead of dwelling forever on the girls, I will, as an equal opportunity observer and commentator, shift now to the boys. Earlier this week I received a phone call from a teacher at Irish Town School. That teacher had called me on two previous occasions for the same reason. Vandalism. Classrooms at the school had been vandalized. Three boys were suspected. I visited the school, and was horrified to see the extent of the damage, and also very disturbed at the thought that so much anger could be allowed to fester in the heart of the perpetrator(s).

This was clearly the work of a troubled mind, or troubled minds. And immediate action was needed. I was told that one of the boys now attended Project Strong, so I immediately went to see Washington 'Washie' Archibald. Washie was very helpful and insightful. I thanked him and moved on. Shortly after leaving Washie, I visited the father of one of the boys. The father threw up his hands in despair and begged for the boy (who is 15) to be locked up. He said that he couldn't get the boy to attend school, and that the boy had been taken from him and placed with the mother. He felt that the mother should be locked up too. I then moved to Camp Springfield, where the same 15-yeaqr old boy and a 14-year old boy who lives in Buckley's but attends school is Sandy Point, had just been taken by a couple of soldiers. The Buckleys/Sandy Point boy told me that he did not attend school that day or the day before because sports day was coming up on Friday. I asked him what sense that statement made. He had no answer. I asked him about his mother. No answer. Clearly he doesn't like school, and so he just doesn't attend. His parent(s) are not in control of him. **Their bad! They should be held responsible for him and his actions.** (See comment 8h) The third boy had not been apprehended by that time. But, as fate would have it, the soldiers had picked up the two boys in the Greenlands area, and had discovered that they had just broken into a home there. And guess whose home! **The home of the third boy!** Do you believe that? I said to one of them: "It's bad enough you all stay out of school. But you the break into somebody's home and steal things. And then look whose home! Your partner's home! How can you steal from him?" you know what he said in response? **"Well, he does tief from me too".** (See comment 8i) Absolutely unbelievable! These are three boys who, under the law, **must** be in school, and their parents **must** be called to account to the law for their truancy. And the appropriate authorities will have to step in and monitor children and parents in these matters. This nonsense needs to be stopped now. (See comment 8j) By the way, speaking about parents being called to account, remember that the curfew program is on, and children under 15 found wandering or loitering on the streets after 10pm and failing to show to the satisfaction of a constable that he or she is engaged on an urgent or unusual errand may be stopped and taken to the nearest police station and held until released to their parent or guardian. Remember also that the parent or guardian can be fined up to $200 by the Court. I personally believe that the age should be raised to 16 and that the fine should be raised from $200. I invite public discussion of this. But the general public ought to know that loitering and vagrancy laws do not apply only to persons under 15. Police, and this is a worldwide thing, can always ask people to move on and to stop loitering in public places, if the police reasonably believe that to be the right thing to do. In the circumstances. Some people believe that once they are in a public place they can stay there for as long as they like and they can do in that place what they like. That's not so at all. So from time to time police will ask people to move on. It has happened to me many times in my years living abroad. It has happened to me here as well. And I am calling on people here to understand that the law must be obeyed and order must be maintained. (See comment 8k) I get upset when some citizens of this nation would act so disdainfully and irresponsibly towards the law here at home, yet they are so meek and respectful towards the laws in another man's land. They get on like 'dut bikes' when given an instruction or asked a question by a police officer, but when they are in New York, they put their tails between their legs, and obey. (See comment 8l) Remember, it's not only charity that begins at home. Respect and order do too! Let's get back to the boys. A significant number of boys in the age group (10–16) in St. Kitts & Nevis are engaged in a wide range of antisocial and illegal behaviour. They do it for fun, as a lifestyle, 'to follow company' and to raise money. How do they raise the money? They steal, rob and burglarize. Some of them sell drugs. Then they sell the ill-gotten items, either directly or through someone who acts as a 'fence' for them. Usually it's the fence method that they use. In fact, these youths are often used as gofers in thieving rings organized and managed by big men and women. Yes, women too! The young boys are smaller, more lithe and agile and can get into and out of small spaces and tight situations quickly. And these attributes are exploited fully by their managers'. And the 'managers' handle the boys much the same way as pimps handle prostitutes. They pay the boys a mere fraction of the price that they will fetch when they sell the item to someone else. And they pay them for selling the drugs. Sometimes when things are slow, the managers provide the boys with a stipend to keep them on board. And when they aren't looking to steal something, they go around begging people for money. They like to go to Porte Zante, the beaches and elsewhere to beg tourists, or to hustle drugs. Some of them, as soon as they get a few dollars, run to the game arcade on Bay Road, where they blow the money in as matter as minutes. Then they go to beg, and if possible, steal again. Except for the few 'freelancers', the rest are under the strict hand of their 'managers' who are constantly on the lookout to recruit new boys to replace those who may have run out of luck, one way or the other. The boys use the money to buy cloths, food, booze, CD's, DVD's, weapons, drugs, jewelry, sex, and so on. A number of these purchases involve the 'managers' who seek ruthlessly and relentlessly to extract every ounce of energy and every penny possible out of these youngsters. (See comment 8m) Of course, the more items the boys steal, the less they would have to buy, although, as I have indicated, their 'managers' keep a close eye on them and pressure them to report on and account for every item collected in a heist. Remember, the 'managers' oftentimes select and target properties and victims for the boys. This thing is a business. Another thing the boys do is gamble. Oh yes. They congregate at various locations throughout the island to gamble. Sometimes there is over a thousand dollars in the collective pockets of these boys sitting in on the gamble. Their hours are usually 7 pm until midnight on schooldays, while there is no time limit on weekends. I say 'schooldays', but school is the furthest thing from the minds of these fellows. Yes, many of them are boys under 16, who are **supposed** to be attending school, and who live in homes with adults who are **supposed** to be responsible for them. (See comment 8n) The gambling takes place in little 'casinos', located at the backs of shops, in people's yards, under a tree somewhere, in a derelict property, etc. The casino operators collect $5.00 a hand, sometimes less. They provide food and drink (liquor too, if you please), and other goods and services, including 'fencing' services for stolen items. (See comment 8o) Some of these boys have guns. Some use 'lighter guns to scare their victims. Sometimes toy guns are used. Those who don't have guns, use knives, ice-picks, etc. The 'managers' and the 'casino' operators contaminating youth who are already vulnerable because of poor parenting, and certain institutional and systematic shortcomings in our communities. The situation is **desperate.** One of my major concerns is with the parents. I know of situations in which parents of children **known** to be involved in these activities swear to high heaven that their children are innocent little angels. I am also aware of situations in which parents have actively induced and encouraged their children to act antisocially and illegally, including sending them out to steal things to bring home. Parents **have** to be **called** to account. They **must** take responsibility. These 'managers' and 'casino' operators need to be brought o justice. And any adult caught gambling with these children or encouraging it needs to be severely punished. (See comment 8p) Tell me. What the heck are all of us fathers, mothers and other adults so busy doing that we cannot spend some quality time with our children and with the nation's children? What is it that has us adults so preoccupied that we cannot pay attention to raising the nation's youth. (See comment 8q) I caution, as I conclude, that if we do not take immediate, deliberate and concerted steps to fix this problem, we run the risk of deteriorating and degenerating to the extreme lows which have been reached in other islands in this Caribbean of ours. It can be avoided, but we must act now. And each one of us can help by taking little steps. Let's start by speaking to the boys when we see them in their school uniforms with their shirts out of their pants and their pants down over their bums. Let's tell them that they are princes and must behave accordingly, while we tell the girls that they are princesses. Let's speak to them in a loving way. Let's tell them that they are selling themselves, their school, their family, their ancestors, their generation and their nation short. Let's tell them that they can do better. Much better. (See comment 8r) Let's **insist** and **demand** that they do **better,** but we must be as respectful and compassionate as we are firm in so doing. And we can't call upon them to behave in a certain manner while we are behaving in a contrary manner. So let's give them the chance to live out their childhood and adolescence without trying to pervert and corrupt them. (See comment 8s) **Until Next Time, Plenty Peace.**

Comments Eight:

a. *Correction: you did not address the problem as claimed; you invented a situation, as you yourself called it: a nancy story. The situation was dreamed up, to which your panacea were applied. There was no reason to accept what you then wrote had any reference to real event. It was very fictitious!*

b. *Have to admit to great suspicion about these stories of yours. You are such an inventor of great tales and the speed of this one, so soon after that article does nothing to dampen my skepticism about those supposed interviews. Truth is I do not believe you!*

c. *As already stated: these tales of yours are to me very suspicious as to their originality. They sound quite plausible and if it is that there is some authenticity to them, then it is very sad that such things should happen in a minuscule society such as this one. On the other hand, we as a people are still recovering from the trauma imposed upon us by your ancestors to be 'breeders' of children stock. These inbuilt cultural traits take many generations before they are eradicated if at all that is possible Although the individuals involved are despicable, if in fact these things did occur. Nonetheless, from a sociological standpoint, we are not as bad as some of the developed countries, where sexual exploitation is a daily occurrence. Alas, in spite of the nature of such happenings, there are worst things happening to this society that are much more devastating than this preferred subject. There apparently is not a lot that you can or want to do about the complaint. However, there is much that can be done about the on going malaise that affects most. Why do you not focus on those things?*

d. *The pattern is reminiscent of happenings in the wider society: You permit certain individuals to use the law for their own benefits, others follow suit, then from among that group of law benders, some get away with it and others get perse-cuted. Those who get away with what they do tend to be so called party faithful. So called because they pay lip service to the party, but in terms of material sup-port, they fall well short. Whatever magic recipe they have, it works for them over and above the real stalwarts. For example: one contractor fellow robbed the state social security system and the workers whose contributions he took and did not pay in is on the brink of or has been forgiven his scamp-ish, criminal activities; yet others have to run the gauntlet of court hearings and fines, while the Labour party darling—boy gets away with his criminality. Thus the sexual voyeurism is well mirrored in your unfair practices!*

e. *Keep telling you that these speculations of yours about people's future prospects are somewhat like 'mouth washing' on outcomes that you do not know about or have no control over. You have to stop trying to play god! Yes, at the moment, you are a successful politician in the sense that people have voted you into office because you have a supposedly labour tag hanging on you but that does not make you into some kind of prophet or endowed with more than your fair share of wisdom. The long and short of it is that not you or anyone else knows what any person's future will be. Regardless of your tendency to think that God is in your pocket!*

f. *Anyone reading this article and do not know what goes on here might swallow that fanciful idea. If it is that the idea of society stepping in to rescue 'children at risk' is being waved here. That myth has to be instantly dismissed. It does not happen. If it was; the present abysmal state of unruly youth criminality would not be the case. For too long, the present regime has not bothered with the blatant abuse and ignorance of the state of our youth has been ignored. Therefore, the bit about society will be faced with the burden of the errors for the young girl, is just more fictional clap trap.*

g. *I am not depressed! Why should anyone copy your example and work themselves into a state, based on some 'trumped-up' situation, more likely than not, formu-lated in your own head? No, my dear writer, There is no depression, brought on by your invention going on in that head!*

h. *It is all very well making such damning observations. If the objective is to turn around these youngsters, so that in time hopefully, their energies can be acceptably focused, then surely, a more helpful and constructive approach is needed. If the animosity between the parents is at the level implied. How could it be reasonable to expect them to cooperate? That situation clearly needs some mechanism where*

Government officials could step in and take control, using whatever levers are necessary, not merely to punish, although there should be some of that! However, the ultimate aim should be an educational one!

i.   *Have you not heard that there is honour among thieves? Seems that you got a 'kick' out of getting into that detective exercise. That though is not your function. Probably, because of who you were and if the story is real, looks like some form of result was the end product. The start of the process should not have been with you. For all occurrences of that type, an arm of some authority should be available as part of a social system, which when operated would yield an outcome similar to the one you described. Instead of you meddling in juvenile crime; there should be proper machinery!*

j.   *The system goes to 'pot' when people like you who were put into office, to right the ills, as and when they show themselves. Your indignation would be more understandable if your team was more in tune with doing the right thing. What you have discovered is in fact, the result of years of neglect and by you lot. There are many examples where you personally could have given more support to officials who tried to enforce existing rules; instead, you joined the remainder of your cabinet friends to 'pull the ground' from under that individual. If the law enforcement officers felt the same about past relationship with you lot; no wonder your discovery was so revealing! It would not be at all surprising if your misguided indignation were traceable, right back to your groups' ineptitude! You guys interfere with processes all the time! Thus, when things go wrong, there is not anyone to blame but yourselves.*

k.   *I don't know where this came from or its connection with the original theme. The development is pointless, since most persons here are respecters of the law and helpful to the police, even without them knowing at times. Indeed, it is sometimes necessary to tell the police themselves what the law and their part in enforcing it should be. However, while you are admonishing us to obey and respect the law. How about leading by example. There is a law against billboards being on display after an election. You have many on display, after the last election. Every day that passes, while they (eyesores) remains on display; you are breaking the law! What about obeying the law! Or, does that law only apply to ordinary mortals and not you?*

l.   *What do you expect? Of course when anyone is in a strange land, they behave themselves. If only because of the uncertainty of their situation and rights in the guest country. When one is in their home land, they have a better idea of what their rights are and if necessary know when to stand up and defend what the freedoms of that home land entitles them to. Your getting upset with those who ask why instead of asking the police how high they should jump without thinking, that is your business. Since you show little respect for the law yourself, getting upset with others when they behave like you do, shows the level of hypocrisy some politicians harbour!*

m. *There is at least one confliction evident here: first you say that these youngsters blow their ill-gotten gains in the amusement arcades; on the other hand, they spend them on the list of acquisitions given, If they blow their cash quickly in those arcades? The addiction being what it usually is, would they not head for the amusement arcades as soon as they lost cash was replenished? It is thoughts like that which suggest that most stories are inventions. One of your experience and style would have come across that type of story in a detective magazine or comic. Why not regurgitate that kind of entertainment in this back wood?*

n. *I do not believe that! I refuse to believe that any responsible guardian will allow that sort of abuse to happen under their roof. If anything of the sort happens, then those guardians cannot be classified as responsible! In such an event, as stated already, there should and ought to be government sponsored mechanism to deal with that malaise, instead of bellyaching in the newspaper about it!*

o. *I do not believe that I am reading this! A preposterous piece of writing by a minister of government and the minister responsible for law and order at that! Instead of painting such a sorry picture of this tale of woe and assuming that your information has any credibility, the details relating to the story should be passed to those whose function it is to enforce the law and they should take action to ensure that these infringements are curtailed with the greatest possible speed! On your part; you are guilty of gross negligence for effectively condoning such outrageous carrying-ons! Do your job man!*

p. *Maybe if the parents in question, assuming that they exist, after they read this article will stop their bad practice and those with really guilty consciences, would hopefully, give themselves up! Perhaps you have forgotten what your portfolio is! IT IS YOU WHO MUST ACT!! Stop hiding behind a newspaper article. Remember this is a paper that does not find fault with you jokers! Thus, not much in the line of constructivism is going to be found in these pages and your nemeses chronicle is completely destructive where you are concerned. You are a highly paid elected official! Get your head out of the sand and start being productive!*

q.   *It is wake up time again. Firstly, the children of the nucleus family are the responsibility of the guardians or head of that family; no outsider can or is supposed to intervene, it is even frowned upon for grandparents, aunts, cousins to interfere; much less unrelated adults. It is probable that you are remembering a bygone time when grownup strangers would correct miscreant youths on the street if that were deemed necessary! The current propensity to sue or cause difficulties for any stranger rash enough to indulge in that practice in very firmly with us today! Therefore, your admonition about raising the nation's children is out of sync' with the times. Secondly, it is your function to lay the groundwork for parents and guardians do take responsibility for their wards. Therefore, to use your vernacular: what the heck are you doing about that? I can answer that question! The answer is: not much, if anything at all! When, you really should be doing more, instead of trying to pass the buck; it is your job! Why don't you do it?*

r.   *And what do we tell them when their response is unprintable? Make no mistake that the young people today, male or female, do not hesitate to tell anyone, regardless of age, where to get off when they have a mind to, especially if unsolicited advice is being offered. Even teachers who have classroom interactions with these young people in school cannot have the audacity to give unsolicited advice outside of school confines. It has to be recognized that the atmosphere you are assuming no longer exists and won't come back. Move on by leading, using tools that are relevant to this age! Discover first what tools are needed and supply the nation with them. If you do not, you will be bleeping until kingdom comes and still get no where. Do your job! PLEASE?*

s.   *From the context, the term used for corruption implies straightening out the suggested problem. Have not noticed much use of that word from your desk throughout your series and have often wondered what the reason for its avoidance might have been. Could it be that the practice implied by it is too close to home? If that was/is the case, it would not do to be pontificating about the practice, when signs of it pervade the neighbourhood! In recent times the 'grapevine' buzzed with reports of one of our ministers of Government having to dash to an island, not so far away, in order to rescue a regular cabinet attendee who happened to be carrying a briefcase, loaded with US dollars. The grapevine has the count' to be in excess of US$8 million. If there is any truth in that piece of news; then your reluctance to fly that 'c' word or any of its derivatives is understandable. Be* *assured though, that a close watch will be kept on that aspect of what comes out of your desk, or anywhere else for that matter.*

26 March 2005

Gavin Gilbert, a.k.a. 'Magilla', a man in his early twenties years, is dead. He received multiple gunshot wounds on the night of Monday, March 21st just next to his home in Saddlers Village. He was one of those at-risk youths to whom we have been trying to help stay out of an early grave. Alas, Magilla didn't make it. In a matter of days his mortal remains will be buried. He is gone. But he must not be forgotten. He must be remembered for what he was as a person, as a symbol of the very daunting domestic and social circumstances which defined and also as a symbol of these troubling times for young people and society. (See comment 9a) Magilla's short life could not have been an easy one. He seemed to rub a number of people on their wrong side. Shots had been fired at his home a few months ago. And he has been involved with melees with people on a regular basis. In short, he seemed to be a magnet for trouble. He also showed signs of intellectual clarity and sharpness, which only served to raise my hope that he would be able to ride out the difficult and shaky short and medium term of transition from the bad boy and gangsta role to solid citizen. He was a complex and contradictory person. Of all the young men whom I had initially approached in my efforts to create and build **the 'circle of peace'**, I had found Magilla to be amongst the most challenging. He had a sharp mind, yet he did foolish things. He did not excel in school or in socially accepted activities, yet he was a leader amongst similarly marginalized and neglected youths. He was shy, yet he was bold, and at times outrageously so. He had low self-esteem, telling me on one occasion that teachers and other persons in his community had often referred to him with pejorative terms such as "scum", "worthless", "good for nothing" and so on. He was earnest in his efforts to attract young females and tried to compensate for what he considered to be his limitations in the looks department. However, in our last conversation he told me that he was in love with a 16-year old schoolgirl whom he wanted to be his wife, and that he was now a one-woman man. And in my limited exposure to him, he seemed keen, even desperate, to assert and show himself to be a brave person, always, however, denying that he was anybody's leader. (See comment 9b) I remember a town hall meeting that we held at Sadlers some months ago. We had to patiently coax him into it, as his shyness seemed to be holding him back. Yet he did eventually come inside, and to my utter astonishment and delight, he rose to his feet and made some very useful comments. Not with the oratorical elegance and artistry of a Bob Bradshaw, Paul Southwell, Lee Moore or Willy Dore, but his delivery was passionate, understandable and worthy of applause (which he got from the packed 'house'). Not only that, but at the end of the meeting he approached me and said that he was sorry we had ended the meeting so soon, because he wanted to say more things. I felt very encouraged by what I saw as possibly the beginning of a turn around in the life of a very, very troubled young man. And like a number of other at-risk young men with whom I have come into contact from all areas of St. Kitts over the past five months, Magilla called on me from time to time to seek advice, guidance and reassurance on a range of matters. And like all the others, he gave me moments of great inspiration, hope and gratification, as well as moments of deep concern and anxiety, like the worrying, doting person that I am. (See comment 9d) He was at my office last week, and we looked at pictures with him and the Honourable Louis Farrakhan taken at the Prime Minister's Gala at the Marriott at the beginning of the year. Magilla had presented Farrakhan with a local painting, and had said a few words before a large and sophisticated crowd. (See comment 9d) He had acquitted himself remarkably well, notwithstanding the fact that he had been asked to do the presentation on the spur of the moment, and that he was clearly nervous. (See comment 9e) As he looked at the pictures in my office last week, I told him that the photos with Farrakhan would be part of his legacy to his children and grandchildren. He beamed with pride, as he accepted the pictures from me. As fate would have it, he left no children (at least, as far as I'm aware). (See comment 9f) And so he is gone. Of course, all kinds of theories and explanations are swirling about the place. It is for the police, assisted by citizens of conscience and a sense of righteousness and civic responsibility to make sure that the perpetrator of this heinous crime face justice. Because all of these foolish feuds are killing people. With all of the problems that people may have had with Magilla, can his killer(s) tell God and man that they did the right thing? You mean you can get up and shoot down a man just so, because you hate him? Let me tell you: this killing of individuals, first of Raffique some months ago, and now of Magilla, and the others over the past few years, are the seeds from which large scale multiple murders and massacres are sown. You know the old saying: "One, one does full basket"? Well, it's the same with these senseless acts of violence and homicide. One, one also kills a generation, and a nation. (See comment 9g) You don't have to go beyond the Caribbean region to get my point. Just look at Jamaica. Nearly 300 people slaughtered over the past 83 days. That's nearly four murders a day. Look at Haiti. Worse! Human beings, children of God, being killed like ants. Brother killing brother, sister killing sister. **We are so damned angry!** We are angry, so we kill. We have a gun, so we kill. We are we angry? And why can we not manage our anger? And as the anger goes unmanaged and unabated, the killings and maimings increase, and the value of life decreases. Remember Ruanda and Burundi? Remember Kosovo and Chechnya? What about the Sudan right now? (See comment 9h) Let me remind us that the First World War was triggered to some extent by the assassination of one man. Life must always be revered, cherished and appreciated. It must always be seen as a gift from God and not a mere something that a man can end just because he is angry and has a gun in his hand. (See comment 9i) I am hearing more and more people calling for a return to hanging. I am hearing more and more quiet, unassuming well-behaved citizens saying that they are not prepared to live in fear, to have their lives put at ransom, or to have their children harassed, beaten, threatened, and intimidated by a bunch of persons who have strength to steal, kill, hustle drugs, gamble and play basketball but no strength to do a hard day's work. More and more people are saying that the trouble makers are not going to be allowed to take control of this society. (See comment 9j) I am discouraging it, but I must confess that I am hearing more and more talk about people taking private measures to deal with this thieving, robbing, beating and killing style that has infected the minds of some members of our population. (See comment 9k) We don't want vigilantism reigning in our land. However, at the same time, people are becoming increasingly vocal in the cause of the safety of themselves, their children and their property. What we really need is for the peace forces to continue stepping up their vigilance and pre-emptive capabilities, and for the public to **partner** the police, the Defense Force, in bringing the offenders to heel! When will the men and women of this country take a stand against this? Or are we waiting for a miracle from the police, the Defense Force, the Prime Minister or the poor Minister of National Security? May Gavin 'Magilla' Gilbert' as soul rest in peace and may his life and death not be in vain. (See comment 9l) For those of us who would wish to soon forget this killing and take a hands-off attitude, I ask: **who will be next?** You? Me? Your son or daughter? Mine? The thought is frightening and troubling. Let's rise up as a people in the name of God and in the cause of peace. (see comment 9m) Until Next Time, Plenty Peace.

Comments Nine:

a.   *How on earth could you decree that he will be symbols for your wish list? It is sad that the young man should die the way he did. However, regardless of your thoughts on affinity to divinity, no magic wand could be waved to turn him into something after death that he was not in life!*

b.   *Of course, after a short interview, you knew better than he, what his leadership situation was: even though he said he wasn't; you decided that he was. Is that a strategy to tailor him into your iconic vacancy for him?*

c.   *Do you mean worrying in the sense that people are caused worry by the things you do, thereby causing them anxiety? Do you mean that you worry on other's behalf? Do you mean that you are a worry to others?*

d.   *It has to be mentioned that this was a time of year when that self same hotel took space in all the local papers, effectively banning black people form using most of the facilities there, even blacks from up north visiting for the season were turned away from the disco, on the pretext that they were full. A position that was defended by the Prime Minister and other ministers. Personally, such a ban in our own country was despicable and worse that our own Prime Minister should at that same time hold a Gala there! Was that not a flagrant disregard and disrespect for all black people within our shores then? I think it was! That was the event that Dwyer described at the section of comment!*

e.   *Was he one of the prisoners who were released to you from their prison cells at your request to the Superintendent of Prisons, so that they might attend the Prime Minister's Gala and one who you photographed clicking glasses with? Or, was he one of those who corporate St. Kitts was asked to finance so that he could enjoy the same 'Gala? It must be a real pain to be so good to those self proclaimed gangstas and left with nothing to show for it? Talk about a bum rap!*

f.   *You are always creating legacies which are without relevance. Even if the guy left children; what good would that have been to them? Would it have provided milk for them? Would it have clothed them? How would that have helped in their upbringing? Having a picture with Farrakhan, who most people here do not know of care about is not worth anything at all. Especially since, in time to come, no one will equate his contribution to humanity with any real significance. Indeed, a faction of the US Congress named Farrakhan as "an agent of intolerance". You are the only person who seem to go 'weak at the knees' at the mention of his name and my guess is that you are looking for a worthwhile mast to nail your colours to. Question is: what is that particular mast worth?*

g. *That is why, some mechanism must be put in place to stop the malaise which you are complaining about. It has been said before and most probably will again: you are paid to do the job, it falls to you to sort it out! So why don't you sort it out before your oblique prediction becomes a reality.*

h. *Pray tell: what is the relevance of remembering your padded list of countries? The relevance escaped me and I am sure that it will put off most who brave the ordeal of reading your article. St. Kitts can never lower itself to the level of your list of countries. Yes we have different races here, but not a s sectionalized as in Kosovo or the other countries. All who have populations many hundreds and thousands compared to the size of we here in this country, we tend to know each other, which in itself is a deterrent to the kind of vengeance and other related killings. Not that there is not vengeance and vindictiveness here but that cannot slip into the scale of those countries mentioned. Of course, all is not lost as yet. If you were to find the necessary courage to do your job properly, the sad situation could well be corrected!*

i. *Life is certainly valuable. There is no doubt about that. However, I will not allow you to get away from the fact that you and your cabinet bunch were elected for the third term, even though one could be forgiven for thinking that those who voted for the likes of you, did not know what they were doing. The point though is that you guys were elected to instill societal atmosphere that should make residents feel safe. Certainly free from he kind of fear that your writing is trying to introduce!*

j. *There is still a problem with the pronouncements of these general claims that are part of the 'toolkit' that politicians like to bring out and wave about. Simply because people just do not go around making convenient noises that you guys like to hear. However, the sentiment are understandable: sensible persons would not be in favour with oppressive anarchy, even though they put up with your financial anarchy, does not mean that they like it. Yes, it is true that the people feel helpless and thereby accepts the abuse received from you elected persons; it would be intolerable to accept control by gun waving others. It still remains though, that it is your function to halt the malaise now!*

k. *You are making that up! I do not believe that you have heard any such talk, regardless of the wording or vernacular used. No one serious or even loony is thinking that way! It has been noticed that your mind seems to be spring loaded towards that type of idea, even to the point of wishful thinking!*

l. *What do you suggest by "may his may his life and death not be in vain? What else could it be? The poor guy did not spend very long on this earth; apart from the way he was killed, not many people knew who he was; What was his achievements apart from posing with Farrakhan and looking at pictures in your office? It is a hard pronouncement to say something like that, especially when it cannot be specified, even approximately what the fellow did while he was alive! This has to be another example of you making up the rules to suit what you want history to believe!*

m. *What in heaven's name do you expect the public to do? Form vigilante groups? It is you who have the tools of government! It is you who have the leverage to control society. Therefore, it is you and the minions of people in your pay who must take the necessary action to do your job! Perpetually 'harping on' in your excuse for a newspaper is not going to do the job. For a start, a significant proportion of the population do not read your paper and of those, an insignificant percentage of that paper readers do not read your desk articles. As I said, these articles are meaning less as far as getting the job done is concerned. It is for you to pull your finger our from where it is normally kept and do your work!*

2 April 2005

Step by step, the agencies of law and order in this country are raising their levels of efficiency. Of course, they face a wide variety of challenges, but I am convinced that with the right attitude, and a commitment to ongoing training, education and professionalism, our Forces will steadily increase the joy and comfort of our residents and visitors alike. (See Comment 10a) It is for me, as Minister of National Security, to do all that I can to nurture and sustain the appropriate enabling environment, both in the Forces and in the communities of this nation, and to help encourage and mobilize a national sense of purpose to resist the influences that relentlessly threaten the fabric of our already fragile society. The process calls for us all to address, not only crime, but also any activity that is **not** in the best interests of our nation. It calls for us to act responsibly and ethically. (See comment 10b) In recent articles I have been addressing youth delinquency and crime gangs, drugs, gambling, guns, break-ins, and other issues that fall generally under the heading of 'blue collar crime'. Today I would like to take a brief look at commercial naughtiness and 'white collar crime'. It is common in most societies to hear the private sector calling for ethics, transparency, law and order, compassion, partnering, and all of that other good stuff. Indeed, it is heartening. And I pray, sinners that we all are, we will continue to strive to achieve and sustain best practice standards. All of us. Meanwhile, let's look briefly at matters such as insider trading, false invoicing, evasion of company tax, consumption tax on services, trader's tax, hotel tax, island enhancement fund and other taxes and levies, willful non-payment of Social Security contributions on behalf of their employees, willful non-payment of utility and other bills to Government (threatening with downsizing or closure when pressed by the authorities to pay up), and so on. These, and other situations, can fall under the heading of 'white collar crime'. (See comment 10c) I want to start out with a reference to Martha Stewart in America. I am not here to judge her, but if she is guilty of her charges, then she is a lucky lady, because that short jail term was a mere rap on her knuckles. And the jail itself where she was sent was a bit of a joke, as jails go. You know, this is something that I say all the time, and when I say it, some persons become upset. But imagine that it wasn't Martha Stewart and it wasn't corporate fraud. Imagine it was 'Joe Blow', an ordinary guy, and the charge was burglary. Joe would have gotten maybe 10 years to life. Martha who 'robbed' a whole corporation with thousands of shareholders, gets 6b months at a minimum security, while our imaginary Joe Blow pulls 10 years to life in a real 'pen'. But that's not the end of it, because while Martha is in 'jail', her company stocks are increasing in value. She is getting richer. Then her 'jail' book will sell like hot cakes. So everything goes her way. When she is wrong, she is right, and when she is right, she is righteous. As old people say, hers will be a straight case of **put 'pon put.** Joe on the other hand, has neither **chick, chick nor come, come.** So he goes to the 'pen' a poor, desperate sucker, takes his 10 to life rap, and ends up worse than before, difficult of that may be to imagine. But that's still not all, because you will hear people saying that Martha is a "victim" while they see Joe as a scum and a scourge who needs to be removed from society for keeps. Of course, Martha and Joe are not the only examples of the double standard and the injustice in justice systems. There are many others. And don't for a moment think that this inequity exists in America only. No, man! It exists everywhere. Right here too. (See comment 10d) And if we want to be serious and honest about having a **real** justice system, then we must be committed to ensuring that it is exactly that: a **Justice System.** Which means a system which strives steadfastly for fairness and justice to and for all. A system in which due process is observed in the case of **everyone,** and, at the same time, a system which is tempered with mercy. A 'system' which wields a big stick at the blue collar criminals but gives lip stick at white collar criminals is **not** a system of justice. And as we try to improve the efficiency of our Forces of law and order in our country, we have to ensure that we train as many persons as possible in the various fields of expertise to detect and deter 'white collar' as well 'blue collar' crime. We need to increase and expand skills among our police, soldiers and coast guard in the areas of law, accounting, banking, finance, information technology, telecommunications, electronics, psychology, etc. Because its not just the blue collar brigade who are clever and cunning. The white collar crooks are no fools, and they often enjoy the added advantage of more dollars and 'higher' social status, which means that they have an 'insurance' which their blue collar counterparts do not have. (See comment 10e) Hence the Martha Stewart/ Joe Blow example. But that must stop. Let me deal with some hypothetical situations. Mr. A., Mr. B and Mr. C are the principal figures and owners of Company X. Company is a trading company. It imports and sells a wide range of goods, and it provides a wide range of services. It buys a great deal of its stock in trade through a company registered in the Cayman Islands. For that 'service' the Cayman company receives a fee or commission. Does Company X need that Cayman company? **Heck, no!** But Messrs A, B and C certainly do. Why? Because they **own** the Cayman company. (maybe not in their own personas, but through a maze of offshore, asset protection schemes designed to hide their connection to the Cayman company). That is illegal, and immoral. They and they alone, benefit, using their privileged insider status to make an unfair income as a result of their involvement in the Cayman company, while the additional cost to Company X is, of course, relayed to you and me, the consumer. (See comment 10f) Is such a thing happening in St. Kitts & Nevis? That's for you to decide. I'm being hypothetical. What about the scenario? Let's use the same Company X. It acts as agents for a number of overseas principals. In this agency arrangements it receives commissions. How are the commissions paid? They are paid into an overseas account, probably registered in the name of another company in which either Company X, or a subsidiary or affiliate, or a couple of its leading figures, would have an interest. The funds, or much of them, remain overseas, and the relationship between Company X and that other overseas company into which account the money goes, is justified and explained in terms of a brokerage, agent or some other arrangement. And so, our Comptroller of Inland Revenue and her extremely hard-working and devoted staff would never get even a whiff of that money because it would be kept out of the range of her radar, which further means that Company X's **declared** gross income for that particular year would be less than its **actual** gross income, and its net, **taxable** income would also be accordingly reduced, because of the reduction in gross revenue and also because Company X would have spent some extra money to invest in **hiding** the commissions and fees and that expenditure would probably be recorded, in Company X quest to pay as little tax as possible. (See comment 10g) It is their own greed and arrogance which most often leads to their detection, because the more they try to hide, the more suspicion conspicuousness they attract. And when the forensic hounds move in. Seeing that we started with Company X, let's stay with it. Like the astute business people that its guiding minds are (remember, all of this is hypothetical), they want to pay **small** duty and make **large profits.** So they arrange with suppliers, through their agents in Miami or directly, to send two sets of invoices: one with the real pricing, and the other **"for local customs",** as they say. The invoice for customs is paid here through a local bank, and the difference might be paid from an overseas account. Maybe the supplier would even 'break' up the invoice and spread some of the funds due and payable into future invoices, as requested by Company X. Duties and other tariffs are calculated on the invoice sent **"for local customs",** which means that Company X would pay less for the shipment, because of the lower Principal figure presented on the "invoice for local Customs". The difference by the overseas 'agent', which could be that same Cayman company to which I referred to earlier, is repaid to it on an invoice presented to Company X for consultancy and other services. No mention whatsoever is made on **that** invoice of the goods for which payment has been made by the overseas **accomplice in this crime.** The net effect of this arrangement is, yes, Company X makes a saving. But a dishonest and illegal one. (See comment 10h) But does that saving get carried over to the consumer? I leave that for you to decide. You will no doubt be already seeing, from the scenarios which I have outlined, how a company might clear the Comptroller of Customs and the Comptroller of Inland Revenue respectively, and the nation by under-invoicing, concocting high operational costs, income shifting, reducing gross and net incomes, etc. And the menu of opportunity for cheating and corporate and commercial taxes and tariffs is as diverse as that of a Chinese restaurant. (See comment 10i) Lets turn to some of these other taxes. Consumption tax on services is charged to lawyers, doctors, accountants, architects, engineers and other professionals, and is payable as a percentage of their monthly gross income. Some professional have argued that the abolition of income tax in the early 1980's extended to this. Respectfully, I think that they do so conveniently. I want us to imagine a situation in which all of these professionals paid this tax and did so on a timely basis. Wouldn't that be nice! Likewise there is a Traders Tax for enterprises that are **not** companies. They are also obliged to pay a small tax, equivalent to 3% their monthly gross income over $8,000, I think. So on the first $8,000 they pay nothing. After that, 3% of the gross. Wouldn't it be nice if they too paid up in a timely manner? I hope that they do. The present Comptroller of Inland Revenue is extremely tenacious, and it is difficult to imagine her allowing serious levels of commercial delinquency in relation to these taxes. Hotel Accommodation tax (which includes the 7% tax paid at restaurants) and the additional 2% Island Enhancement Fund (which is added to the 7% to bring the figure payable to 95 of the hotel or restaurant bill) are two areas of potential substantial revenue earning for Government. The Island Enhancement Fund payment is also due from car rental firms (US$1.50 per day for each car rented) and certain other businesses. It also includes a US5.00 fee to be added to every airline ticket originating outside and bringing a passenger. Do relevant business pay up and on time? I can say for sure that not enough of them do. And all of the cheats should be made to pay. (See comment 10j) When you see some restaurants which, reasonable observation will show, must be $70,000 to $100,000 a month, some **$250,000 and upwards a month during the tourist season,** and only declaring gross monthly sales of $30,000, you will appreciate the extent of their irresponsibility, their dishonesty, and their contempt for the law and for the people of this country. (See comment 10k) Another area of concern is the ongoing, stubborn failure of commercial consumers to pay their utility bills in a timely manner. I have no problem if they are cut off or rationed in some way, until and unless they can come up with a way to get their balances down to reasonable levels. (See comment 10l) What I find most irksome and 'gutless' is when employers deduct Social Security and Social Services contributions from their employees' wages, then simply do **not** turn in the money into Social Security. Well, whose money is it? Not the employers for sure. It's the worker's money. So when a worker makes a claim on Social Security for maternity benefit, sickness, or whatever else, only to find that no payments were made by the employer, so that no benefit is there for the worker, through no fault of his or hers, as the case may be, then we have an employer who needs to be dealt with. (See comment 10m) What amazes me about white **collar arrogance** is how very quick it is to extract its pound of flesh, and to impose all kinds of interest charges and penalties (including debtors jail) when customers (who, after all are **the people**) owe, but how very slow and reluctant to pay its proper duties and other tariffs, taxes, utilities, etc to the government (which is the institutional embodiment of the people). (See comment 10n) I have contended and continue to contend that white collar crime causes severe financial and fiscal damage to governments, and, in the process, wickedly denies and deprives the people of a nation of the facilities, opportunities and benefits that they would otherwise have received in a fairer world. Indeed, white collar arrogance and crime are a major cause of the blue collar crime, because deprivation often leads to desperation, depravity and antisocial activity. And the anger of blue collar folks is further aggravated when they see white collar arrogance and crime going unchecked and unpunished. (See comment 10o) It is my fervent hope that we will see a diminution in white collar arrogance and crime. To be frank, I detect more than a little hypocrisy in self-declared bastions of corporate rectitude calling for, indeed, demanding, responsibility, transparency and accountability from the public sector while they and their corporate interests devote so much time and energy cheating the public purse and the people. (See comment 10p) Until Next Time, Plenty Peace.

Comments Ten:

a.   *One year later and your convinced state is still way off: there is no joy based on freedom to move about as one pleases, neither is there the predicted comfort anticipated. The Forces, especially the Police Force is not functioning properly. Reason being: they suffer too much political interference from you politicians. There are many stories which illustrate that point. We hear of recruits mouthing off their trainers, including a one time commissioner. That recruit was subsequently dismissed. Within days the recruit was back on the job; having been sent back to work by a politician. A recent Commissioner was heard to say on radio that he cannot weed out the bad policemen because he does not have authority to dismiss anyone. By implication, he has not got that power because you politicians keep it for yourselves. How in heaven's name can any commissioner perform properly if they are denied an obvious lever like that? Once again the root of the problem is shown to be squarely at your cabinet's feet!*

b. *"to act responsibly and ethically" You have to be laughing at us by writing stuff like that! Do you for one moment think that people in this country do not know what is happening? When those acts of yours are called for; do you not think that we should be led by example? In particular, you elected persons ought to set the standard for us ordinary mortals to follow! That though, is another unreachable expectation. Your cabinet is so fraught with greed that sentiments of responsibility and ethics have to be long out of reach. If that be the case, where or how could the country generate them? If the head of the fish is stink then the rest must smell bad!*

c. *Is 'corruption' not a 'white collar crime'? Why did you not mention that one? Perhaps it's too close! There are members of your party who could be identified in your listed categories, even it is claimed, a regular attendee of cabinet. It is also claimed that you have or are about to forgive a heavy offender of passing on Social Security deductions. That figure when last published was quite significant. There was at the time a ruling that no Government contracts would be given to that type of offender; yet that person won most Government contracts! We are now years after the last publication from Social Security. It would not be surprising to find that Social Security has been prohibited from naming names. The skeletons ought to be cleaned out before your vague accusations are slung around! There is so much baggage in there!*

d. *You bet it exists here! Why only the other day, so the report goes, one of you non-political cabinet buddies, was stopped at another country's airport with a large sum of US currency. The report claims that one of your political cabinet colleagues flew, post haste to rescue the guy who escorted the large sum through another country's borders. If there was any truth in the story, then there is an example of the double standard; for Kittitians were not officially reported to on the incident; just oblique references in a local newspaper and discussions about that on a radio program. Imagine if that were me or some other poor slob! Your representative would have locked the miscreant away, the minute he or she landed back here after being apprehended by that foreign authority! Instead of talking about an imaginary 'Joe Blow'; your 'bugle' would blast the name across its headline! Too right about the double standards: one for you elites, another for your 'hanger's on'; another for the outcasts and many more for who knows? Something that might help to give a little redress: 'There was once a Prime Minister named Panday; he rode high and mighty in his day; and now that once great man is locked away!' The morale of the story is that every dog, has their day! All those who rip this country off to shreds, by creaming off her best resources, driven by whatever level of greed which could be mustered; will in time pay for the damage they are doing now. Internationally, corrupt people are being marginalized and made to answer for their actions. One day St. Kitts also will round up its corrupt ones and history will extract what belongs to it!*

e.   *Before you rush past revising the legal system. Do not forget the legal crooks who masquerade as officers of the courts but in effect are in league with many institutions, including the banks, to exploit poor people. Calling themselves lawyers, they overload themselves, past saturation point and then cannot remember their clients' situation and as a consequence clients fail to receive the service, paid dearly for in advance. Any fair justice system will most certainly need to clean that up. Any justice system will have to tackle the so called small court system, relying on inept magistrates, who show little regard for small individuals, do not understand simple logic or even care about those they hand down grossly unfair sentences to but are moved by fancy and looks of those who should be treated fairly. They cannot or will not keep proper time, goes overboard in expecting instead, undue and outdated courtesy. The new system must not be a mockery but should dispense justice efficiently.*

f.   *But that is stupid. If they involve that Cayman company. It will also involve the government of that country and attract all relevant taxes relating to whatever the line is. There has to be some form of staff to generate the necessary paperwork, plus of course overheads connected to those extras. You are trying to paint a picture that this sort of operation is shunted in and just so that scamp-ish business practitioners invent such procedures just to cheat ordinary people out of a few cents? I do not believe it! Then there is the competitive element: While your business rogues are busy organizing such scams; the competitors who play straight will be able to sell their products for much less, thereby cornering the market. Effectively leaving the rogues with un-sellable goods. With such an outcome, what will be the point of your example? It is ridiculously stupid.*

g. *Sounds like 'open sesame` time. Even though you have returned to that fantasy land of yours. If such a situation did occur. Logical individuals would be sympathetic to those shrewd enough to go through the described hurdles. They will perhaps conclude that with ministers of Government screwing the country dry; why should we not take as much as can be got and whenever we can. Thereby, joining the greed brigade. Greed, like laughter, is most certainly catching. If the widespread perception among the populace was that of an honest Government, your apparent intolerance for those who avoid paying taxes might have found some sympathetic reception. However, with the 'rotten-egg' syndrome being what they say it is, crocodile tears have no effect!*

h. *Dishonest and illegal indeed. There is a saying that people who live in glass houses should not throw stones. You belong to a group of individuals who make laws from which that group benefits. You make those laws early enough during the period over which your reign of greed lasts, so that by the time election re-emerges, the electorate will have forgotten about them. The acts you pass take on the mantle of legality but they are really greed based, beguile the masses and they are very dishonest in many ways. That, is no better than your image of the corporate fraudster. Indeed, your combined acts that legally set up swindles of the people from the country's resources is in my view contemptible and contradicts any semblance of the word you ministers love to prefix before your names. You can hide behind their legality, that perhaps make you feel good, kid you into thinking that no reproach can be reflected your way, because you have made a law or laws that will see to your well being for as long as you may live, but some of those conditions are disadvantageous to the country and that may be legal in your eyes but to some of us they are immoral! Thus, before you see white collar criminality behind each transaction; examine your own actions! Some of your gains were made legal by your group and that makes them legal, but they are dishonest, unfair, unjust and despicable!*

i. *That explicit example was not one of your best ideas. Painting a picture as you did, could be seen as an example of how to do those stunts outlined. It could also be argued that for those importers who have hitherto-fore not thought of that scam; now have full instructions of how to go about implementing something similar. Showing yourself like that also has side effects which might stretch far beyond your wildest thoughts. It was a daft idea!*

j. *It is noted that you are very quick off the mark to call tax payers who do not perform to your specification: 'cheats'. It should be noted however, that these compa-*

nies and others who you are so quick to 'slag-off', are doing your work for you, in monitoring, calculating, collecting and processing your taxes at their own costs. Therefore, they have to manage their time between their business management and that required towards collecting your taxes. There really ought to be some recognition to their role in your tax collection processes. Wish that you were as hard on those close to you who could be branded as cheats but from different dimensions? Do you have knowledge of some sharp practices which occurs amongst your colleagues? Or, do you turn a blind eye when you see them? Or, do you pretend they do not happen? What about those known to the whole country? Whomsoever cheats Social Security? Whoever attempts currency smuggling? Do you also call them cheats when you all meet in corridors of power, or sit around swapping tales? When you clinked glasses with convicted criminal at Marriott, what did you call them? There certainly is a case for a more even distribution of your 'slagging' offs. Especially when those enforced tax collectors, doing your functions could well be doing their best! In any event, you should not have to rely on managers who have their own businesses to organize to do your work; a machinery for that purpose should be implemented by you!

k.   There you go again: attempting to hide behind "the people of this country". You tend to do that when you are in search of some kind of moral high ground. It does not work. It is the fault of your Government to pass laws without the mechanism to enforce them. In any event, you are using your hunches once more as if they are factual. The Figures banded about in your article is as fictitious as most of your literary inventions. However, your appetite for bullying business has branched into a different sphere of imagination. The thought that your current fixation with this subject is related to greed and access to even more resources in the sense that the more businesses which can be bullied into raising more funds or increasing more sums for Government, regardless of the validity about what you say; provides the more resources to make you guys drool over!

l.   Does that apply to supporters of your party? According to one of our newspapers: one top ranker of your party does not even bother to open his. If you are serious, as opposed to blowing 'hot air'. Why do you not make an example of your party' buddy? Thereby, demonstrating to the nation how serious you are? The country is waiting!

m.   You also have at least one such Social Security fraudster of high rank in more than one sense as a member of your party. One who, in spite of self imposed punishment by Labour (not to award Government contracts to that type of cheat), *manages to get more than his fair share of Government contracts. He is one of your comrades, once more then, are you going to create an example of this one? Or is it once more that you are talking for talk sake?*

n. *Only if they are fairly and legitimately elected! Last time I looked there were three (3) Court cases outstanding. Where the legitimacy of some of your colleagues are to be tested.*

o. *The knock-on effect cries out to me here. If as you say the white collars influence the blue collars. What do you think the effects of the political criminals are? Does it perhaps also influence everyone else? Does the size of returns for favours to politicians who plays 'fast and loose' with the country's resources have influence on the way business persons behave? Does the perceived preferential treatment given to persons who are in positions to make life easy for politicians have any influence, do you think? May I suggest to you that generally, when a fish stinks, it is from the head down! When a politician fly's home on a private jet how do you think those who pays the 'bulk of the taxes' see that? You want to punish somebody? Look in your own closet or cabinet as the case may be!*

p. *It is also my fervent hope and perhaps that of other citizens, that this country will see a diminution in the advantages taken by those of our political regime on the wider population, regardless of their nature and that they the elected officials devote more effort and energies towards looking after those who elected them to high office, in every regard; instead of treating us as property that can be used and abused at their whim, including allowing others to trample over our national dignity and integrity. The impression is strongly suspected that akin to the hypocrisy that you detect, is one of your own: reasoning for the noise you made about cheats; is the desire on your part to generate enough will among those who might feel that they are in your sights, so that they in turn will be motivated to produce more resources; thereby rendering increased accessibility by those who make rules to help themselves to more, in the name of the people! And to have the audacity to talk about Cheats!*

9 April 2005

I was very concerned. On Friday April 1st, I attended the funeral of Gavin 'Magilla' Gilbert, age 23, at the Church of God of Prophecy at Saddlers Village. It was the saddest, most unsettling funeral that I have ever attended. It would have been heart-breaking enough if Gavin had died, at the tender age, as a result of some terminal illness or a vey unfortunate accident. But that's not the way it happened. Gavin was shot outside his home on the night of March 22nd. As I stood over his dead, young body lying in the coffin at viewing time, I was overcome by sadness. I tried hard to resist the tears that welled up in me, tugging on me to join in the piercing chorus of weeping anguish that filled the church. But I failed, and I sobbed. Lord, it was sad. The finality of it all. There he was, lying stiff in a box, dead to this world. And nothing could bring him back. I wondered about that chilling, final moment of his life when he was gunned down. In a snap, a physically healthy, robust young man was reduced to a bleeding corpse. Who could have done this? And why? How much anger and hatred can a human being allow to fester in his heart that would move him to slaughter another human being? How much does it take nowadays just to kill a man? (See comment 11a) could it have been avoided? If so how? How could Gavin's family, especially his mother, Patsy, handle this tragic and sudden loss? Lord, if it was so hard for me, how on earth could they muster the strength to manage this tragedy? Just before my turn came to say a few words, a relative of Gavin's named Naomi Gilbert sang a beautiful, mournful, soulful song in a husky, velvet voice. She moved me and, as I was next up after her to say a few words, I faced the microphone and the church in a shaky state. I remember asking who and, more importantly, **what had killed Gavin,** and blaming it on the materialistic, instant gratification, violent lifestyle which we have adopted in the Caribbean. (See comment 11b) I also remember saying words to the effect that there was a great amount of sadness and anger in and around the funeral, that I felt somewhat at a loss as to what all of this cruelty was all about, but that I would take refuge and comfort in the hymn 'Farther Along' which we had sung earlier, especially in its chorus: **"Farther along, we'll know all about it, Farther along we'll understand why; Cheer up, my brother, live in the sunshine We'll understand it all by and by."** I said that

nobody should seek to avenge Gavin's murder, because was for God, not for man. And I expressed the hope that Gavin's death would not have been in vain. (See comment 11c) And in order to make sure of that, we have to **assess** (because, although **farther along** we'll surely understand why, **right now** we have some big problems that need solving) if we are to **progress.** Following me were some of Gavin's friends who sand and spoke in tribute to him. The last words of tribute came from a young man who obviously was feeling the pain and anguish of Gavin's death. As he spoke, it was clear to me, by his choice of words, that we are faced with an identity crisis, and a lifestyle crisis among our young people throughout the Caribbean. The young man referred to Gavin as his "dawg", and as a "West Side nigger". What is this West Side story? Is there an 'East Side'? You bet there is. And where do these terms come from? Well, I am told that not too long ago in America, **a war of words** began among some hip hop artistes from the US East and West Coasts. They began '**throwing wud'** at each other. Have you ever heard people sy that "sticks and stones can break my bones, but words can never hurt me"? Well, I am here to tell you that **they lie!** These **tough** guys, calling themselves and their friends **'soldiers",** were going around the country bedecked in a tattoos, and bling bling can't done, cussing and 'dissing' in raspy voices and showing irreverent, war-like attitudes, were not **that** tough, because the words pierced their paper thin skins. (You cannot be a really tough guy if you have a thin skin.) This caused war to break out in the ghettos of the US, with Tupac and Biggy, two of hip hop's superstars, and central figures in the war of words, being among the more notorious casualties, gunned down as if God hadn't created them and mothers hadn't carried them, birthed and nursed them. Murdered by individuals who decided that they would be police, judge, jury and executioner of persons who were so brazen to **'throw dem hard wud'** at their friends and at themselves. (See comment 11d) These 'soldiers' would defend themselves to the death. And losds and loads of them did 'defend' and die. It wasn't just Tupac and Biggy. But the mind-set of war went beyond East Coast and West Coast and, coupled with man's natural territorial instincts, the war was transformed from being a straightforward East Coast, West Coast thing to being a war between and among individuals in and between **neighbourhoods,** or 'hoods'. So things escalated to the point where large numbers of youths in America were going around the place vexed with everybody and everything, and looking to 'defend' against any aggression or what they perceived as even a sign or hint of aggression. All of those drive-by shootings and other acts of mad, wanton, extreme rage, all of them were 'defending'. **'Defending and avenging friends, 'defending' turf, 'defending' the hood.** And don't fool yourself. There are some people who made large blood fortunes out of this warring and killing, through video productions, sales of CD's, guns, clothing, drugs and other paraphernalia. (See comment 11e) And those who have made, and are making, money from it couldn't give a damn how many of these hip hoppers or their fans wanted to **engage in rage** and kill off each other, because all of that only brought more media hype and more anger, more revenge and **more money!** The bottom line was that for the most part young black and Latino men were killing off each other and bringing endless anguish to their families and communities. If the Serbian version of 'ethnic cleansing' was atrocious, this one is a thousand times more so. And many of these young men are from home situations either with very cruel and uncaring fathers, or with no fathers at all. Too many men seem only to enjoy **'dining at the table'**, because when the time comes for them to help **'wash up the dishes'**, they can't be found. However, lest some of us think that this is only a 'fathers' problem, we need to note that there are some mothers who encourage their children to do all manner of wrong things, and who themselves set terrible examples for their children. (See comment 11f) Indeed, some of the violent behaviour and failure to manage anger that we see among the children comes from their mothers. Now, don't go off and say that I said that all or even most mothers are like that. What I am saying is that a number of them are like that. Why? To a large extent because they have not completed their education, that they are overburdened, that they are frustrated, that they themselves were not given sufficient attention in anger management and personal development, and so on. So they act out all of these negative energies on the children. Don't forget: the children, and even the mothers, see less of the fathers than they should. So the major impact is very likely to come from mothers and, of course, in the absence of the fathers, the other youths in the area, who are in the same boat. (See comment 11g) Now, we all know that there is economic poverty. However, economic poverty is not an invention of the 20th century. And it should never be perceived, especially by the poor, as a permanent condition or as cause for self-pity, lawlessness, a victim mentality, desperation or despair. You see, brain power is not reserved for the rich. So everybody has a chance, once the spiritual strength, commitment and perseverance and the other basics are there. (See comment 11h) I have referred to this hip hop war in the past tense, but I can assure you that it ain't over yet. Because, as I have said, it has gone down to the 'retail', in the 'hoods', and the subculture of destruction won't easily disappear. Trust me. As far as I am concerned this may be the most dangerous **weapon of mass destruction** facing the world to day, especially Western societies where we seem all-too-eager to sacrifice tradition and values on the alter of instant gratification. Let's face it. The souls of the young people are being torn out, as a result of the constant hammering of these destructive influences into their minds. And once the process of soul destruction is completed, even begun, then the stabbing, the robbing, the drug selling, the murdering are less difficult. (See comment 11i) So generations are being decimated. And in this terrible genocide that is taking place, the souls of the victims are dying first, then the bodies are following. In a sense, then, these young people are **dying twice.** And guess what! We all know that when those folks up North sneeze, we down here catch cold. It seems that we just love to follow people. (See comment 11j) So **copycat** wars have sprung up throughout the Caribbean, as we have copied all of the other destructive habits that afflict Northern society. Among the Caribbean territories where this copycat behaviour started were Jamaica, which was already struggling with its violence and crime, Puerto Rico, the Bahamas, and the Dominican Republic as young people, especially marginalized ones (who feel they had no identity), and to a lesser extent wealthier ones (who are confused about their identity), found easy acceptance of, and attraction to, this decadent and deadly subculture. Remember, young people are generally rebellious and anti-authoritarian, and very much driven by hormonal influences and by peer pressure. Even more so those who are not given steady guidance and support. They are the most vulnerable. All of that makes them ideal candidates to be sucked into this whirlwind of destruction. And it is happening Right here in little St. Kitts & Nevis. (See comment 11k) St. Kitts has an **'East Side'** which includes places like Newtown, Conaree, Cayon, Ottleys, Lodge, Mansion and Tabernacle, and a **West Side** which includes other parts of Basseterre, and going westwards to Saddlers, but also includes Phillips and Molineaux. So, like in the US, it's not simply a matter of geography. Personal connections and specific grievances also play a part. Within these groupings there are a number of 'crews'. For example, Gavin's friends included KMS Crew, West Moreland Crew, Tek Life Crew and others. Members range in age between early teens into the thirties. They all see themselves as **'defenders'** and they will all tell you that they didn't start anything, they're only 'defending'. A number of them speak to me from time to time. **Not one of them has ever 'ratted' on anybody else.** Yet, they accuse each other of coming and 'ratting' to me. Even some of those who speak with me accuse others who do of 'ratting'. A number of them tell me how others call them **"punk"** for joining the circle of peace. And they say how angry they get when people refer to them as "punk". I invite them to define themselves, rather than allowing themselves to react violently and foolishly simply because somebody called them "punk". For God's sake! If you are a tough guy, and you know who you are, why would you be so thin-skinned as to allow a man to get you off simply by calling you "punk". That is what I ask them. How can you be tough but have a thin skin? And I keep preaching to them that any weakling can get into a fight, and pull a trigger, but that it takes a brave warrior to walk away, 'to tek de wud dem', and to maintain peace. Of course, I also appreciate their troubling circumstances and I know that this approach of tolerance is easier said than done. I know that this has to be a patient process. Many have not finished school. Many have low self-esteem. Many cannot claim an 'impressive' job in the community. Many feel that they have a lot of catching up to do. Many feel that if society doesn't care about them, they won't give a damn about society, and if they cannot survive and thrive one way, they will take it the other way. (See comment 11l) These are our children, our nation's youth. Now the night Gavin's earthly remains were buried, another young man was shot outside a night club. Thank God, he is still alive. I pray that he will recover totally. But these two shootings have set tongues wagging, have caused accusations to flu about left, right and centre, and have upped the tensions among these young people, and in the communities of this island. And the weapons of destruction that are at these youths' disposal is troubling, if the word on the street is anything to go by. Yes, somebody is making big dollars selling guns in this country. Somebody who doesn't care about life, and selling guns that are probably made in one of the 'developed' countries which like to scrutinize us so closely for our crime rate, visitor safety and so on. (See comment 11m) Somebody who has no problem selling guns to the 'defenders' and to whoever else has money to buy the guns. As Minister of National Security, I will expect the Police and the Defence Force to continue and even intensify their stop and search exercises (and to do so professionally, consistently and respectfully of people's rights); I will expect these youths to find ways of making peace among themselves and to try to set right their lifestyles; I will expect the adults and the institutions of this country to have every measure to guide these youths by example and instruction, to love them but to let them know in no uncertain terms that the time has come to end this madness; I expect us adults to take these youths to church. (See comment 11n) I expect that those who continue to hold onto guns will be man and woman enough to live with the punishment under law that comes with it, because while the hand of peace continues to be extended (with the willingness to receive 'clean' weapons from willing individuals under an amnesty and anonymous arrangement), anybody convicted of illegal possession of a weapon will have to face their own music. People cannot have their cake and want to eat it too. (See comment 11o) I appreciate that people are willing to give up what they have, but they are too concerned that while this would have them vulnerable, they cannot be sure that their enemies would do the same. So they are worried about this. I understand. This thing ain't easy. Pastor Ron Collins, who preached a powerful, stirring and unforgettable message at Gavin Gilbert's funeral provided what, for me, was the correct cause of all this trouble and tribulation we see affecting our youths and our society: **Satan.** (See comment 11p) He said that with all of our efforts, all our talk and all our goodwill, we will **never** lick this problem if we don't realize that it is more than us, because it is coming to us under the auspices of Satan who is far more powerful than we could ever be. Pastor Collins did give us hope, however, by telling us that there **is** a solution, and **only one** solution, to conquer the problem, and to conquer Satan, and that we **have** that solution. All we have to do, he said, is to **use** that solution, which is our Lord and Saviour. Pastor Collins told us that Satan is a foe who was defeated 2000 years ago by the death and resurrection of Jesus Christ and all we need to do is keep Satan defeated. Of course he recognized that that is a difficult task, but eminently doable, because and only because we have our Solution. God. (See comment 11q) Why throw away a win that you have in your hands, that you can guarantee by simply playing it right and tight? Now, more than ever before, we need to bruise our knees, make our sacrifices and show some tough love. Before I end I wish to send this special plea to radio station personalities to be more watchful in terms of what they play on the air, especially up to 10n o'clock at night. I am also calling on DJ's and owners and operators of nightclubs and other entertainment facilities to simmer the music down and make every effort to provide a peaceful musical atmosphere at their functions. If this can't be done, the police may have to reduce the operational hours of these facilities. (See comment 11r) We all have to make an effort to fix this problem, and seeing that the music and the entertainment industries have been and are being used as vehicles of death, I am praying that they will now be used as vehicles of redemption. (See comment 11s) Until Next Time, Plenty Peace.

Comments Eleven:

a.   *Suppose that the same type of question could be asked about some of the things you do? Maybe yoru deeds do not directly kill people to the extent that one could utter the words: 'Dwyer killed so and so'; however, we never quite know where the indirect consequences of the things we do to others lead. Questions such as: how much spite can, any politician store? What limits of vindictiveness are there? You see the results and pain for those on the receiving ends of actions inspired by such qualities can have the effect of the receiver 'wishing' they were dead! Makes one think about individuals such as: Scratch Ward; Fidel O'Flaherty. Was it possible that their life-ends and that of others, results of knock-on effects?*

b.   *Blame could also have been ascribed to the example set by our leaders and the magnitude of greed that they display to society in general. Another aspect of 'blame' could quite legitimately have been attributed to the failure of our elected representatives to devote enough time, effort and resources to the problem which have been around for some considerable time now and has failed to attract the requisite priority. Another way that sentiment could be stated is that they, the elected leaders, do not know what to do about the problem but talk their way around, bluffing the people into believing that they know what they are doing; when of course, they do not!*

c.   *Gavin's death most certainly would not have been in vain, since none really is. However, it is felt that the manifest reason might take considerable unraveling; the latent cause on the other hand, subtle though it may be, should not be wasted on those with responsibility for the good order in society, who perhaps, do not have a clue as to what they should be doing but is talking and writing drivel about the subject. Certainly, there are those in society who do have ideas about necessary solutions for the subject but because of the political tribalism that sours the quality of existence, are left out of the equations needed for effective solutions!*

d.   *Is that what the police conclude as a result of their investigations or are you off into your fantasy world again? Your danger is that these fictitious answers are provided, with probably no trace of reality attached, thereby encouraging some in our country to buy and most likely, swallow your concoctions, thinking perhaps that you have some kind of insight, when all the while they are results of your thoughts running amok! Your guess is no better than anyone else! Once more: it may well be that some of the causes could rest in your lap!*

e.   *Is there any situation in your dreams where you do not visualize people making money? Is that talent hatched out of a propensity towards greed? Or does it come naturally?*

f.   *That philosophy could be extended up the line, all the way to those who run the country. E.g. There are many examples by ministers, which most certainly are not good for the grass roots. Many have already been mentioned and in the fullness of time, others will no doubt come to light.*

g. *Could those dire circumstances of family groups emerge from the social conditions in which unfortunate individuals have to exist? Whether or not fathers are around to your satisfaction. In the hard and difficult atmosphere allowed to pervade, the environment has to be to the cost of those elected to shape our lives. In such environs, even among the responsible, both partners have to go out and earn. In an age where the extended family has more or less vanished and with both parents or guardians out at work; who is going to supervise the 'kids' at home? There-in lies the crux of the problem; not in your fictitious creations!*

h. *Someone who never knew poverty, much less hunger; cannot really pronounce on their effects properly. Whether it is a modern invention or otherwise, when one is hungry, the effects are immediate. Depending on the severity of pangs and regardless on how much brain-power one has; the focus is inescapable with a net result that other capabilities shut down until that hunger is satisfied. Thus, your fanciful notions about the functional capabilities in the face of hunger cannot have any basis in fact!*

i. *It's not just the souls of young people which are being torn out! It's most of us who are suffering some degree or form of malaise, which is a consequence of the prevailing conditions of life and manifests itself in one form or another. When you newly molded aristocrats, who really were elected to lead us out of the mire get focused and perform as you indicated: focus more on working for the people and less for yourselves; maybe, positive things will begin to happen!*

j. *Is that why so many people voted for the Labour colours that you wore when election results came your way? Was that not the reason why our masses "just love to follow people"? Look where that got this country? Truth of the matter is that people are like sheep: they follow and like sheep, stopping them from following stupidity is not an easy matter! They cannot be expected to be followers around elections and something else at other times! The 'proof of the pudding' lies in the fact that the Labour disguise that you wore, got elected thrice!*

k. *Only because you politicians fell down on the job! Conditions have been allowed to deteriorate to such a state, allowing the ground for such traits to germinate. You have this annoying habit that perpetually attempts to lay blame elsewhere, when all the time, the cause for the problem is right in your face! The greed aspect of your political existence blinds you to what is really going on!*

l. *I suspect that, like most of your philosophical pronouncements, this one is unscientific and based on your hunches. No wonder you cannot make much 'headway' because that is exactly what you are working with! May I suggest that instead of meddling in areas where you are not competent to practice, social workers, police and other relevant trained persons in that field be given the task of professionally investigating the root cause, analyze the resulting data, extract careful conclusions, make and publish findings. That would release you to do what you were elected to produce: Actions to make the conditions within this country softer for people to live their lives in!*

m. *Your tone suggests a certain amount of indignance. Methinks the point is missed that developed countries do not control the outflow of illegal items, especially since some of them do not have prohibitive laws against the sale and use of firearms. The relevance is how free those who like to use such items are? As minister over such an area here; it is your function to control that aspect of life. Therefore, your indignation is symptomatic of somewhere there is someone who keeps an eye on whether you are doing your job or not. It is obvious that negative would be the result. Since that is the situation, one has difficulty in seeing what those onlookers can do to make you perform better: Visitors still come and the people still vote Labour. Question: in the end does it really matter? Seems not! So what are you bellyaching about?*

n. *You go to church as does, a number of your colleagues (not often in some cases). What good has it done them? Some of your church going cabinet are married but still have children outside. What kind of example is that? Practically, what are we supposed to do? Round them up; beat them up if they do not come with us to church? Clearly there are problematic spin offs from that daft suggestion of yours! What is needed really is prescription for firm action and then application of it by those sanctioned to apply it!*

o. *That is one stupid phrase. How can anybody eat cake if they don't have it first! Therefore, once cake is in one's possession then of course the temptation to eat it will be there and in any case: what is the point of having cake if it is not going to be eaten? Thus, to eat your cake; you must have it first!*

p. *Did he also share with you the view that Satan come in many guises! There are those who see the devil in the guise of politicians. The manifestation, depend who is looking!*

q. *It is no good for you to hide behind the pastor and God. The Bible says: "God helps those who help themselves". Just cannot sit back with folded arms crying for the good Lord to do your work!*

r. *If that is not an attempt blackmail, then what ever is? That is really out of order! Ordering the business community to operate according to your wishes, just isn't the way things are done in any democratic society! Quite honestly, seems to be another of your attempts to 'pass the buck' relative to your failures or inability to do the work you are overpaid to do. It is most certainly unacceptable that threats of this sort should be published in any article; much less that of a politician. Poor, very poor*

s. *This is still a free country, at least during the time of my writing this, and in any democracy, dictatorial utterances or writings are not supposed to feature. You are well out of order, dictating via your columns that places of entertainment should follow your directives. If anything that should be in the province of quiet diplomacy and even then, it would be a dodgy endeavour! You go too far!*

16 April 2005

Prior to the general elections of 1980, there was a billboard up at Welling ton Road in the area of the Seventh Day Adventist Church carrying the biblical question: **"What shall it profit a man if he gains the whole world and loses his own soul?"** That billboard had stood for many years. In fact, I don't remember life up to then without it. It was a key part of the landscape of the area. And, remember Wellington Road is one of this island's busiest thoroughfares. So everybody saw that sign. Some children even used it to practice and to show off their reading skills and biblical knowledge. That billboard and its powerful **message** were therefore important components of the island's physical and spiritual landscapes, firmly embedded in the psyches of all who read it. (See comment 12a). Mysteriously, almost immediately after the PAM-NRP coalition government was sworn in following the general elections of February 1980, the billboard disappeared. That was an omen of what was to come under this new era of **DISRESPECT and DECEPTION,** in which every effort would be made to irreverently blot out the past, and to introduce a new culture of drugs, gangs, guns, violence, lawlessness, freeness, and the wanton destruction of our traditional spirituality and value systems. The first act of the new Premier and his famous Ambassador Plenipotentiary was to drive a motorcade the wrong way down Fort Thomas Road. That was **disrespect.** (See comment 12b) Around this time, PAM launched a vigorous campaign promoting themselves as a **"nice, honest, decent, three-piece-suit government"**. That was the slogan they splashed all over the Democrat and every where else. **Disrespect** and **deception.** This propaganda created somewhat of an impact on gullible persons, but it only served to underscore the concerns and, in some cases, skepticism of thinking, analytical folks who wondered aloud why would the nation's new leaders felt that they had to try so hard to convince or even **fool** us into thinking that they were decent. **Disrespect and deception.** It didn't take long before the first assassination of a police officer took place. A young man named Stafford Grant was posted at the wrong place in Frigate Bay at the wrong time. In those early days, it is widely said, drugs used to come in at Half Moon Bay, right in front of everybody. Except that few persons were aware, and fewer watched, back then. The assassination was followed by all kinds of bogus stories and cover-ups. **More disrespect and deception.** In the midst of these and other happenings, and like a bolt out of the blue (at least to those who had not been reading the colonial endgame), Simmonds said that he was proceeding to independence. He had fought feverishly **against** the former Labour Government's dignified and elegant drive to independence during the 1975 elections (said drive getting a powerful mandate of support from the electorate). And he had spoken out **against** independence in the 1980 election campaign. At least Bradshaw had properly sought, and had received, a mandate in 1975. Simmonds, on the other hand, had opposed independence in 1975 **and** in 1980. So he in fact had not obtained a mandate from the people to proceed when he announced his 'intention'. **Total disrespect and deception.** (See comment 12c) Remember, we're talking about a leader who would later provide a government guarantee of over **US$ 25** million to the Italians for a loan made to a private company which was purchasing three hydrofoil boats, one of which never showed up and two of which disappeared, leaving the taxpayers of this country with a debt for which the Italian Government still demands payment, even to this day. And he signed the guarantee without seeking Parliament's approval. So you can understand the extent of **disrespect and deception.** (See comment 12d) In 1975 he had been talking a load of foolishness to scare, deceive and deter people. For example, he said St. Kitts & Nevis were too small to be independent, and independence meant that if you had two TV's, the government would take back one. More **disrespect** for people's intelligence, and more **deception.** Nothing had changed in this country between 1975 and 1981-2, except for the fact that 1981-2 Her Majesty had become more blunt and more adamant that we move on. (See comment 12e) Of course, by then also. Great Britain had almost completed its program of 'unloading' its former banana and sugar colonies in the Caribbean. Other than Anguilla, BVI, the Cayman Islands, Montserrat and the Turks and Caicus Islands, we were the only one left for Her Majesty to 'unload'. And Her Majesty was in no hurry to 'unload Anguilla and the others because they all had an **offshore financial services sector,** which, for Her Majesty, was the 20th century's version of banana and sugar, and which was putting some serious bread into the pockets of Brits who had influence on Her Majesty's government. So we didn't need to be brain surgeons to work that one out. (See comment 12f) The rest of us, however, had to go. And anybody who was truly and genuinely reading the game even before the 1980 elections would have realized that St. Kitts & Nevis simply had no choice but to proceed to independence. And I must presume that Billy Herbert and Kennedy Simmonds, two very intelligent men, would have understood that. But instead showing statesmanship and altruism, and holding hands with Bradshaw who was taking the dignified and elegant path to independence (as we could have done following the 1975 elections), Billy Herbert and Kennedy Simmonds chose to be deceptive and obstructive (to serve their own narrow and selfish political purposes), and caused the process to drag along for another eight years, by which time it had become embarrassing. (See comment 12g) As if these islands had not endured sufficient ignominy over the centuries. As if the people's voice in 1975 was not sacred, or the timing not then right to advance to independence. So rushed and embarrassed were they that they didn't see the need to put the matter to the country in a referendum. Her Majesty was hurrying Billy and Kennedy, she they were offering a very attractive 'golden handshake'. To hell with the people, to hell with democracy, put on a big show, glitz and glamour. The people would not pay attention (and those who might, would soon forget), and away we would all go. (See comment 12h) So instead of striding with honour and in full command of our own destiny in 1975, we were made, through the machinations of selfish and malicious deceivers, to endure the insult of being told to get lost by Her Majesty in 1983. And for that, the PAM "honest, nice, decent, three-piece-suit government" wanted to be declared as heroes for delivering us to independence, and for the new Prime Minister to be called the Father of Independence. (See comment 12i) That's deception taken to sacrilegious extremes. Remember, these are the same 'disrespecters' and deceivers who scoffed at history by declaring that there had been no attempted coup d'etat against the duly elected government of this land on **10th June, 1967.** (See comment12j) And to add insult to injury, and to show their utter contempt for righteousness, they paid compensation to some of their 'friends' who had actually been involved in the 1967 coup attempt, saying that their 'friends' had been wrongly incarcerated. If I recall correctly, some of these 'friends' got EC$18,000 each. That money came from the pockets of the very same poor people who could have perished on the night of 10th June, 1967, if they resided anywhere between Pond Pasture La Guerite, Such was the destruction that PAM had planned to upon people of Basseterre, and the country, on that shameful day in our history. (See comment 12k) The same very poor people, and their children and grandchildren, who PAM keep wooing and trying to **disrespect** and **deceive** today. Incidentally, 10th June, 1967, was the date when Her Majesty's birthday was celebrated: Queen's Birthday. That would be a grand occasion for them. And for obvious reasons. **What better time to attempt a coup d'etat?** They had even began the celebrations in the issue of their newspaper coming out just before the holiday, by declaring that **"Monday (coming) is Freedom Day".** You couldn't ask for a clearer message.

That's how bold and brazen they were in their callousness. **'Nuff disrespect!** (See comment 12l) Disrespect for peace, for people, for the law, for democracy, and for life itself. Disrespect especially for the **truth.** PAM is a party whose roots lie in the plantocracy. Before PAM, there was the Democratic Party which was driven by the Boons, the Wigleys and other leading families among the planter class. These are the people who owned and dominated the sugar industry, and so the economy and the politics of this land. (See comment 12m) That party was the parent party of PAM, just like the St. Kitts Workers League was the parent party of **LABOUR.** (See comment 12n) PAM's political connectivity has always been to a small, privileged portion of our society. And their only method of attracting popular support has been by use of **disrespect** and **deception.** From the very early days of Manchester, Sebastian, Halbert, Challenger, France, and others following such as Bradshaw, Southwell, etc, and right through until the present, Labour leaders have been faced with a steady onslaught of abuse, vilification, mockery, ridicule, and disrespect, as the planters and their minions of yesteryear and the present have sought zealously to create a disconnect between the masses and the leaders of Labour. (See comment 12p) It's the old 'divide and conquer' method that PAM and their forebears learnt so well from their planter bosses and in London. They had told Manchester that they would punish and destroy him for casting his lot with the poor. **And punish him they did!** G. P. Boon, who was the big man among the planters of the day, influenced the banks against bridge-financing Manchester for his estates when crop was 'off' and in a short time Manchester was finished. By the way, the deceivers in **PAM** are now peddling the line on their platform that Labour was founded by a white man, and that **PAM** was founded by a black man. Thomas Manchester wasn't a white man. He was a mulatto. He was an ancestor of Cosbert 'Panis' Manchester and Ricky Skerritt, to name just two persons. But what does the colour of Manchester's skin have to do with anything? Bob Marley's father was a white man. Manchester and Bob Marley were the same colour and both were light skinned. Does that diminish Bob Marley's genius in any way? Of course not. What is important is that Thomas Manchester was a man. He believed in the cause of the masses, and he stood up for his cause. He believed in social righteousness, and he lived to his belief. (See comment 12p) In my book, that is the stuff of which heroes are made. And look at what flowed from his beliefs, his efforts and his sacrifice! Study the history of 20th century St. Kitts & Nevis and you will see. It is the struggles and successes of the Labour Movement which, more than anything else, have driven social, economic and political development in this country over the last 73 years. And Manchester must be credited and respected for taking those early and bold initiatives. (See comment 12q) But I realize that PAM is keenly and callously aware of the caution that we must know our country's history, lest we repeat the errors of the past. And, as I've argued, they continue to presume that we would be sufficiently ignorant of our history, and that they can propel themselves to power on the basis of that ignorance. (See comment 12r) And who is the black man that founded PAM? Was it Billy Herbert? He was fairer in complexion than Bob Marley and Manchester. And he was the man who orchestrated the attempted coup d'etat 10th June, 1967. Was it he who founded PAM? Was it Billy's father, Willy? He was very dark in skin colour but 'boasted' that he had the heart of a white man. (See comment 12s) In fact, he was the errand boy for the Sugar Producers Association, which was the real 'government' in this country for a long time. He was their secretary. One of his major claims to notoriety was to discourage the said Association from granting a Christmas bonus to sugar workers. Was it Willy who founded PAM? It surely wasn't Kennedy Simmonds, because they drafted him in after the fact. Was it Richard Caines? Was it Michael Powell? Who was this black man that founded PAM? Again, with this foolish and wicked 'nancy story about a white man being the founder of Labour, PAM is seeking to **disrespect** and to **deceive** our young people. Perhaps the most succinct illustration of this PAM credo of disrespect and deception can be found in an unforgettable comment that Billy Herbert made to me in the early 1980's. He said: **"Politics has nothing to do with the truth. Tell people what you want them to believe and tell them again and again. They will be gullible enough to believe you".** Nobody could have put it any better and here it was, coming straight from the horse's mouth. (See comment 12t) Other possible examples of the implementation of this credo of disrespect and deception by PAM follow. Lindsay Grant published his statement of net worth some time ago. **His motivation in publishing such a** piece of thrash was deceive people into believing that he was open and transparent, and the contents of the statement revealed Grant's utter disrespect for the people's intelligence. (See comment 12u) Here is another to think about: the general elections of 25th October, 2004. Grant and his gang had been going around screaming for voter I.D., accusing Labour of planning to cheat, and threatening to do all manner of thing. On election day, they posted some of their supporters at strategic locations to intimidate and discourage Labour supporters from voting. They tried to stir up confusion almost daily during the campaign and on polling day. In this they had a couple of very willing friends in the media. In the months leading up to the elections, a number of their less visible supporters, who were already registered to vote, went to the Electoral Office and re-registered in the names of non-existent persons. If they were registered in a particular constituency, they would make up a name and go and register under that name to vote in another constituency. (See comment 12v) They misled the people at the Electoral Office. Their aim was to pack up the voters' lists and to engage in multiple voting. Their motto was: **Vote PAM and vote often!** A lot of these persons got their wish, voting more than once on election day in different constituencies. A number of persons also voted in the names of other, actual persons. And, of course, there were those non-citizens who entered the jurisdiction from nearby to impersonate duly registered Kittitian voters, or to vote as some of those non-existent persons whose names they had gotten onto the voters' list. Most of them succeeded in voting, and all who did, voted for PAM. Some of them were able to vote twice. The deal was: airfare; comfortable hotel or villa; transportation arrangements; and some cash in the sum of $1,000 per person. Some very generous supporters/promoters of PAM had set up the deal, and the "demolition crew" had been put on the ready well in advance. They came in on LIAT and Caribbean Star. PAM had been cautioning about the loopholes in the electoral system, and saying that Labour was keeping the loopholes (PAM loopholes, you know, because the system has been in place since they introduced it in 1984) to cheat. (See comment 12w) They had said that without Voter I.D. people could vote more than once. And every time they sad this, I remembered a man, now doing time in an American jail, who told me that he had voted three times for PAM in 1989. And everything they had cautioned about, and accused Labour of, they did. Was this yet another case of **disrespect** and **deception?** Totally! But that's not all. A number of young persons have been targeted by PAM to make false statements concerning voter registration and election matters. Some time ago, I told you all about the 17-year-old lady from Ottleys area who was called to a meeting with a certain PAM fellow and told that they knew Cedric had arranged for her to be registered under age, and that they wanted her to swear an affidavit to say all manner of lying and bad things about Cedric. The young lady came to me and told me that she didn't even know that her name had been registered, that she hadn't been approached by anyone, and that she had never spoken with Cedric. (See comment 12x) What had happened was that someone slightly older had impersonated her and registered in her name, unbeknownst to her? The poor girl was scared to death. This weakness in the system was once again dishonestly and unlawfully exploited by and for the benefit of **PAM**. There are some other affidavits which I may wish to discuss with you at a later date. I can assure that they reveal in no uncertain terms the **disrespect** and **deception** that I have been talking about here today. Then there is the sugar industry. We all know that there have been difficulties with this over the decades. After extensive and exhaustive consultation and research, it was decided that we would phase down the industry as we have known it, and evolve the entire agricultural sector. This is an historic, and critical exercise. One that requires a national, concerted approach. One that has no place for petty politics. Just like the independence issue in 1975. (See comment 12y) But what is happening? An unprecedented number of cane fires, and an instigation to people to take lands, because is their time to do so. The identities of the fire-setters will be known publicly in due course. Suffice it to say, that masked individuals have been seen, high day, from a distance, in areas where fires may have been set. And the identities, if any, of their sponsors will also become public knowledge in time. However, in the matter of the instigation to grab land, let me say that this is something that PAM is guilty of. This instigation has the potential to destabilize this country. And they know it. Indeed, it seems that they want instability. What is interesting about all of this is that their big friends are, as always, totally mum and silent, although those same big friends have so much at stake if instability sets in. I, for one, will not hold my breath waiting for their friends to scold PAM for its misbehaviour. If the transition and the continuing empowerment processes are traumatized, it will have been as a result of **disrespect** and **deception,** which, we know, are the two components of PAM's credo. Again, the leopard are showing their ugly spots, and seeking to push the country into conflict and instability, all because the leopards want to run things. We know that the leopards are eager for the lands to end up back in the hands of their big friends, who are today's version of yesterday's plutocracy, and looking grabbaliciously at being returned to an even higher plutocracy status in the future. (See comment 12z) Here we have history repeating itself, where PAM are being used to carry out the mission of their bosses. Just like in 1967 when the mission was to remove Labour at all costs. To hell with the consequences. **Disrespect** and **deception.** And just like the process of acquiring the sugar lands. PAM like to say that it is they who made the sugar lands available to the masses, as if ordinary folks in St. Kitts and Nevis don't know that instead of paying the planters the $9 million that the lands were valued at, or even the $12 million that Bradshaw had offered, PAM had paid their 'boss men' a whopping $23 million for the lands, as payback for the massive contribution the 'boss men' had made to the PAM's election effort in 1980. Don't forget, today's 'boss men' paid a hefty sum top try getting PAM elected last October too. This was yet another example of PAM robbing the poor to make the rich richer, using **deception** to mask their **disrespect.** Now they want to fool off poor people again with this instigation to grab up the lands. Yes, folks, the PAM credo is alive and well.

What shall it profit a man...? (See comment 12aa) Until Next Time, Plenty Peace.

Comments Twelve:

a.   *Here we go again with your psychological 'clap trap'! The vast majority of those who read the sign, forgot about it immediately afterwards! Everyone were acclimatized to the double standards, practiced by the elite, even back then. Thus to the masses they were just meaningless words that those greedy at that time ignored and the people were powerless to do anything about that situation. The same as things are today! You the current elites have access to the best and most resources. High lighting the old adage: 'the more you have is the more you want' and in your cases: no one can stop you taking it! You guys simply legislate to suit your wants!*

b.   *Pray tell: how could driving along Fort Thomas Road be considered as disrespect? Even if it was from west to east. As long as the route was announced to one and all. If no prior warning to the route was given; the worst that it could be described as: is driving down a one-way street, the wrong way! Incidentally, was that a period coincident with your days of being a PAM supporter? If you ever were!*

c.   *Looks like you are getting carried away with yourself again! When the people give their consent to any action by government through the ballot box. Any new regime can 'follow through' on the actions of the previous executive of that same entity. Thus, if as you say: Bradshaw obtained a mandate previously, to go toward independence. If he died or was succeeded by another leader; that new replacement had the legitimacy to continue the movement, as it were. Thus, Simmonds did nothing wrong in moving towards independence when he did!*

d.   *Looks as if power corrupts absolutely and all of you get to be tainted by it eventually! Look, for example at some of the things you guys are reputed to be doing right now! As a member of cabinet, an expectation is that you are familiar with most if not all of the bad practices some of your colleagues get up to. Especially since there are no public reports of the financial operations by Government owned institutions.*

e.   *It is doubtful if Her Majesty were as personally involved as your comment suggests. More likely to have been the actions of Her Majesty's Government and that is if your interpretation is a reliable one!*

f.   *It is a good job that there are those of us who know what went down are still around for history's sake, to put right your misguiding slant on what happened; it certainly is not related to the facts as portrayed. Movement towards independence for those who wished it had nothing to do with the wishes of speculators as implied by you. Her Majesty is only a 'figure head' and had no personal motives, nor was she manipulated by speculators as you implied. When the Federation of the West Indies failed for reasons of jealousy among the leading players. Each significant island group went alone to independence. When it was the turn of the colony. Comprised of St. Kitts, Nevis & Anguilla. The latter wanted none of it with Bradshaw at the helm. He terrified them in more ways than one. Anguilla created 'holy hell' because they dreaded a future with the First National Hero at the helm. Such a fuss was made that British law enforcement officers and all other kind of peace keeping machinery had to be dispatched from England and it was not because of any* **offshore financial services;** *it was sheer dread of a future under the then local politics. That is why Anguilla is where she is today: An overseas dependant of Britain and the European Union. It has to be admitted that Anguilla was correct in the move made then. Look at her today. She is much better off than we are. Her people have a higher quality of life than our citizens and they do not have selfish politicians either! If you are going to dabble in historical events about this country; then write it right!*

g.   *Another version might be that prior to 1980; those holding seats of power, were wasteful, cocky and sure of themselves that too much was taken for granted. Like now, the then Labour administration thought they would rule a misguided people forever. They spoke and did a lot of stupid-ness, including frightening the people, with examples of retrograde movements. Thus the country got scared of going into independence with such persons at the helm, changed the leaders with different time-table and impetus!*

h.   *Is that not what your government now does? You make election promises that you would or would not do such and such; then closely after you've won, the opposite is done. Does that reflect the same sort of attitude you are claiming in the article: 'to hell with the people'? Your hypocrisy is so transparent: it is okay for your side of the political divide to break promises; when the other side does it, you label that* **'disrespect and deception'!***

i.   *Your suggestion that our independence was orchestrated to suit the taste and interests of personalities in PAM could not be further from the truth. What really happened that after the death of Bradshaw, who had independence in sight, the*

Labour regime went into 'in-fighting', loosing view of progress altogether. It was a period when members of the government were so wrapped up with their own welfare that they forgot about the country. In truth and in fact it is only after their political demise that the new leaders re-focused the country's course and that contained Independence!

j.   *The judges of the day agreed with them. That they spent no time in prison for what you are claiming must be in their favour and against yours! However, you perpetually labour the claim, which has to be bogus but yet, you will not let it go. Ironically, it is suspected: during that period, the PAM was your preferred party. If that was the case? What shall we call this? Historically denouncing, your own team?' It was once stated that with a friend like you; those who fit the position do not need enemies. This could well be a case in point!*

k.   *"That shameful day in our history." According to you, looks and feels very much like another of your creations because the official records do not support your claim as already explained. The attempted creative dramatic effects by placing 'the people' in your usual framed backdrop has long ceased to work. Indeed, this article is turning out to be another of your attempts to fan flames that did not exist, nor is there any ashes to raise your hoped for 'phoenix' from!*

l.   *You speak of disrespect for the law etc... You and your colleagues have been disrespecting the law for some time now. Look at the litter that is your election billboards which are still posted all over, years after the last election and some were there since after the 2000 general election. Paraphrasing the law: all campaign material in the form of posters should be removed on the eve of the election. That, in my book is willfully showing contempt for the law and if that is not disrespect? What is?*

m.   *Astaphan and Sahaley (your ancestors) were families who certainly had a strong hold on commerce within this country once. They conspired with the whites who connived and exploited black people. Fooling the blacks into believing that they were sympathetic to their cause, when all the time those poor people were being used. So it was that as far as history is concerned, your ancestors were bad; does that make you bad? If not, your current point is stupid!*

n.   *Point of information: the Universal Benevolent Association was around before the Workers League and so it is the Universal Benevolent Association is the real beginning of the Labour Party. In any case, it is very doubtful that any of the founders from either movement would recognize 'Labour-ness about what you are calling 'LABOUR'. Those leaders were concerned about the disadvantaged masses; you lot are only concerned about your greed. Man! They would turn in their graves if they knew what you guys were up to! Now that you have taken over the role of being the "small privileged portion of our society". A role that you were accusing PAM of!*

o.   *The 'disconnect' you speak of, has its translation and commonality in terms of exploitation. The present leaders, masquerading as 'Labour' in essence. They have in common with the old plantocracy, the unquenchable greed for the most and best of everything local. Consequently, the result, since there is limited resources to go around, that the masses are exploited by those elected to defend them! Talk about sheep in wolves clothing.*

p.   *Note the qualities of Manchester and those who struggled alongside him. Contrast those qualities with the leaders of this day: Manchester lost what he owned as did others of his genre; the leaders today take, take and take more! What ever is left can be thrown at others below them.*

q.   *In reality, the present Labour surrogates cannot really be counted, simply because in their case, the word Labour is a name rather than a definition of quality and style. If that ethos be taken into consideration; the real time value will have ended with the demise of the previous Labour Government, in 1980. Thus, the time value of the drive would have been just over 40 years; not 73 as you claim! Really, no one in their right mind could describe the members of your cabinet as anything resembling a Labour party. Take for example the new executive of your party. How many of the masses are among them? The answer is: NONE. Look of the venue for your conventions: Marriott Hotel. How many of your 'grass roots' members are moved to attend those!Calling yourselves 'Labour' has to be a modern contradiction!*

r.   *Now how are they going to do that? Power can only be attained at the outcome of general elections. The result of which is a function of 'current affairs' combined with elements of recent history. Longer term history, diminishes in importance with time as does improvement in education. From your performance, both relevant variables ought to work against you. However, unspeakable forces seem to be having damping effects on the way the theory should work. One day though, the proper effects of the theory will 'kick in', then: watch out!*

s.   *What is it with all this colour fascination suddenly? You are a white man in a black man's environment; (well, half-white, half-Arab). Nobody holds that against you. It is your attitude, conceit, arrogance and condescending ways that puts people's backs out. Education is a good thing, it is never too late to acquire and we never stop learning as we go through life. It is good that you learnt something from your earlier connection with PAM and the repetitive venom with which you now write, indicate that whatever memories of those bygone days are now sorely regretted, perhaps even wished to be forgotten. However, it is just possible that the only person who is screwed up about the nonsense written form your desk, could be seen by looking in a mirror!*

t.   *He was right and you know it. otherwise how else can your party's continuing success be explained? Is that not the philosophy which you have practiced ever since that conversation with Billy? Was the 1980's the time when you were part of the PAM organization? Was your transition to the ranks of 'pseudo Labour', motivated by PAM's lack of interest in making you one of their 'big shots'? Was that move initiated around the time of your reported conversation with Billy? Or, was it much later, after several attempts to attract the leadership of the then ruling party?*

u.   *There you go again hiding behind the people. You are the one who did the sums and it was based on your arithmetic that the decision by you to denounce Grant's figures was made. No one else, just you! A reasonable guess would be that less than one hundred persons in this country read your article regularly. As a percentage that is less than one quarter. Additionally, not every one who reads your article agrees with what you say. Therefore, that makes your writing even less credible. With that kind of logic, there is absolutely no basis for claiming that the peopl is in your corner with that claim!*

v.   *How did they get the stained ink from their fingers? That ink is pretty hard to remove. Thus, if those persons voted more than once, as your claim suggests, the electoral ink would have been on their fingers. Unless the officials at polling stations were asleep or crooked, it would not really be feasible. However, that is another plus for the idea to introduce voter I. D. cards.*

w.   *That is so stupid! Your party wes in control for just under ten years. You knew that such loopholes existed, if they at all did? These accusations would have been more credible if the other party had the reins of power! It does not make any sense for you to write like that when it was you who were in the driving seat, unless, of course, there is no truth in your story. I am not surprised though, since a lot of what you write are fictitious!*

x.   *Why come to you? Why did the young lady report a matter involving Cedric to you and not the man named in the story? Is it that you are so approachable? More accessible than the guy whose name was supposedly taken in vain? The logic escapes me here. It would make sense if it was not a true story but another of your creations, designed to fill the page of your column.*

y.   *How was it that the public was not informed about the so called "extensive and exhaustive consultation and research" which you claimed went on? It was generally known at the time that one of you said on a public platform that "the sugar industry will close over mydead body!" It is known historically that when the people feel betrayed or lied to or fooled; their reaction has been to light cane fires. That has been the practice since slavery days and it still is. The people felt that they were let down and lied to by a party that is supposed to be on their side. Thus they reacted in a familiar way. They burnt cane fields! It is firmly believed that there was no instigation or sponsors of any cane-field burning! If there is anyone to blame, it is those who tell the people one thing before an election and acts against their promise after it!*

z.   *Once again the logic looks more than a little shaky here. During the October election of 2004, PAM was the only party advocating closure of the sugar industry! Assuming it is they who are being referred to as 'leopards'. Why should they, on the one hand have an intention of closing the sugar industry and on the other hand, desire to return to a plantocracy. Especially now that parts of the sugar lands have been disposed of, in a number of cases, at ridiculous give away prices to foreigners! Ostensibly orchestrated by your party.*

aa.   *Your theme of 'disrespect and deception' appears to have struck out on all counts! The 'what shall it profit a man….' Quote, would appear to be more applicable to you and your mates' performance than the PAM so far. The jibe written would appear to have been badly invented as they fit your 'loyalty base' more than any other entity in our 'goldfish bowl'!*

23 April 2005

Some people argue that the independence of Haiti was the last nail in the coffin of the Caribbean sugar industry, while others claim that for the better part of the next 200 years sugar provided much economic and social sustenance to the people of the Caribbean. What is unarguable is the fact that sugar cane production was discontinued in a number of Caribbean territories in the 20th century. Indeed, with production costs rising, prices falling and preferential treatment fast disappearing, it is virtually impossible to see hope for those remaining in cane sugar production. Let me put it more bluntly. The sugar industry as we have known it for the past hundred years or so is finished. I say "as we have known it" because some cane production will continue and because there is a silly fellow in this here land who would have closed down the industry just so, and give three, four and five acre plots, and some money, to the workers, but they don't really say much more. (See comment 13a) His plan is obvious. Put the freehold title in the hands of workers. Tell the workers they can do as they like with the land. Don't prepare the workers to use the land for the benefit of themselves, their families of today and into the future. Don't train, don't assist, don't facilitate. (See comment 13b) Just give them the lands. Give 4,000 to 5,000 acres of sugar producing land to 1,000 sugar workers. Jus give the land like that. Don't bother about any system or plan. Don't bother about prioritizing what are the ideal sizes for small farming or other operations. Don't worry about what are the target crops and other uses to put the lands to. Just give them away. (See comment 13c) And, as fate would have it, the silly fellow's plan is being aided and abetted by an unusual amount of cane fires. The wicked thing about these fires is that they are shortening the crop, causing the workers (for whom the silly fellow has found great love and affection) to lose money. The fires are also stretching the resources of the Fire & Rescue Services, the Police, the Defense Force, the Electricity and Water Departments and so on. They are causing sickness and inconvenience in the schools, in the homes and everywhere else, affecting productivity and running up costs to the government. Sugar workers are very, very important. Their contribution to the development of this country has been enormous. And whatever arrangements are to be made in relation to the transformation of the sugar industry as we know it, or anything else in this country, must, as a first priority, take into account their past and present tribulations and contributions, their future, and the their general well being. (See comment 13d) It is that sense of appreciation, respect and commitment that drove the present Labour Government to introduce in 1996 the Village Freehold Lands Act under which sugar workers received legal title to estate lands on which they lived. And the government did not see this as a gift to those sugar workers. Rather, it was seen more as part of the country's repayment of the debt which we all owe these folks. (See comment 13e) But as important as the sugar workers and their families are, we have another 40,000 plus people in this country, and many more residing abroad. They all have a stake in this land, and if 40,000 to 50,000 acres out of the 75,000 acres to which that silly fellow is referring are passed over to 1,000 sugar workers just so, what is to happen to the remaining sons and daughters of this country, not to mention a master plan for the sustainable development of our land assets? Is he saying that the remaining 40,000 and another 40,000 abroad will have to share the remaining 2,000 to 3,000 acres? (See comment 13f) We have to make lands available to them too, whether for residential or commercial purposes. And we have to consider future developments, public access areas and facilities, recreational and community areas, reserve areas, roads, and, yes, continuing cane production. We have to look at the whole picture. But none of that matters as far as the silly fellow is concerned, because he is a strict believer in the PAM credo, which is to bury the truth six feet deep and tell the people what you want them to believe and to keep repeating your message, because they will be gullible enough to believe you. And being the believer that he is, he has absolutely no interest in sharing the truth with sugar workers or anyone else for that matter. (See comment 13g) I mean, for goodness sake, didn't he try to fool off the nation with his pappyshow declaration of personal net worth, didn't he? And didn't he tell a public meeting at Feinnes Avenue on the night of Thursday, April 14th that "in 1930 they had the Buckley's Riot (the poor fellow doesn't even know his history, because he got the year wrong), and we want to see something happen in this country on Labour Day"? Didn't he tell the public meeting that he wanted "all of you hearing my voice in Central Basseterre, all of the sugar workers, all of the stevedores, all workers in this country...I want to see your placards and I want you to talk with your machete too." However, and conspicuously, when he spoke to his party members three days alter at PAM Headquarters, he told his supporters not to walk with their "tools". Look at that! The people on the road are asked to walk with their "tools", and to make sure that and to make sure that something happens on Labour Day. They are reminded of the Buckleys Riot. They are even told: "**So, they accusing me of inciting people to violence. Well, I want the people to be violent come Labour Day**". They are asked to conduct themselves in a certain way that would put their lives, the lives of countless others and the stability of the country at risk, but the supporters up at PAM headquarters are told not to walk with their "tools". One set o rules for the masses on the road, and a next set of rules for the people in PAM. (See comment 13h) Wanting once again to fool the people. The PAM credo at work once again, in all of its ugliness. Trying to 'hoots' the masses on their Labour leaders while he and his silly acolytes watch and wait for a chance to step over the carnage and into power. Shades of 1967. And true to form and character, they are trying yet again to use the sugar lands as a stepping stone for their own elevation, regardless of the damage and destruction that are caused. (See comment 13i) Remember the deal leading up to the 1980 elections, and the payoff with the Simmonds government giving the barons $23 millions for those same sugar lands? Never forget it. Don't be fooled, you know. They have no interest whatsoever in the sugar workers getting any land. The silly fellow himself is part of a family arrangement that has sought to deprive poor sugar workers of significant acres of sugar land. How can he expect to fool sensible people into thinking that he is now on the side of the sugar workers? (See comment 13j) It is they who want the land, and they feel that if the sugar workers get the lands, they can come along in a matter of months, dazzle some dollars in front of the poor workers and get all those lands back in the hands of the persons from whom they were taken 30 years ago. The idea is to turn back the clock. (See comment 13k) That is why I refer to PAM as Robin Hoods in reverse. They want to robe the poor to make the rich richer. That was Wigley's game. It was Billy's game. And it is Lindsay's game. And the more you listen to the rhetoric of PAM you are convinced of their trickery. (See comment 13l) They must know that this step which the country is now taking is the culmination of the process that began thirty years ago when the labour Government acquired these sugar lands, and which was accentuated when the present Labour Government gave Village Freehold Lands to workers living in certain estate areas. (See comment 13m) They must know that this process is one that is intimately between the Labour Movement and the sugar and other workers of this country. With respect, I am constrained to say that PAM are interlopers here. They represent what Labour and the people together have, together, been fighting against for the last 73 years. They represent the problem. They cannot therefore be part of the solution. Not then, and, for sure, not now. Not Billy and Consie then, not Lindsay and Consie now. Of course, they have the right and, indeed, the responsibility to participate in the national debate, and are expected to contribute to the process. But they can't push themselves between the sugar workers and Labour. That would be the worst type of abomination. (See comment 13n) Don't forget, That it was their political, economic and social 'ancestors' who killed off Manchester when he stood up to be when he stood up to be counted with the poor and down-trodden. (See comment 13o) It was they who fired Paul Southwell when, as a time keeper at the Factory, he made the mistake of taking a few minutes to write a letter seeking a raise in pay, only to be told by his boss, a Mr. King, that if he (Southwell) had the gall to take time out during working hours to write a letter, he would have to go. And King fired Southwell on the spot. (See comment 13p) Now remember what work Southwell was doing. He was a time-keeper. He noted when people entered the workplace, and he noted when they left. His job didn't keep him that busy, but he was diligent and dedicated. So he had time to write that brief letter. But King would have none of it. He saw from Southwell a letter better written than anything he (King) could write. And he was outraged. So he used his power to wrongly dismiss and spite a man who he knew to be brighter and more able than he. A man who had done nothing wrong. It was they who helped finance and who participated in the attempted coup d'etat of 1967. It was they who refused Bradshaw's offer of $12 million, later $16 million for the sugar lands which had been valued at only **$9** million. Not even an additional **$7** million would make them budge. They felt that they could afford to sit on the lands for a while longer. After all, they weren't exactly starving. They could wait. And they did wait. Just like the owners of land at the Southeast Peninsular. (hey, aren't these some of the same people?) who raised their land prices big time as soon as they heard the road was coming. They kept out hotel developers for a long time because of that. But they speculated and made more and more money, while the country waited. Even now, getting some of the owners down there even to trim the 'kosha' bush pushing into the road from their lands is like pulling teeth. One owner even sold a large piece of land to the same people who bought the land in Nevis and developed the Four Seasons Hotel. Why did the developers buy the piece at the Southeast Peninsular? To block out anyone else from building a hotel in the SEP that could compete in the short to medium term with the Four Seasons. And the government of the day gave their blessings. Another classic and ugly example of collusion between PAM and the barons to deprive the poor people of this country. (See comment 13q) I am talking about the backbone, the heart and soul of PAM. I am talking about the real members of PAM. No, the owners of PAM. The big land barons. That's who I mean. They and their high level errand boys. The rest are "friends" or followers. You know they speak about their members and friends. That is the caste system upon which

PAM is built. (See comment 13r) So back in the 1970's, they waited for Bradshaw to die. When he did, they made their move. Sensing that there might be a bit of a struggle among the younger leaders in Labour, the barons and PAM set about their joint task. (See comment 13s) They had of course, engaged in another joint task in 1967, when they tried to knock the then Labour Government off. This collusion between PAM and the barons propelled PAM to its coalition with NRP in 1980. And no had the sun set on swearing in day bin 1980 than the barons called for their pound of flesh. In good time we heard the announcement that the PAM Government had agreed to pay the owners $23 millions for the lands. That is $14 million more than the assessed price and $7 million more than Bradshaw's offer. One of the things that they were mortally afraid of back then, as they are now, is that with their stranglehold on the lands and on the economy broken, they would no longer call the major shots in what goes on in this country. **And they can't stand that!** They fully know that with the game opening up, and international players coming on board here with us, our small man and woman automatically get opportunities that were withheld from them before. And the whole dynamic changes. The average man benefits. Those who held and supported the stranglehold lose. And their trickery over the decades is bared open for all to see. Ironically, it has taken us all these years, and it will have taken the inward movement of foreign investors, to help relieve the masses from the stranglehold in which the barons and their members and friends have held them for so long. (See comment 13t) And the barons, and their members and friends can't stand that! That is the main reason why that foolish little man is behaving so desperately and so lawlessly. (See comment 13u) He and the barons see the country moving up to a next level, and they aren't in the driver's seat. They are playing a driver's game. By the way, as at 6:30 pm on Thursday, April 21st, 2005, has anyone heard a comment from the Chamber of Industry & Commerce on Grant's Fiennes Avenue statements? I also recall a certain radio station making a Federal case out of something that I had said at a public meeting about how someone had described a certain program on that station. Now suppose those comments by Grant had been made by Dr. Douglas or one of his ministers! We would have heard screams of righteous indignation and outrage from these folks. It is situations like this that show who is who and what is what in this country. Some people like to make rules for the rest of us, while no rules must apply to them. (See comment 13v) Let me finally say that the government has exhaustively and caringly engaged all stakeholder groups here and abroad. We have not been hasty. We have taken, and we continue to take, all necessary steps to ensure that the best interests of the sugar workers and the whole nation are safeguarded. (See comment 13w) It is the canefield arsonists and their paymasters who are the enemies of sugar workers. Not us. (See comment 13x) And it is they who keep screaming out about the rising SSMC debt, when their own acts are causing that debt to rise even higher, and in the process cut down the sugar workers money. We are confident that history is on our side and that we will make the people of this country proud of our work in carrying out this very difficult and historic task. It is sad to see a political party which, when in power, lacked the moral fiber to take on the task, but now that it is out of power, it comes with all of its mischief when the party that is in power is taking the step. (See comment 13y) And it is important to note that while PAM is saying that we should get rid of sugar cane completely, we are saying that we are finishing with the sugar industry as we have known it for the fast 100 years. We are not saying that we are getting rid of the sugar cane completely. Our approach means that people will be still employed by SSMC or whatever the entity may be called later on, and that work on cane and other produce will take place. That means that people will be engaged in doing that work. And that they will be paid. This must be taken into account in addition to the array of benefits that will go to the sugar workers, and, indeed, to the entire population of this country. It is important to pay close attention, because the deceivers are on the rampage. The purveyors of the PAM credo are on the loose. (See comment 13z) Until Next Time, Plenty Peace.

Comments Thirteen:

a.   *What you are accusing the "silly fellow" of planning is what you eventually did and your party leader said he would do it only over his dead body! The man who uttered those words is still alive but the industry is closed anyway! If you called the man who said he would do the deed silly, you guys said you would not but did anyway. What does that make you?*

b.   *This critique portion of your article lists a number of assistance points suggested as necessary before the sugar industry workers were released from work at the closure of the sugar industry. Since the article, the industry closed on the decision of your government and none of those attributes were evident in the run up to closure. Yes, there were monies paid but nobody seemed to understand what the formula was. To this day, there are those who feel cheated. Thus, in spite of your critique, when it was time to act, your cabinet did not meet any of your criteria.*

c.   *Is there much difference between what you are sarcastically telling them not to bother with and what you are actually doing! It would be silly in the extreme to accuse you guys of giving the lands of this country away. However, it looks like the situation is pretty close to that: the land of this country is going 'dirt cheap' to foreigners and expensive to citizens. There is a suspicion though, that the cheap land is the paper value, the real value to the purchaser would include 'overheads' and/ or 'under the table' values. The talk about is that it looks like some politicians are collecting more than their salary. Why don't you talk about that? Or is it that oath you took when you were sworn in? The people would love to know, since you are so concerned about poor people. Tell them what is really going on with the post sugar-lands of our country!*

d.   *The present tribulations as far as the ex-sugar workers are concerned, is identified within members of your political organization and corresponding greed element that is contained therein. Thus, how could that be treated as any 'first priority', when to you guys, greed appears to be working against that! Conflict of interest cannot even be cited as relevant, since whenever the greed attribute raises its ugly head; putting the workers first does not stand a chance!*

e.   *Admittedly, that was just after you guys were first elected and there was then some semblance of idealism in the eyes of the new Labour team. That was a time when you had the 'good will' of the people and it was your first response to that global bonhomie. It was a beautiful time, when your errors were forgiven readily. However, cynics would say that it was a sweetener of things to come and that all along the kernel of the greed-seed was hatching! Your emotional anecdote could be just a poetical after-thought!*

f.   *Don't forget those who will finance the "sustainable development of our land assets!" The source of much private wealth to those of our countrymen who should be placing 'country above self' but have got themselves confused and reflected that motto to self above country*

g.   *There is a massive exaggeration in this text! It is not a matter of telling the truth or implied lies. It is more to do with planning! True there was never a complete plan of land distribution advanced by PAM when they declared the proposed land gift to sugar workers and as a result we can never know the extent to which their planning went. However, to delve into the realms of truth and its connotations is going over the top somewhat!*

h.   *These articles of yours appear more and more to be aimed at creating emotional alarms. Clearly occurrences which are disjointed and nothing to do with each other, according to you have high significance and relevance. Additionally, utterances are obviously taken out of context from their natural settings, put together in ways to suit your designs and arranged to create images that were not there or intended to be there.*

i.   *Is it not true to say that all politicians try to use whatever circumstances fall to their disposal for personal advantage? Isn't what you are doing now amounts to the same thing they are being accused? If that be the case; then what is the point? It would appear therefore, that your venom knows no bounds!*

j.   *Well you did! You managed to persuade the head of the Labour party that your sentiments were in that direction; in turn those who voted for Labour in the constituency which carried you must have been so moved and after that it was down hill all the way. As you implied earlier: politics is about fooling people for as long as is necessary, until the desired outcome is achieved! Thus, your 'silly fellow': his day will no doubt come.*

k.   *My question to that idea, would be: why? What would be the point of returning sugar lands to sugar planters and others in a defunct industry? Unless they would then go into realty speculation. Ironically, as I write, some persons are suggesting that is what members of your government are now doing. The talk is that sugar lands are being sold exceptionally cheap to foreigners who in the process of acquiring those lands are greasing the coffers of those in positions to sell same lands with sweeteners that do not necessarily pass through the books. Why in recent months, there has been report of a high official with 'big-up' party connections, who was detained in a neighbouring country, carrying lots of US currency in a brief case. It was rumoured at the time that the cash belonged to a minister of government here.*

l.   *And what is the game of those of your colleagues who cream off resources for their own benefit? There appears to be a mixture of the Robin Hood effect and that of the highway robber! Perhaps the term 'Robin-the-people' might be appropriate.*

m.   *The lands which were offered to persons living on old estates' lands, must have amounted to a very small proportion of the overall total land mass which became available on the demise of the sugar industry. Metaphorically, it is less than a drop in the ocean. The quantity distributed does not merit the weight you have attributed to that act! Thus, that reference has to be a gigantic, exaggerated spin!*

n.   *If that abomination is as implied, also in the minds of workers, if it is true that your cabinet and friends take advantage of the embedded trust which have been readily given by that same set of workers and their off-springs. If that advantage taken amounts to enrichment of elected representatives at the expense of the country, then the ensuing crime surpasses anything that 'those you target' could ever aspire to!*

o.   *Point of interest? Where were your ancestors when that was happening? Were they perchance fooling black people? Trying to make our ancestors feel as if your fore-parents were on their side; while they were really helping the 'white' man to keep the masses of this country down? How do you explain the speed with which your ancestors acquired great wealth? Have you done an inventory of the land holdings and other assets in your family's possession now? Compare that to what any offspring of those who were oppressed and/or disadvantaged now possess! Including members of the PAM!*

p.   *It is rather interesting to read a text of this nature written by you. The reader could be forgiven for concluding that you would not be capable of behaving in similar style as Mr. King with regards to Paul Southwell. How wrong anyone with such thoughts would be. You see there is not much difference between your behaviour and Mr. King's with regards to firing people.*

q.   *If there is any truth in your claim about the game of the 'land baron' over at the Southeast Peninsular. I wonder how that compares with recent practices that occurred during Labour's watch? That is since you guys assumed power in this country: Conaree Sports Field was taken away, transferred to a foreign millionaire, they say for a pittance. The replacement land that Conaree was supposed receive in place of that they lost is still on its way. In the mean time the colossus built on the old Conaree sports field has turned into a 'while elephant' and is currently serving no purpose. A perfectly useful hotel has been allowed to slip into decay suspiciously because it was a nuisance to a more massive organization who has brought your leader home on their private jet! I wonder who calls the shots in that relationship. In recent times your party convention has been held at the grand Marriott, creating increased difficulty for the poor to get to their party annual gathering! How does that fit in with the fact that you are supposed to be the natural party of the poor people? Can anyone spot the contradictions?*

r.   *It is interesting that you should introduce this type of analogy. Especially since your team has turned the social structure of this country into a sort of 'caste' arrangement. With you the elite being equate-able to the 'Brahmin Caste' (top of the heap) and the masses rapidly devolving into the 'untouchables' (bottom of the heap). And you are supposed to be a 'Labour party'. Something has gone terribly wrong somewhere along the line. History will most certainly not forgive you lot for that deterioration caused basically by your greed and lack of focus to what should have been a more equitable society!*

s.   *Were you a part of that equation? It is suspected that your poisonous venom for the PAM boys and girls is related to bad experiences or rejection from the inner circle of the group when power was being fished for. If that is true then the saying 'hell hath no fury' should be extended to scorned men as well. By the way, their implied anticipation of new labour infighting would appear not to have been far off the mark: there was a rumble that your hero Paul was killed by a member of his team. If that was true, then what an in fight it must have been!*

t.   *But for the quoted foreign investors, even now, the country would most probably be moving backwards. Thus, as you say thanks to foreign investors, there is some progress in living standards. That though, is more due to luck than design. Underlying that progress has to be the fact that it could have been more rapid and pervasive if we did not have to survive a leadership buried in political tribalism, cronyism and creaming off the top. One which has been overtaken by greed and suspected corruption. If only the resources which have been siphoned were ploughed back into the system, the people or masses would have enjoyed a quality of life that would have been more conducive to better and more accelerated development! Meanwhile, it is difficult to see any sign of the empowerment, so frequently claimed!*

u.   *I lost concentration there for a while! Help me to re-focus; who are you referring to as "that foolish little man who behaves so desperately and lawlessly"? That could either be your boss or the leader of the other major party? In various context they both could fill that bill.*

v.   *Would not use the word 'no', instead the phrase should be: "Some people like to make rules for the rest of us, while 'different' rules apply to them." Reason being: ruling politicians do it all the time: one rule for them and another for the people. For example: the most latest nest of pay increases: 3% for pensioners; 10% for public workers; 34% for ruling politicians! Ruling politicians and their chosen ones enjoy duty free concessions while the rest of us have to pay full price on everything. Even when there are specialized incentives available to encourage certain activities, your operatives select those with party affiliations over others. The list goes on and on.*

w.   *A number of ex-sugar workers do not think so or share that opinion. They felt that payments made to them only happened once in some cases, when they were led to believe that three payments should have been the norm. Others received less than earlier promises led them to expect. There is a suspicion that the monies reputedly intercepted by a neighbouring country came from that bundle which should have gone to the ex-sugar workers. If there is any inkling of truth in what is suggested here; then it cannot be true that the "whole nation are safeguarded"!*

x.   *There are many who differ with that view. Many, many!*

y.   *It is difficult to understand your point when you say that: "when their own acts are causing that debt to rise higher". They are not in government; you are. Thus more explanation is needed before that comment moves into the realms of under-standing. If it is that there is any truth in the multiple tales and rumours circu-lating. There is no way history will be on your side! How can history be in favour of any group of leaders who it is said of, creams off the resources from the country into their own pockets! How can history be in favour any government who aban-dons the philosophy that is supposed to be 'Labour', of looking after the people, putting the country first and replace that with selfish goals! How can history be in favour of a so called 'Labour Party' have an executive from which the ordinary man is excluded and holds its conventions at the most 'plush' establishment in the land? However, the system is so corrupt, that in time, some of you will end up as national heroes.*

z.   *Looks like the deceivers are in similar positions as the various candidates for the position of the 'anti-Christ'. Those likely candidates pointing fingers at others with the truth staring at them, straight in the eyes, whenever mirrors are encoun-tered. At the time of writing there is no sign of any replacement activity for the sugar cane that is growing around the countryside. 'People are not engaged in any kind of sugar related work and it follows, not getting paid for any associated work. Thus, it looks very much like the writer of that yarn is the most likely can-didate for the position of deceiver.*

30 April 2005

As we approach Labour Day, it might be useful to look back at the achievements of the Labour Movement over the past 75 years. I wish to thank the union, the Labour Party, Mr. Washington Archibald, Mr. Stanley Franks, Mrs. Josephine Huggins, Mr. Sam Nathaniel, Mr. Vincent Inniss, and Mr. Cyril 'Puntan' Webster who have all been consulted on some of the matters mentioned here. By the beginning of the 20th century, conscious men and women of St. Kitts and Nevis had begun the move towards trade unionism and worker empowerment. (See comment 14a) They also began to seriously lay the foundation for the path to power for worker-based political organizations, holding the admirable view that is wrong and dangerous, and not in the best interests of workers, for the reins of government to be held by the same people who privately and personally occupy the commanding heights of the economy. (See comment 14b) Seeing that no political parties or trade unions could be formed back then by and on behalf of workers, these folks started the St. Kitts Benevolent Society. That organization did tremendous work in the cause of worker empowerment. In 1932 the St. Kitts Workers League was formed, with Thomas Manchester as President and J.W. Blackett as Secretary. It was established to uplift the downtrodden, to achieve social justice, and to build a strong and united Caribbean. (See comment 14c) It's motto: **"For The Good That We Can Do".** In that same year a delegation was sent to Dominica top discuss a West Indian Federation. In 1935 the workers took a stand against the low pay and other oppressive actions of the planter class, headed up by the Boons, the Berkleys, the Wigleys, etc. That said planter class controlled the economic and political arrangements of the country, and were among the formers and shapers of the Democratic Party (whose chairman at one time was a man called William Herbert), and later the People's Action Movement. Similar circumstances existed in other Caribbean territories, where the masses were also reeling under the oppressive hand of colonialism. The British Government responded by setting up a commission under a man named Moyne, to look into matters. In quick time, changes started coming at a rapid pace. (See comment 14d) In 1937 **minimum wage and workmen's compensation** laws were passed. Trade unions were made legal in 1939, and in 1940, the St. Kitts &

Nevis Trades & Labour Union was established. In the same year, the efforts of the workers and their union led to a change in the **working day from 12 hours to 8 hours.** Two years later, estate workers annual bonus was restored, after the workers and their union had gone on a one-week strike. The Workers League and Union worked very much together, as sister organizations, to uplift the cause of the masses. As they do today, although over the past 25 years or so, the Union has not been attracting workers like it should. (See comment 14e) In 1945, **rent restriction** measures were introduced, providing protection to tenants of certain premises. These measures are to day still available, but not sufficiently used by tenants. In 1948, the **slum Clearance and Housing Ordinance** was passed. CHA was born. In 1949 a system of registration and rotation of **waterfront workers** was introduced. Two years later in 1951, the **factory workers' bonus** was restored (some eight years after their counterparts on the estates). In that same year a system was established to provide **free medical attention and sick pay for non-establishment workers.** When 1954 rolled in, a **minimum wage** rate, with a minimum 3-hour guarantee, was successfully negotiated for water-front workers, and non-establishment workers received a Christmas bonus. In 1958, **meal allowances** and **protective clothing** arrangements were negotiated for waterfront workers. In that same year the ill fated West Indies Federation was established, with the great Robert Bradshaw going down to Trinidad to serve as Minister of Finance. In his absence, the great Paul Southwell took up the leader-ship here at home. Around the same time **the Industrial Bank** opened; **the new police headquarters** at Basseterre was being built, as were the **Basseterre High School** and **the War Memorial.** Also around the same time what was then **Pall Mall** (now Independence) **Square** was upgraded. Around 1960 **the leveling of Warner Park** began. This was completed about a year later. The first interna-tional cricket team to play on the new, leveled Warner Park was India during their 1962 tour of the Caribbean. It is interesting to note that **the first One Day Cricket International** was scheduled in 1979 (when a labour Government was in office), and that a new international stadium is **now** under construction (with a Labour Government in office) at Warner Park to host The **Cricket World Cup 2007** for which we have been awarded venue status. By next year, 2006, God willing, we may host **our first One Day International.** (See Comment 14f) (Curiously, the One Day International at Warner Park in 1979, which was rained out, was a Packer fixture between Australia and the West Indies, while Warner Park will be the home base for Australia in the 2007 World Cup opening fixtures which will also include South Africa and two other international teams). Mr. Bradshaw was long back home, with the quick collapse of the ill-fated West

Indies federation, when in 1965 important legislation was introduced in relation to **Holidays with Pay,** and a settlement was reached in the negotiation for **protective clothing** for airline attendants and brewery workers. (See comment 14g) One year later, we saw a revision of the **Labour Ordinance,** allowing the inspection of premises where people were engaged in work, and we saw the introduction of extra pay for stevedores handling refrigerated cargo. The period 1966 and 1967 was very busy. It brought PAM's first attempt at elections, the **J N France General Hospital,** the **comprehensive system of education,** and, of course, **the infamous attempted coup d'etat of June 10th, 1967,** by PAM, Ronald Webster and a small number of Anguillians, aided by a couple American mercenaries and financed by some sugar barons here in St. Kitts. (See comment 14h) I think it was also around 1967 that we saw the opening of the **Sandy Point High School** (the first high school in the smaller islands situated outside the main town). By this time we were already seeing the **emergence of a tourism industry,** with Golden Lemon. Fairview Inn and Ocean Terrace Inn coming into their own and a small **manufacturing sector** with Curtis Mathis. In that same year PAM provided financial support for a full-page advertisement in the New York times, no less, urging business people **not** to invest in St. Kitts. Those who doubt this may wish to check the archives of that newspaper. 1968 was also a major year in our national development. It brought in the **National Provident Fund,** as well as the standardization of wage rates for non-established workers in Nevis, extra pay for port workers handling steel, and "dust money" for tally clerks. In 1970 wage rates were standardized for port workers for handling cargo from all ports, and the **Technical College** was being completed to open its doors for its first batch of students in 1971. In 1971 **risk pay** was introduced for non-established workers, and **protective clothing** agreed to for sugar workers and for non-established workers in "ice-rooms", the Apprenticeship **and Tradesmen Qualifications Act** was passed, and **government acquired majority shares in National Band.** In 1971 also, the **Cayon High School** was built. In 1972 weekly **sick pay** was increased for sugar workers, and **grant of leave** paid on occasion of death in the family; **"callout pay** was agreed for crane operators at the Government warehouse pier when no work was provided; and additional wages were agreed for crane operators handling cement bags, acids, steel rods, etc. (See comment 14i) But that's not all, because in 1972, government also undertook the rescue of the sugar industry **(SIRO); Holiday Inn** (Fort Thomas) Hotel was opened; **ZIZ TV** was introduced; and The Frigate Bay Development Corporation Act was passed, ushering in **the Frigate Bay Development** with the **Royal St. Kitts Hotel, Golf Course and all the rest.** The action continued hot and heavy in 1993 when the

Central Marketing Act and the Fiscal Incentives Act were passed, and the **Gingerland High School** was established. These two acts pf Parliament set up the legislative frameworks respectively for the operations of **CEMACO** and for the **industrial estates** at Bird Rock, Pond Pasture and Sandy Point. And in quick time we saw a number of **garment and shoe manufacturing** and light **electronic operations** being established. In 1974 government introduced a levy on the sugar industry and paid over $1 million in bonus to the sugar workers. In that same year the **new runway at Golden Rock Airport** (now Robert Llewellyn Bradshaw International Airport) was completed, and government increased **the minimum wage** for shop assistants, cashiers and domestic workers. It will be clearly and definitely understood by one and all that **the foundation, the framework and the 'flesh' of the economic diversification of the country were laid and established through the efforts and successes of the Labour Movement back then in the 1960's and the 1970's** (See comment 14j) Now we're into 1975, which was another big year. All **sugar lands were acquired by the government,** pensions, salaries and wages were increased by 40% and 50% for civil servants non-established workers; (See comment 14k) a special 29% bonus was paid to sugar workers; **Newtown Health Centre** was opened; housing projects were built at Bourkes, Boyds and Cayon; a new Education Act was passed; and an act was passed setting up the National Agricultural Corporation **(NACO)**, to replace SIRO. Having acquired the sugar lands in 1975, government proceeded to **acquire the sugar factory in 1976.** (See comment 14l) In 1977-8, in addition to developments at Boyds and the Abbotts, we saw ongoing construction of **low income homes;** the transfer of Basseterre Junior High School to new premises; **a new administration building in Nevis;** the introduction of **Youth Skills** and the inauguration of the Social Security Scheme (with **you know who** complaining like crazy and telling people not to allow their money to go into the scheme). 1979 saw the introduction of **jetair service** into St. Kitts by KLM; an **increase in minimum wages** for shop and domestic employees; the opening of the **Road over at Molineaux/Phillips;** and the commencement of the **Deep Water Pier Project** at Bird Rock. When the government changed hands in February, 1980, a great blow was struck against the workers of this country, because the new incumbents did everything they could to destroy the idea of collective bargaining and worker representation. (See comment 14m) And this ought to have come as no surprise to anyone, because the movers and shakers of the new dispensation were the same persons who had so cruelly and calculatingly opposed and oppressed the Workers' Movement in this country for all those previous years. (See comment 14n) Am I saying that no progress whatsoever was achieved by workers between 1980 and 1995? No, I am not. But I am confident in saying that the strides which workers may have made during that period would have occurred in spite of those who now had control of this country, economic and political. (See comment 14o) And I will also say that under that totalitarian type arrangement the workers were subjected to the same divide-and-rule and other scare tactics which the British colonial bosses so callously and effectively practiced and which their 'heirs and successors' so enthusiastically adopted. (See comment 14p) These tactics frightened workers away from the Union, and obstructed them from continuing on the path of steady empowerment that had been laid down for and by them over the previous eighty (80) or so years. (See comment 14q) I must also say that in the late 1970's there were persons associated with the Union who did very little to help the cause of the Union. And they would have been at least in part responsible for some of the difficulties which the Union encountered then and thereafter. To be more specific, after the deaths of Bradshaw and Southwell in 1978 and 1979 respectively, not only the Labour Party, but also the Union seemed to go into a bit of a tailspin, and personality clashes and attitudes caused more damage than good to the Movement. (See comment 14r) These things, no doubt, contributed to Labour's defeat in the 1980 elections. And so with a Union in a tailspin, and a government in place that represented interests that were anti-worker and anti-union, things would not have gotten any easier for the workers. In their 15 years in office, PAM deliberately cut down on the opportunities for poor people to be empowered. (See comment 14s) One of their first acts was to pay the sugar barons a whopping $23 million for the sugar lands which had been valued at only $9 million, thereby depriving the poor people of this country of much need funds to build and fix schools, homes, hospitals etc., and to provide for the education and other social development of the poor people. (See comment 14t) That extra $14 million could have gone a long way to assist the country's poor. Instead, it went into the hands of the already filthy rich. That act represented one of PAM's most callous and cruel acts against the poor of this land. (See comment 14u) And speaking of land, look at what they did with it. They shared up Bird Rock Commercial Development among themselves. Simmonds took three lots for his children who were at the time still in school, Billy took the big lot on the corner, and other 'members' all got big pieces. (See comment 14v) Then Roy Jones grabbed up large acreage at 8 cents a square foot. Sidney Morris grabbed his big chunk, etc, etc. It was patently obvious that they had set their eyes grabbaliciously on the people's land and couldn't wait to get their hands on it. The more they grabbed, the less was left for the workers. Look at the thousands of house lots and homes that have been distributed to the workers of this country, both Labour and PAM, between 1995 and today. And don't forget that the distribution of lands and houses means that small builders, painters, electricians, masons, carpenters, plumbers, etc will make money. (See comment 14w) PAM built some houses, but very few, and only a small portion of their diehard supporters got. And even then, the quality of the houses was poor. After all what would you expect from a company. Solid Construction Ltd. Which got the contract for many of the houses, a company owned by Simmonds' campaign manager (the late Romig Phipps) who had never even built a shoe box in his life, far less a house? (See comment 14x) To add insult to injury, some of these houses were sold on a hire-purchase basis, so that if an occupant was to pay 100 monthly payments out of a program of 120, and then run into default, the house could be taken from him just like Courts, TDC and Horsfords do when they send the trucks to take back beds, TVs. Living room sets, and so on. Yes, **hire-purchase houses.** 'Only in St. Christopher', as Lord Kut the kaisonian might say. Some people never saw even one house built in their communities for the whole fifteen years. Ask the people of St. Pauls, Phillips, Molineux and Keys. Roads were built and fixed in a very selective manner. For example, having resurfaced the island main road between Sandy Point and Cayon, passing through Basseterre, they absolutely refused to resurface the other half, putting the people of Ottleys, Lodge, Phillips, Tabernacle, Mansion etc, right through to Newton Ground, and everybody else who used the road in those areas at an unfair disadvantage. (See comment 14y) Even if the housing projects that they built, they failed to put in the roads and in some instances, other infrastructure. (See comment 14y) Some people also got scholarships, but relatively few. And the yardstick used in the distribution of scholarships, like everything else under PAM, was: **Is he one of us?** So many poor people's children wanted a university education and couldn't get it, because the grabbers were hawking everything for their members and friends. Asim Martin had told them that he could get seventeen (17) scholarships for poor people's children to attend university in Cuba as he had done. They laughed at him. (See comment 14z) Since the change of government in 1995. I would guess that maybe 100 bright poor young Kittitians and Nevisians have been able to go to Cuban universities on full scholarships and become professionals. In addition, a number of others have taken advantage of university scholarships in the USA since 1995. Scholarships that had been available before 1995 but which had been essentially ignored by the PAM administration. Further, in 15 years I office, PAM had issued $15 million in student loans, while during its **first five years alone** (1995–2000), the present Labour government issued over $18 million. (See comment 14aa) And these opportunities in tertiary education have gone to young people of all political persuasions. Opportunities for the workers and their children to be elevated and empowered, at first squandered and neglected by PAM and made good use of by Labour for the people and their children. And what of the health care? Remember how JNF Hospital was left to deteriorate under PAM? Remember how it used to run out of toilet paper and other basics? Do you recall how many health centres they fixed or built? Do you remember how many schools they fixed or built? (See comment 14bb) Compare (or should I say "contrast"?) their 15 years with the 10n of the present Labour administration. All of these aspects of social development are geared primarily for the benefit of the workers of this country, because they are the ones with the greatest needs and the least means. (See comment 14cc) How many times in 15 years did PAM raise the minimum wage? What was the minimum wage when they left office in 1995? I can tell you. It was $3 per hour in the industrial sites. In ten years since 1995 the minimum wage has been more than doubled, to the present $6.25 per hour (brought into law by an instrument which I had the personal privilege to sign in December 2004) (See comment 14dd) And have you noticed that every time the poor workers get a raise in minimum wage the owners and bosses of PAM raise the prices of their goods? As if they 'grudge' the poor workers the little extra nuts change in their pockets. (See comment 14ee) And did you notice how much trouble they and their bosses gave me when I was trying to introduce price control? Of course you did, because you recognize how contemptuous they are towards the poor people of this country and also towards the poor people's government. You can rest assured the price control battle isn't over, and sooner rather than later they will understand how serious this government is with regard to fair pricing and fair treatment of consumers. (See comment 14ff) Do you know another atrocity they committed against the workers of this country? They brought in international criminals to do business, causing great harm to the country's image. In so doing they chased away a number of reputable investors and, in the process, depriving the workers of a fair chance of being further empowered through economic and social development opportunities. (See comment 14gg) Of course, you know about the culture of guns, drugs and violence that was introduced in the early 1980,s, the ugly and deadly legacy of which still haunts us today. Have you ever paused to think about the amount of human damage that this has done to the workers of this country and their children? (See comment 14hh) **Not one major hotel** was built in St. Kitts under PAM. The Royal St. Kitts, which they sold for a pittance after a fire, had been built by Labour back in the 1970's, as had been the Fort Thomas Hotel (then Holiday Inn). Compare and contrast then with now. A Marriott, and other hotel, villa, golfing and other tourism and related developments sprouting up all over the place. Look at the number of craft vendors and small entrepreneurs, including farmers, then and look at what we have now. Look at the facilities then and now. Look at the number of taxis, new taxis, the number of new vehicles, and so on. Look and see who are the people driving them. Did they do any good for the country while they were in office? Yes, of course they did. But their philosophy (I think I am being kind here) and their actions were not geared towards the empowerment of the small man. Their mission was to further enrich a small group of elites, which was and continues to be their essential constituency (the 'haves' and the 'wannabees', which includes some persons who have come out of poverty mainly because of social programs instituted and opportunities created by Labour and have sought to forget their past) rather than go to spread empowerment equitably among the people of the land. (See comment 14ii) Today, we stand on the step to the next level of growth and advancement. More hotels, more jobs, more investors in all sectors, more entrepreneurial opportunities, a juicy package of benefits and new, better opportunities for sugar workers (who Grant is trying to fool off), more universities coming to set up shop here, more financial service and telecommunications service providers, World Cup 2007, and on and on. (See comment 14jj) It is clear, even on the basis of this very brief overview of the last 75 years, that the essential steps in the empowerment of the workers of this country have been taken by the workers in tandem with the Labour Movement. (See comment 14kk) That is why so much more has been accomplished in the cause of the workers when Labour has sat in government. And we have only just begun to scrape the surface of opportunity and empowerment for the workers of this country. With God in the front, our future looks very, very good. Pause and reflect on it for a moment. Everybody is looking at St. Kitts & Nevis. Everybody is looking to join us in our development. And everybody wishes us well. Everybody except a small band of persons including the present leaders of PAM and their bosses, who seemingly would rather the country and the poor people perish than see a Labour government continue to empower the workers. We have problems, but we also have solutions. And the country is definitely on an upward thrust. Those who keep screaming about the national debt knows how and why the debt has been incurred. (See comment 14ll) Congratulations and thanks to the workers of St. Kitts & Nevis for your great service to this country. You have been the backbone and the cornerstone of every aspect of economic, social and political development in this country. It is in your honour, and in your honour alone, that I march on Labour Day. (See comment 14mm) **Blessed.** Until Next Time. Plenty Peace.

Comments Fourteen:

a.   *Some conscious men tried but were frustrated by persons who belonged on one side of your racial mix, aided and abetted by the other side. However, the spark which lit that particular fuse began on January 29th, 1935 at Buckley's Estate.*

b.   *The foundation laying for your path to political power, it has to be stated was not a conscious plan. That the direction worked out that way, evolved from true 'social concern' in a greed based environment. In the early days of NATHAN, MANCHESTER, SEBASTIAN, CHALLENGER and others, there were genuine desires to improve the quality of life endured by all workers but more particularly, those in the sugar industry. It was during that process that men like Bradshaw realized the nature of the beast he was riding and its potential for the future. That was the phase where concern for the downtrodden masses began to evolve into greed based hunger for power, for control and desire to be of an elite class. Since then you guys have turned it into a fine art.*

c.   ***Wrong! Wrong! And wrong again!*** *The main objective of the Workers League was, as you would call it 'the upliftment' of the exploited workers in the sugar industry. That was its only goal, vision and desired outcome! Nothing relating to the wider Caribbean was envisaged then. That part of your writing is the usual habit of yours: putting spins on most things you touch. In this particular context that spin is offensive to those with interests in the history of our people and those who sought to help rather than exploit them!*

d.   *The impression given by the continuity of the sentence beginning: "In quick time, changes started coming at a rapid pace." That is misleading. The reason for the changes which followed was not due to 'Moyne's visit'. Those changes resulted from the January 1935 riot's, which spread throughout most of the island.*

e.   *To take the last point first: The Union is not attracting members because they are perceived as being overawed by a government which pulls the strings of its Union puppets. That those who run the Union absorbs what ever the government ministers signal, regardless of the effect those dictates have on the workers. The Union will never stand up to the so called Labour Party ministers. Thus, having a Union with those qualities is a waste of time. Therefore, why would any sensible person join such a toothless organization? Secondly, The 'Workers League' no longer exist and cannot be uplifting the masses' causes. Perhaps you mean the so called Labour Party and the Union working together? If that be the case. Such a bold statement is very erroneous. Neither the Union or the political party mas-*

querading as a labour party has as top priority, what you suggest might uplift the "cause of the masses". Any up-lifting that filters through to the masses is secondary or knock-on effects of something else. Especially the 'greed' element, which appears to be the major motivator. The Government begs a lot from friendly, more developed nations and it is clear that some of the receipts from begging gets through to the ordinary guy. It would be interesting though, to find statistics which would reveal what proportion of receipts from begging gets through to the people at grass roots and the proportion that sticks to the elites? Alas, I fear that such a revelation will never happen! Not in my lifetime!

f. *What is interesting to note about that? The opportunity arose and you guys were in office! Any political party governing would have accepted the same opportunities which you guys took advantage of. A party in power at such a time would have been idiotic in the extreme, if they did not take advantage at such an event, together with the built in opportunities to beg. Your party even managed to turn an ex-Windies manager against his natural party, orchestrated him to influence that process. If your boast is that your party will stoop to any level to influence events in your direction; then, congratulations! However, knowing how persons are discarded after their usefulness evaporates. I hope that the convert minister, ex-cricket manager does not live to regret his service to you guys!*

g. *Since Bradshaw, who you appear to claim at times as your personal adopter, was such a phenomenal brain, as you once said! Why did he not single handedly, rescue the West Indies Federation of that time? The speed with which your new 'labour'? party made him national hero no.1 has confused me since then and the reasoning is difficult to fathom. No clear explanation of that has to my recollection, been given. Maybe it would clear things up if one of your desk items could spend some time on that. In any event, a long time tale or rumour had it that he was part of the cause for the federation's demise. Perhaps one day that subject could be the subject of some form of historical PHD research.*

h. *This monotonous clam and re-claim of yours keep reappearing with regular boredom. In case my responses to them have been missed by any reader: None of what you claim has been supported by the court which heard the results of the subsequent investigations. Everyone indicted for the coup you quote were dismissed by the court. Therefore, the proclaimed coup did not happen and has to be an indoctrination attempt. Something you give the impression that you would like to be good at.*

i. *Let's look at this: ""**callout pay**" was agreed for crane operators at the Government warehouse pier when no work was provided". The question is: why did anyone call out workers if no work was there to do? If the situation was as you described it; then something had to be wrong!*

j. *Yes, your list meanders on and the unenlightened might swallow that conclusion. However, close inspection shows that most of those listed were 'bread & butter' legislation and had to be brought in as a matter of necessity. In other words, the actions were enforced upon the country and by extension, which ever party was ruling at the time, even a party of chimpanzees could not have done less. Those acts still alive are not necessarily working according to their definitive plans and none of you made any adjustments to ensure correction. Seems to me that the bottom of this particular barrel is being scraped in order to find cases about which Labour chests could be beaten to plant the view that the party has done so well! The reality could well have been much different.*

k. *It is much different now! Pensioners receive 3% increase; civil servants @ 10% but you, the elite politicians in power get over 30%! What happened to the equity element that was present in the previous Labour treatment of the people? You guys certainly lost that! Indeed, it could be argued that you lost 'Labour'!*

l. *And since then the place was allowed to deteriorate! No effort at all was made to modernize or efficient-ize the buildings or processes therein. It was like the initial owners of the Sugar Factory saw you guys coming. If not immediately, certainly, not long after buying it, that action must have been regretted. It is certainly fair to say that had more effort been put into the Sugar Factory, immediately after purchase, perhaps that place would be functioning to this day and producing more diversified products. Bottom line has to be that yes our historical Labour Party Government acquired the means of sugar production but immediately after neglected it!*

m. *It is necessary to remind that the change in government occurred because the people wanted that. It is also true to say that the masses desired that change because they were growing increasingly frightened and scared of the then crop of Labour leaders. With regards to collective bargaining, if your attestation to that was true, the question is: have we got a different situation now, under your watch? It does not look that way to some of us!*

n. *That is blatantly untrue. Those persons who aspired to office in 1980, were members of PAM, negro citizens of St. Kitts & Nevis. The party that it is claimed who preceded them was the Democrat Party and that was a different organization to the PAM. On that one criteria alone, your logic, claim and assertion are all defunct. PAM or the Democrat before it, did not have the power to control anybody before attaining power. However, it was also claimed by some workers that once Bradshaw assumed absolute power, many persons were victimized, put out of work and generally disadvantaged by him. Why do you think that so many working class persons flew into the arms of the then infant PAM? Because they were persecuted by your number one national hero!*

o. *What you have just managed to do was to say a lot of goggle-de-gook! The best sense which can be deduced from that bunch of nonsense is: it does not matter who ran the country during that fifteen year period, progress would have been the same. That is a ridiculous utterance for a minister to make. It would have sounded better if you said nothing*

p. *To call what is generally practiced when a new government takes over the reins of control after being newly elected, divide-and-rule is ridiculous. All governments prefer to have persons they can trust heading their establishments and in key positions, especially when that government is very young. After your government won in 1995, you fooled yourselves into thinking that if some of the 'old guard' civil servants and others were left at their posts; they would think more kindly about your party, perhaps even vote Labour next time and look what happened? To this day you still have 'mole(s), even in Cabinet! Some old Labour felt that the PAM remnants were used as tools to get at them. After, when complaints were made, you guys pretended that nothing was known by you!*

q. *You are off course again! What really frightened people was the sight of a government minister, taking off his suit jacket, rolling up his shirt sleeves, grabbing a machete and proceeding to cut sugar-cane, thereby demonstrating to all citizens what was in store for them: The white collar workers were scared because they had no idea what kind of work the future had in store for them; the sugar workers were frightened that they might not have work in the future. Thus it was the remnants of the Labour leaders-after-Bradshaw who really put the frighteners on the people and they were happy to have a PAM to escape with!*

r. *There nearly was a sense of excitement at what looked like some refreshing honesty showing through the 'poker faced' pretext that have led to a phenomenal vol-*

ume of drivel hitherto-fore. There is still a long way to go before I can really get excited though! Another factor which contributed to Labour's defeat then had to be the sinister image portrayed by the leaders of those days as they went about oozing airs of invincibility. An attribute that is rearing its ugly head again as you guys get more bolder and arrogant. However, as the mighty always fall. Watch out!

s.   Do not agree with the 'deliberate' aspect of your statement. What probably was true is that PAM being new to controlling the reins of power, was more focused on consolidating and perhaps planned their position with views to lengthened their tenure, perhaps lost sight of the motto: 'country above self'. They lost it for a while and got bogged down in trying to steady themselves. However, you guys have been blown off course for such a long time that it has to be you are in control of the deliberate path being followed. But, time is going to catch up with you. I mean look what happened at ENRON!

t.   The fixation with welfare of poor people do not strike as genuine. It feels more like exploitation. Every time the opportunity to score points over the other party, 'poor people' are thrust forward as if they are some form of shield that gets struck first in any eventuality. When any perceptive onlooker will readily see that the writer uses the term 'poor people' as a moral bashing device.

u.   If the destination of that extra $14 million was such callus and cruel act? What would you call the failure to account for those missing millions, under your watch from institutions like NHC, Power Plant and other places, which have reputedly found their way into private pockets? How are poor people affected by that? These vanishing funds are apparently still happening. A report circulating on the 'grapevine' suggests that foreign law enforcement officers have apprehended a high ranking official from this country carrying a brief case, loaded with US currency and at the time of writing, no one here has been made to account for that reported incident. This is your party in power. So what of the poor people now? Or, is your concern only activated when some other party is in charge.

v.   What the old PAM's greed amounted to has been displayed through two commissions that were on show here during the late nineties when you guys made national spectacles of the old PAM brigade. History will deduce that a political charade was orchestrated by the government that was in power at the time. Your party has certainly learned from the manifestation of the PAM greed, in that you do not take land of groceries from national institutions! The question is: what do *you take? You see, people are wondering about the 'rags to riches' almost universal story, that fits a number of Cabinet members. It is suggested that ownership of resources is well beyond what your collective earnings adds up to. Ironically, it is the same poor people who would be disadvantaged if there is anything in what the general belief suggests.*

w. *Will politicians, motivated by greed also make money? It would make an interesting study to evaluate and compare who makes more. If the value of benefits, immorally attained by those ministers and other parasites of the previous regime were equated with those of the present! After allowing for inflation, I wonder, which set would work out to be most lucrative?*

x. *When all is considered, that twisted loyalty is no worse than you guys giving building contracts to your party operatives who cheat workers out of their social security payments; who influenced minister(s) to desecrate Warner Park with a monstrosity that was derelict in under a decade. What did that cost the people? Seems to me that all you politicians who have tasted power must answer to history for a lot!*

y. *Seems extremely picky! Especially, when after nearly eleven years in control a number of thoroughfares can be selected. Roads and pathways that have not been repaired, much less re-surfaced in all that time. A high proportion of the accommodation built by your side, cannot in any way meet the specification of what could be considered homes. In some cases, they are not big enough to swing a cat in; others are presented to owners, completely without internal fittings, they are unpainted and over costly to poor people. The problem with bleating politicians is that they very often fail to 'pick the beam out of their own eyes' before attacking others!*

z. *Although it was not very nice to laugh at Asim, some leaders have moral standards. Since it is felt in some quarters that a country which abuses its citizens in the ways of Cuba, may not be a country to get too close to. Such a country may seek to indoctrinate those sent to them with scholarships, in ways that may not be appreciated in the home country. Your government, however, welcome their ambassador here, court that country in all sorts of ways. But you see, as a begging government, you are prepared to lie down with any government, with potential to beg from. It could therefore be said that the previous administration had standards, which you appear to be ridiculing.*

aa. *If that is true, it is explained by the ageing process. Since the Development Bank has finite resources for lending towards education, it would have been necessary to await payments from existing borrowers, before such income were recycled and so on. Thus as repayments accumulate; the bank would be in stronger positions to lend more!*

ab. *To be fair, it could be remembered that when New Labour assumed control, there were some projects nearing completion or were just completed. Like most projects' development, the various parts would be at different stages. Thus it would be expected that the 'pipe-line' time for a number of projects that occurred under 'New Labour', could have been planned before then and actually began life under the previous regime! With regards to functional health comparisons. I know that the cost of medical services today is prohibitive to the masses. Things were not so difficult for the sick or casualties before. However, medical tests and other essential diagnosis are so expensive that poor people's health are suffering. Even the aged, have to make choices between eating and seeking medical treatment when needed. It would be a good idea to do some meaningful checks before stupid claims are courted. Toilet paper indeed!*

ac. *Explain how those with the least means are helped when the cost of water is multiplied six fold. Electricity has been massively increased a number of times under your watch. More recently there has been the appendage of 'fuel surcharge', which effectively adds around 80% to the standard costs of all, including those with 'greatest needs and least means'!*

ad. *It would be interesting to compare what prices of necessities were 12 years ago, compared to now say. It is possible to find cases where individual price of some commodities have risen by a factor of more than 300%. If that turns out to be an average, then your comparison will be meaningless.*

ae. *It's not quite as simple as that. Most price increases are more closely related to fiscal and other government changes in charges of: water, electricity and customs. It is estimated that these have gone up by some where close to 1000% since New Labour, if all the various increases are accumulated. Of course that multiplicity of costs have to be passed on to customers, or business would be run at a loss. You guys ought to have more concern for the 'knock-on' effects from your actions.*

af. *The word 'fair' to you must mean something other than what ordinary use suggests. You use that word like an illusionist would use a rabbit: now you see it;*

now you don't! I can suggest numerous instances where the word 'fair' is contradicted by your actions, the most recent being salary increases of 3%, 10% and some where in the region of 34%-35%. Fair! Don't make people laugh! Since when were you, poor people's government? Only if the word 'poor' was prefixed with the words: 'soak the'. You are your own government, fooling poor people into thinking that you emanated from them. There is nothing resembling Labour philosophy or poor people orientation about your government, so please do not kid yourselves! Your labour-ness vanished, ions ago!

ag. *Explain please: what happened to the investor who built that 'white elephant' at the airport entrance-exit roundabout? What happened to Stevia? Who chased those investors away?. What happened to 'Jack Tar'? Were their owners international criminals? Is that why they had to leave? Were they indirectly or directly chased away? Seems to me that if those questions were properly investigated, it might just be possible that conclusions similar to those categorized as atrocities!*

ah. *Back in 1975, police had guns strapped on their waists, walking around on patrol. That according to my logic was the start of the gun culture. Somebody has to start first and once the police began; the criminals followed. As 'a supposed' student of psychology, you should know that! To this day, in the U.K. police do not carry guns as part of their patrol equipment and although criminals arm themselves in practice. The possession of arms is not as widespread as here, proportionally speaking.*

ai. *By criticizing the party previous for not spreading equitably empowerment 'among the people of the land'. Are you saying that your party has? Because if you are, that is a load of balderdash! It is extremely difficult to identify anyone who has been empowered, by any way, shape or form! You guys look after yourselves first. The best of what ever is left goes to your cronies. There are streets and roads around in worst states than when you first took over. There are schools and other institutions in derelict conditions. What about the many reports of benefits finding their way in directions of some political leaders, not necessarily fairly earned. If there be any truth or parts of truths in those rumours? Then someone with your pretences must know that the practice is wrong and has to work against your claim of equitable empowerment!*

aj. *Your bullish, up-beat attitude about the list of attainments within the country is equivalent to beating your chest for other peoples work. In the main, the list records a high proportion of results from private persons incentives, in some events, they happened in spite of you guys. In most; they would have happened, regardless of who was in power. It is however without doubt that more could have been done. If reported missing millions were properly channeled to ventures that the people benefited from. In any event since you are so proud of your list, why is the production of accounts to show how spending on your darling projects were effected. Produce the accounts and we will see the reality of your claims! Then the country would be in a position to judge!*

ak. *It should be quite clear by now, from my series of comments, triggered by these items from your desk that 'New Labour' lost out in the claim of 'value added' when viewed from the perspective of the workers here in this land or indeed the real Labour Movement. Greed, vindictiveness and personal idolatry got in the way for your group to be seriously thought of as in any way, shape or form to have any labourness about you! Remember the story of the boy who shouted: 'wolf, wolf....' At every opportunity? Your repeated claims of things done by your outfit on behalf of the workers; smacks of much the same bluffs by that boy. The irony is that one of these days you might actually do something worthy of note for the workers and like the case of the boy, nobody will notice!*

al. *Oh how you may wish that national debt problem was easily dismissed. It is a huge problem and deserves more consideration. If your tone suggests that those who know better should recognize that the debt was necessary to kick start or finance some of the projects claimed to be necessary to the level of development of which you boast, then that would be only a partial answer. To be fully appreciative of the veracity as far as any project is concerned, there needs to be supportive documentation to such projects. We hear too frequently of missing millions. How can any concerned citizen be ever certain that your story is true? With so much rumour and other sightings of suspicious operations; it is positively confusing!*

am. *Looks to me as you like to march so that you can bang your mouth as you do. It just may be that is your real reason for marching! Forgive me, if that "in your honour alone" part is just hot air*

7 May 2005

Before I get into the meat of this week's discussion, I want to thank Lynette Pemberton, our Central Basseterre contestant in last weekend's Miss Labour show, as well as folks like Sheldon Isaac, Shelda Webster, Irvin Bart (De Don Trucking Service), Babs Tyson (Barbs Ram PakBar) and other friends who were so very helpful and supportive of the young lady. I also wasn't to thank Sidney Bridgewater and his team with the float for the Labour Day Parade, along with All Dive & Marine who sponsored it. I had a wonderful weekend paying special respect to, celebrating and honouring the workers of th is nation and of the world generally. (See comment 15a) Now let's get onto the other business. The three-person Parliamentarians' and Ministers' Salaries Review Committee of Mr. Brisbane, Mr. O'Max Gardner and Mr. Emile Ferdinand have been engaging Stake holder groups and the general public. It seems that their work has generated much interesting discussion. That's consultative democracy in action. And that's good. Recently I was listening to a radio talk show when a gentleman, obviously overcome by a rush of singular irrationality, put forward the argument that instead of getting a raise, ministers ought to take a pay cut because we have put the government in debt. I also heard a gentleman who works in the tourism industry call in to the same talk to say pretty much the same thing. As I listened to him, I wondered if he knew that as a Minister of Tourism I had spent considerably more of government's money and other resources promoting the establishment at which he works than its very owners, and that the efforts of the Ministry of Tourism and government generally have been responsible in no small measure for that establishment still being in business today. (See comment 15b) I wondered if he knew, but I doubted it. But even if he knew, I didn't think he would be sufficiently open-minded to see the truth. People like that you le4ave at the foot of the cross. I don't want to get into the government debt with microscopic detail at this moment, but some components of it need to be addressed. Firstly, the spate of hurricanes and the flood between 1995 and 1999. The damage and loss were widespread. Hospitals, schools, homes, roads, coastlines, water and electricity supplies, damage to fields, loss of topsoil, flooding decimation of crops, vegetation, forest, hotels, closure of businesses, loss of man hours and so on. (See comment 15c) Enormous losses of revenue! And we had to find money to fix up the country. The economic damage, as assessed by international bodies, was **One Billion Three Hundred Million Dollars.** In addition to finding and spending money to make good the loss and damage, we had to continue our social programs with schools, community centres, hospitals and health centres, roads, housing and other developments, as we sought to continue solidifying the infrastructure necessary to build social and economic wealth for our people. (See comment 15d) And we had to spend money to let the world know that we were very much alive and kicking. So while we were fixing, we had to be spending. In other words, **more expenditure** and **less revenue.** All for reasons essentially beyond our control. Naturally, in circumstances like that the national debt will grow. To make it grow even more, we had a sugar industry which was declining in the face of global economic realities and causing us to lose, in dollar terms, over thirty million dollars a year. (See comment 15e) In addition, the World Bank decided that it would introduce a new practice whereby the debts of statutory corporations would now be included in the calculation of national debt. In that single step, we saw a big jump. It was **not** new debt. Just old debt that had **not** previously been included as part of the national debt. But that's not all. We also had to factor in all of the Nevis Island Administration debt through loans that were guaranteed by the Federal Government (which is about two hundred million dollars. I'm told)… (See comment 15f) Now with all of that, both the Federal Government and the Nevis Island Administration were, and are, still able to service their debts in a timely manner, and are both considered to be reputable and responsible members of the regional and international financial communities. Further, investor interest and confidence in St. Kitts and Nevis over the past ten years have been **higher** than ever before. And that is with the large national debt and all. Do the government and administration not get credit for that? (See comment 15g) And while the Federal Government and the Nevis Island Administration have been facing down this large debt, they have also succeeded in propelling the country to reach Number 39 in the world in terms of human development (Number 4 in the Western Hemisphere behind Canada USA and Barbados, Number 2 in CARICOM, and Number 1 in the OECS). And do Douglas, Amory and their ministers not get credit for that too? (See comment 15g) In the process, a vast amount of wealth has been created in this country. House and land ownership, education, social development, jobs, benefits, and corporate sales and profits have grown exponentially. The number of vehicles has doubled in this country over the past ten years! (See comment 15h) In a nutshell, therefore, we have faced gigantic challenges as a result of natural disasters, a declining and costly sugar industry, and a new method of calculating national debt by the World Bank. Yet notwithstanding all of that, we have still been able to propel the country to the front of the pack, empowering and enriching vast amounts of persons and enterprises. (See comment 15i) We have done a good job of creating an enabling environment for the creation and growth of wealth across the board in this country. Surely, our hard work and our gravely serious responsibilities merit reward. (See comment 15j) Yet, these people who have benefited handsomely from our efforts and who want to keep making their millions and millions, wants **us,** who have been significantly responsible for the recovery and growth efforts, not only **not** to take a raise, but instead to take a **cut** in pay. (See comment 15k) But, you see, natural disasters, the declining sugar industry and the World Bank's reclassification of debt have not been our only challenges. Some of those same people who want all for themselves and want us either not to get a raise or to take a pay cut have also been a big part of the problem. How is that? A number of import transactions in this country are characterized by double invoicing: one invoice which is for the Customs in St. Kitts & Nevis, the other is strictly between the seller and the buyer (this one the Customs don't see). The amounts on the ones that the Customs do see are always **less** than the amounts on the ones they **don't** see. As a result the importer pays **less** duty and other charges calculated against the duty here in St. Kitts and Nevis. That is robbery of the Treasury. And don't forget that duty is perhaps our largest revenue source for the government and the administration. So we are talking big time robbery. (See comment 15l) The **hundreds of millions** of dollars, **maybe billions** over the past twenty years, which these folks have cheated this country of, could have gone a long way to keep down the debt of the Federal Government and the Nevis Island Administration, thereby radically improving the fiscal position of the public sector. Those millions or billions could have gone a long way to help both government and administration ion providing necessary and ongoing social and physical infrastructure to ensure sustained and balanced development and growth as a society, for the good of all, both the cheaters and the just. (See comment 15m) And with the millions, possibly billions wrongly withheld dollars, the cheaters have bought real estate, they have built edifices and projects they have put some away in little and-not-so little nest in many parts of the world, they have put themselves and their children in all kinds of fancy cars, and so on. They have been able to 'put put 'pon put' (See comment 15n) They have contemptuously used the government, the administration and the people of this country as their piggy banks. Whom do I blame? Of course, I blame the cheaters. But they are not the only culprits. All of those who have served in successive governments and administration must also take the blame, because we have not tackled the cheaters with sufficient and sustained aggressiveness on behalf of the public purse and the people. (See comment 15o) Yes, we have done a good job in laying down the physical and social infrastructure. Yet it could and would have been better, and less burdensome to all, had we stopped the cheaters dead in their tracks years ago. But we are changing things, because the Prime Minister, the Premier, the Comptroller of Inland Revenue and the Comptroller of Customs have sent a very clear signal that it is 'hammer' time. Time to make the cheaters pay up. And it is high bloody time! This is not about witch-hunting. And persecution. No, it's about getting people to pay what they are supposed to pay. (See comment 15p) A number of forensic audits have been done and I hear that others are to be done. And some people are 'guestimating that when the punching of numbers on the calculators is over, the total **corporate** tax robbery that has taken place and is to be paid up will **exceed two hundred million dollars. Look how far that money can go to radically reducing the national debt and improving our fiscal position.** In addition to custom duties and corporate tax, of course, there are property taxes (the figure of which must be right up there too), and the non-use surcharge at the Southeast Peninsular which must be around **twenty million dollars** by now. That too can be of great help to reduce debt and improve our fiscal position. There are also consumption tax on services which professionals should pay (some don't) on their monthly gross, which I am sure would add up to a hefty sum as well. So if a vigorous, just and consistent campaign is launched to make all cheaters pay and stay paying their taxes, the government and the administration could find themselves with good and steady money that would dramatically reduce the Federal and the Nevis Island Administration debts, and radically transform our fiscal situation for the better. (See comment 15q) And if the cheaters are going to continue to be reluctant, or at best, slow, to pay what they owe, then it is indeed time for their hands to be put to the fire to make them understand that **their free ride** on the backs of the government, the administration and the tax payers of this country **has ended.** The individuals pushing the argument about no raise or reduction in pay have been able to create and or grow their personal wealth because, in no small measure, of the strong foundation which we in government and administration have been laying and continue to lay. When they are in their leisurely conversations with their friends, both here and abroad (for example, at a party somewhere of at cricket in Antigua) they say how great business is for them, and how much is happening here in terms of economic growth. However, and to nobody's surprise, when they speak for the rest of us to hear, they bawl and complain about high taxes and hard times. They rob the treasury and take whatever advantage they can, yet they accuse ministers of being corrupt and cry out for transparency. And having wrongly and with contemptuous regularity withheld monies owing to government and administration, and having sought to milk the cow from all apertures, they still have the gall to ask whether government has the capacity to pay ministers and parliamentarians an increase. (See comment 15r) They want the farmer to fatten the cow for them, but they also want the farmer to starve. Here are some other arguments that they promote. They state that ministers top up our pay by traveling. In other words, they are saying that ministers travel unnecessarily and dishonestly, as we do so to put money into our pockets rather than to do the government's work. Such statements are as inaccurate as they are unfortunate. Let me list what I get monthly as a minister and parliamentarian: (a) salary……… $6,610.00 (b) housing allowance…$1,500 (c) constituency allowance……. $1,500 (d) entertainment allowance……$300.00 (e) travel allowance……$500.00 (f) GROSS TOTAL $10,410.00. Ministers are allowed a duty free vehicle ever four years. In addition, ministers receive an allowance for local telephone calls. We have to submit our monthly bills to the Ministry of Finance for clearance and approval. Ministers also receive EC $100 a day when they are traveling in the OECS and US $100 a day when outside the OECS. When I travel, I incur certain expenses **at home** which I do not ordinarily incur when I am at home. I also pay for little incidentals when ever I may be overseas for which I do not seek reimbursement by government. Both those at home and overseas expenses come out of the $100 a day. (See comment 15s) Frankly, and simple mathematics would show this, a minister would have to spend an awful lot of time overseas is in order to top up his pay. (See comment 15t) Let us analyze the package which I receive. The $6,610 is my basic salary. That is the figure against which my pension is calculated. The housing allowance is a figure introduced by Dr. Simmonds in 1989 just when his new house was completed. He wanted to increase ministerial pay, but he did not have the political fortitude to give himself and the other ministers a raise, so he called it Housing Allowance. No problem. (See comment 15u) Then there is the Constituency Allowance of $1,500. I don't regard that as my money. And I decided from day one that instead of using up most of it by paying rent for a constituency office, I would have constituency days on Thursdays at my office and put it straight into the hands of constituents in need. After six months in office I had already expended over **$33,000.00** in financial assistance to constituents, and others. At that time I had to make a decision whether I should stick to the $1,500.00 or to simply stop counting. (See comment 15v) I decided to stop counting. It would be scary to learn how much I have disbursed over the past ten years, proud and humbled as I am for the privilege and opportunity to have been able to assist persons in need. The entertainment allowance of $300.00 is a pittance, and the Travel Allowance of $500.00 is just $50.00 more than the $450.00 that permanent secretaries get. (See comment 15w) My vehicle is used in my work as a minister and a constituency representative, as well as for private purposes. (See comment 15x) Let us compare my package with that of a manager in one of the big companies in town. I am not talking about a Chief Executive Officer. No, just a manager. Here is what he might get: (a) anywhere between $8,000 and $20,000.00 a month in salary; (b) possible board membership ion a subsidiary company at about $250.00 monthly; (c) free use 24/7 of company car with a gas allowance of $250.00 up[wards monthly; (d) an annual bonus of $10,000 upwards to very high figures; (e) a health insurance plan in which he gets 80% paid to him; (f) a free cell phone with a $250.00 per month credit (excesses often ignored); (g) an away from home per diem of EC$ 100.00(the company pays all expenses, so that $100.00 is for him to pocket); (h) 20% discount on all purchases, 5% on blocks, cement and steel, 30% on household items, and if he is buying things like galvaloom he pays cost plus 5%; (i) pension scheme; and (j) low-interest loans. (See comment 15y) The bigger boys can get up to $200,000 in bonuses in a year. The really big boys get even more than that. In fact, I recall that a few years ago, one particular company generated over one hundred million dollars in annual sales, and paid its top four executives over one million dollars in bonuses, yet in that same year it declared a net profit of less than $400,000.00, paid a miserly 3.25% dividend to its shareholders, and laid off 35 workers. **All that in the same year!** Go figure that one out. And if you seek, you will surely find that at least one company in town has retired executives who still get their full salaries and company cars, free gas, free insurance, travel allowances, and other perks. Can it be rightly said that these companies have the capacity to so handsomely reward their big bosses and managers the way that they do while at the same time paying miserly dividends and robbing the public purse of taxes justly due and payable? Would it be fair to argue that when they pay these low dividends, cut workers from their payrolls, and bawl so loudly about these high taxes, they should also take a cut in salary and remove their bonuses, instead of topping up and grabbing big 'makko' bonuses? Are these corporate leaders so self-indulgent and 'jepse' as to believe that the primary objective of their companies is to generate large benefits packages for **them,** while sticking it to shareholders, workers, government, administration and the general public? Can spokesmen for these companies speak with moral authority on the rightness of a pay raise for government ministers, who have largely been responsible for infrastructural and economic development and growth and for so much wealth creation, when their own union-hating, income-shifting tax-hiding corporate cronies live like maharajahs. Let me say this. As a minister of government, especially in an environment in which much of the country's economic growth has been driven by **public sector initiatives** and by the public sector's success in attracting big league foreign investors. I believe that my **contribution** and **responsibilities** as a minister, as a parliamentarian and as an elected representative of the people of this country have been as substantial and beneficial to this nation as those of any CEO of any local company. (See comment 15z) And although I know that traditionally ministerial pay packages have been less than those in the private sector, I can see no good and fair reason for such a foolish practice to continue. (See comment 15aa) Why should department managers in TDC, Horsfords, Rams, Cable & Wireless, etc receive a better pay package than someone who is not only a minister of government, but also a law-maker and an elected representative of a constituency in this country? (See comment 15bb) How on earth can their contributions and roles be more critical than mine as a minister, lawmaker and representative? (See comment 15bb) Yes, people come forward to serve in a public capacity, and there is a real element of sacrifice involved. But it is preposterous, rude and insulting for someone who is busting his tail, creating wealth and opportunity for people, making a decent and substantial contribution to his country, putting his life and his family's comfort on the line and making a real difference to the general good, to be told that his contribution is less than that of a private sector CEO. (See comment 15cc) It is ludicrous in the extreme to hear people who claim to be intelligent speaking in seemingly grudging tones about ministers and parliamentarians receiving substantial gratuities and pensions, and pay increases. (See comment 15dd) All public servants got a 10% raise effective January, 2001. All, that is, except ministers and parliamentarians. (Of course, it is no secret that as soon as the raise was introduced just like the minimum wage increase, the cheaters upped their prices). Now some parliamentarians are not doing too badly. For example, our new colleagues gets his parliamentary pay plus a handsome package from TDC. So he gets a fatter pay check at the end of the month than the ministers do. (See comment 15ee) Let me ask you this: how much longer can we reasonably expect good, committed and able people to make themselves available for public leadership if they are not to be justly remunerated. (See comment 15ff) And ask those critics, nay sayers and cheaters if **they** would take up public office at the going rates. Ask people who are, and can be, making $25,000.00 and upwards a month, if they are willing to face the music of public life for less than half of that. If they say yes, tell them to come into the bullring. Some of them are also saying that discussion of ministerial pay must be taken in the context of the size of the public service. Though not irrelevant, this argument needs to be taken in the context of job and economic stability. How many public servants do they want to be sent home? And do they have jobs for these public servants? Are they going to allow them to keep their cars, their furniture and their homes for a year or two until they can get jobs and get their lives and their families re-stabilized? Are they going to be patient with the dismissed public servants until some time as they can start finding money again to pay their bills? Are they going to be able to control the social criminal problems that will most certainly ensue if their asinine suggestion of radically downsizing the public service is pursued? Or are they going to foreclose and send these people to debtors' jail. I know the public sector is not to be treated as an easy road for the lethargic and unproductive among us. But any suggestion by anyone of those cheaters out there that the majority of public workers are louts and layabouts is wrong and rude. The cheaters look like they want to take people out of bread, but don't even have biscuit to offer in its place. I gone see! (See comment 15gg) Until Nest Time. Plenty Peace.

Comments Fifteen:

a. *The workers of this nation need your kind of honouring like they need to be exploited, as reputedly practiced by the leaders of your organization. What they need is a more honest bunch of leaders whose, motto really is: 'Country above self!' In any event, I doubt if its genuine.*

b. *What has that got to do with that person's views? If as you suggest the guy works in the Ministry of Tourism, then he is in a position to know of the wastages indulged in by that ministry including your antics. It follows therefore that if the guy has such knowledge and cannot dispose of it no place else, then why not during the public debate that was current at the time! Was that not the point of the discussion?*

c. *The list may or may not be correct. The extent to which each item reflected serious cost on government would be questionable. A cost analysis would show that some of the items would have been borne by individuals, private companies and organizations. Plus, of course there would have been those inflowing aid, both financial and materials. Indeed, it would not be too surprising if the total value of aid received was not greater than overall cost to government in relation to disasters over the period of your definition! As a minister of government, should you really be leaving anyone at the foot of any cross?*

d. *Firstly, who exactly are those international bodies who assessed the after-disaster damages? Perhaps another of your much-loved list, naming them, together with corresponding reports' breakdowns would have supplied more credence to your vague claim! Exactly who do you mean as 'our people' when you sought to solidify the necessary infrastructure to build social and economic wealth for? Did you mean the Cabinet or Marriott? Because, from where I sit, it looks to me as if both use the masses for their convenience. It certainly does not look as if any kind of wealth is being built for them!*

e. *That state of affairs was known to you even before your team assumed power. You ran for election in 1993 and again in 1995, knowing full well what the state of the sugar industry was. Stands to reason that there should have been, in terms of your strategies for sugar, a plan. That situation was allowed to drag along for two of your elected terms; or should I say 'neglected'. Clearly, action to deal with the sugar problem should have been taken much earlier in the life of your government. It is hardly acceptable now to use sugar loses as an excuse for the country's poor economic state under your watch!*

f. *That though, is your own fault! Allowing Nevis to behave as if it had autonomous international operations. Nevis is a part of the Federation and as happens in ALL federal countries in the world: federal governments are responsible for foreign affairs, which includes financial relationships with international entities and states. However, in this federation, governments of St. Kitts entreat the Nevis Island Administration to behave as if they can do as they please in the international arena. Even if the previous administration subscribed to that practice to appease Nevis for what ever reasons they had; there was no reason for your brand of government to perpetrate that inheritance. You should have exerted control of the Federal relationships the instant power was won back in 1995. Therefore, bellyaching about that now is less than impressive!*

g. *What do you want credit for? You are the ones who got this Federation into whatever 'debt mire' there is! It could be that we were led blindly into it, without the necessary planning that should accompany such ventures. If it is that the nation's head is miraculously being held above water in a sustainable way, then it is our good fortune that there are entrepreneurs and perhaps a few well meaning investors who are earning for this country rather than political skill. Additionally and especially since no accounts has been produced to substantiate claims of 'good house-keeping'!*

h. *If, as you painted, this boom is occurring; then, why are you at the same time penalizing the bulk of the population in the way that you do? Sixtipulating water, continuing with the import tax of $5,000 per used vehicle import and the most recent almost doubling of electricity? Surely if as you say: exponential advancement is the case and your government is such a marvelous social engineer, why do you not absorb some of those social shocks which are readily passed onto the masses who you profess to love so much?*

i. *Exactly who have you enriched? How do you define enrich? I certainly would describe those who have invested in 'half-hog-head' residences at below value mortgages as being enriched, or indeed any other commitment to house purchase on the communal scale! Apart from, to the consumer, below value social house purchase (normally houses are considered to be capital equipment, but these here have to be questionable with regards to that macro-economic definition), more guidance as how exactly the people have been enriched? Fact: people are eating less; spending more on phone cards; getting into more personal debts and stealing more! So, where is this enrichment? Empowerment is another of these catchy phrases that you seem to have taken a liking to! How, I would like to know has this happened. Who has been empowered and to do what? Let's face it, you the elite are the only ones who have the power and you pretty much do with it and with us as you please, when you please! Clearly, you have reasoned that the population of this country is at the moment: putty in your hands and working under the 'Labour' banner, the masses still allow you imposters to get away with waving that myth in their faces. It therefore, seems to me that the most rapidly enriched group is yours!*

j. *I question the term "our hard work". You delegate minions and 'yes-persons' below your hierarchy to do you chores for you and then after whatever is done, come out and claim the glory. You guys spend a lot of time 'globe trotting' or joy riding, sometimes attending gatherings which are not relevant to this country and some claim that these trips are done merely to accumulate travel and disturbance expenses. One has to laugh at the suggestion of hard work being relevant to you lot! Serious responsibilities are another difficult category to associate with you guys. I find it difficult to think of any sort of responsibility that you and your mates take serious!*

k. *Who are these people who made millions and millions? I have not seen anyone who fits into that category. Please show me who they are? Could it be that you are working yourself up to some state that will make you feel the need to convince the public that you deserve an increase in salary, that the people will buy it and per-haps persuade those awards trio panel personnel to give you some form of massive increase?*

l. *Seems clear to me that you are once again slipping out of reality and into another of your fantasy worlds. If there was any thing in the claim of yours, it stands to reason that the authorities would bring those responsible to book and prove their case. However, there has not been many if any such reports announced. This claim of yours seems to be a 'smoke screen' designed to make you and those who like yo,u feel good about convincing the people that you deserve the pay rise being anticipated. You make these 'way out' accusations against vague persons or per-haps companies to add strength to this point about how much you deserve a pay rise. Looks to me like a protracted build up of greed on display!*

m. *If it existed, some of it could also have lined the pockets of some of those close to you. But then we are in the realms of 'pie in the sky' land here and in such a world all this talk is fantasy drivel.*

n. *That is exactly what people are saying about a number of your colleagues! Posses-sions such as condo's; homes in far flung places of the globe are attributed to high rankers in your party. Could it be that your models for the 'far-fetched-tales' came from real-life ones not far from where you sit in Cabinet? Because, quite honestly, similes with recognizable nicknames are reported in other newspapers about some of your colleagues all the time! On the other hand, you are the only one in your newspaper who mentioned such tales and then, they are vague, too vague for recognition of anyone or organization. Thus, it is understandable when disbelief is attached to what ever you say about that subject.*

o. *If it was that some of your colleagues in and out of government were known to take hand-outs, extra to their salaried earnings. What would that make them? If someone in your ministerial position used employees paid by the government to do personal chores and errands for them. What would that make you? Would that be a form of cheating? And if that be the case, would you be classified as a cheater also? If that be the case; then what we have in this country is more cheaters than the rest. Seems, that you live in a nation of cheaters! For, in one sense or another, some form of cheating goes on in most quarters!*

p. *Talking about: 'supposed to'. You and your buddies are supposed to lead this country by example. However, you make it far too easy for yourselves. You are supposed to be citizens of this country and you say that you represent the people. What do you create for yourselves? A tax-free haven, giving yourselves concessions all over the spectrum! Advantages that ordinary people dream of in fantasy worlds. You have no idea what the real world, in terms of living is like because most of the essentials of life is sent to you by suppliers, who then squeeze the rest of us. What is not given to you, perhaps in the hope that you would be kind to those suppliers who keep you well stocked; you make laws to help yourselves to what you want to take from the rest of society and that makes you smug! Makes you feel that you can call those who try to survive and perhaps give employment to poor people, makes you feel that you can be rude to such hard working persons by calling them cheats. It is you elected officials who give the impression of being the real cheats. Just because you make laws to cushion what you do; does not mean that what you do is right. To some of us, your antics are worse than anyone who manipulates Customs to improve their balance, which enables them to create opportunities in other dimensions. Thus, while you political leaders make laws to keep you legal, the moral aspect of the things you do is more despicable than attempting to reduce Customs ridiculously high rates to ordinary folks. In any case, it looks to me as if you are once again, fantasizing up situations in your dreams to find softer easier pickings for your guys. Your blatant display of greed is growing exponentially! And you say that you are for the people! Looks to me like you are more for 'ripping' them off as much as can be done!*

q.   *But what about temptation? Would it not also be more inviting for those of you with opportunities to find ways of digging into those lovely fiscal monies to for your own, extra financial activities that are so tempting, either by drafting new laws that aid the helping of yourselves to the nation's resources, temptation to do more unnecessary globe trotting which automatically swells the travel allowance or employ increased numbers of snivel servants, resulting in less work done by you guys. The list could go on but there is no doubt in my mind that a way will be found to swell the personal coffers of elected individuals if the public purse was fatter!*

r.   *This is really a strange approach! There appears to be the 'build-up' to a case being made for you guys to encourage the public to think that some increase in your remunerations is justifiable. However, your approach is to accuse some fictitious person or persons with 'no end' of wrong doings, coupled with a plentiful dose of repeated hearsay and all that is supposed to be reasons why, we the people should melt our hearts and say: poor hard-done-by minister! Give them the money and the more the better. For you to produce such tripe and expect those of us with the capacity to think to swallow it, is insulting to everyone. Especially since, no one begged you to run for office. It was you who went throughout the land, a few months before and up to October 23, 2004, asking masses and loads of people to vote for you. You asked for the job and shortly after getting it you are abusing fictitious citizens, calling some of them cheats, just so that you elected politicians could get your hands on more money to do with as you please. Additionally, you think that you are so smart: When you pull your fast ones, you do so early in the life of your parliamentary term, counting on the eventuality that by the time election-time resurfaces, the populace will have forgotten about those worthless feats. With such acumen, you really have the devil's nerve to cast such insults, like bait on fish hooks out there?*

s.   *This revelation has the potential to be a 'tear jerker'. It may be that there are those whose heart would bleed for your predicament. Really? On $10,410 per month, that is your take home pay that is about ten times as much as what the masses, who you love so much, earns. Since you are so eager to identify with the masses, to ask for more than ten times what the normal person earns has got to be greed in the extreme! The case you are trying to make for more money at the people's expense is pathetic!*

t.   *Don't you spend a lot of time overseas? Seems to me that there is nearly always one or more of you ministers away from the country. Sometimes troops of persons are taken along on your trips. It is regularly estimated that there are those of your colleagues who accumulate travel allowance and collect at the end of the year as a sort of a bonus. The figures banded about for those annual pay-outs, seem high to me.*

u.   *If this is a 'dig' at Dr. Simmonds, why do you still continue to take the housing allowance? There certainly has been a long enough time for that slight of a pay increase to be eradicated if you wanted it removed. Truth is that you people are out for all that you can get and taking less than your predecessors is not on the menu!*

v.   *It would have been more impressive and convincing if there was documentation to show how those monies were spent. It is all very well to talk and make claims that 'such and such' were done; it is a different matter to convince sensible folks that the claims made are real! You have, in the past, made considerable mileage by calling those defined by you as cheats. Yet, here you are claiming to be so upright. However, we only have your word for that. Surely, someone of your experience should know that documented support of expenditure ought to be available to verify financial claims of the type made.*

w. *"Just $50.00 more than permanent secretaries get"! What kind of comparison is that? Surely travel allowance should be related to the amount of moving around that one does in relation to the job! If it is the case that permanent secretaries travel more than you in the execution of their duties then they should be paid more travel allowance. Using their travel allowance as a yardstick as how much ministers should receive is the same as saying that because any person is a minister, all their allowances and salaries should be above what everyone else receives. A ludicrous logic! The entertainment allowance is more than most people in this country are paid weekly. To call it a pittance is another indication of the greed that is prevalent among you 'big shot' politicians!*

x. *Sometimes that vehicle is loaned to family members. Apart from that, no mention has been made of other perks, such as complimentary gifts or discounts that are not available to the general public, items some would classify as necessities. For the purpose of living, such items are necessities to most people and contribute to the cost of life. However, when they are free, savings are the result. Not to reflect such commodities in your presentation could be considered misleading and so they would be! Is that not the same reasoning used when the word cheats are being slung around?*

y. *This could well be another of your trips to fantasia. Even if the details portrayed by you are near accurate; the question has to be: are the services produced by your fictitious comparison equate-able with yours. The parameters for your model are, to my mind, certainly not equate-able. You may have forgotten that as a public servant there are different expectations. Firstly: you were not recruited by any company for your skills, qualifications and potential for attracting the kind of business that your imaginary manager/s may have been. Looks to me as if you lost your way! It was you, hand-picked by your leader, took yourself to the constituency and for weeks on end, begged the people to vote for you, so that you could serve their needs. Those people trusted you to keep your word! Did you? Certainly not for the same remunerations that were current when you got elected. Next thing you are writing articles, trying to make yourself look pitiful so that you would feel better about taking more resources than you are probably worth. Then you have the audacity to define others as cheats. In any event, the share holders of those who own lots of benefits must be happy with the service they are receiving in exchange, otherwise they would not stand for it. We, the people, on the other hand, are your share holders but we do not get any statement of accounts to show us the scale of your economic or financial performance. Instead, we are verbally bamboozled and encouraged to think that whatever you do is okay. You have not a leg to stand on when you compare yourself to the rewards paid to our giants of industry and commerce!*

z. *Of course you believe all that! It would not surprise many people if you believed that without you the country would fail. However, what you believe is a matter for you. Other factors suggest outcomes that differ from your beliefs. You claim that you attract investors; what you fail to mention is that when you do, they come fully equipped, bring their own resources and they are given mega concessions! Explain how that injects development for local businesses? The public sector is a drain on private enterprise, the people and resources of this country. It is that way because of its inefficiency, wastage, complete disregard for its behaviour and answerability to the people on whose behalf the country functions. Yes, it appears that you do some kind of a job although it is publicly obvious that you abuse your authority with unattractive arrogance. Absurdly comparing yourselves to successful private enterprise! They must show profits to be successful and in the process satisfy their governors and shareholders. What have you accomplished to demonstrate capability? I'll tell you! People are abused fictitiously and you talk or write down to those who elect you, giving bizarre reasoning why you should get more money, when all the while you do not deserve what you already get!*

aa. *Your greed is showing again! It is affecting your logic and reasoning, which was always more than a little suspect in my view. It is not a foolish practice and I'll tell you why. Ministers are in the same category as parasites, they feed off the wealth creating components of society. No special skills are needed to be a minister, the ability to fool people by twisting whatever the truth happens to be. To use, exploit and betray those who serve you well. Wealth creation has to be a myth since you are desperately trying to believe that whatever progress occurring in this country is down to you suits your fantasy world. You create oppressive laws which in effect deter progress. Truth is, those who work in the private sector and investors are the pioneers of growth; you and your friends just find ways to load yourselves with the country's resources, as you are doing within the embedded article. Most level headed individuals would agree that in spite of your creative arguments, you have no case but I expect that your greed will win out.*

ab. *Put another way: why should a minister and what ever else you may be, elected by the people of any constituency, be paid over ten times the average of those who put him where he is. Does that not indicate such a person is not really interested in serving said people but is more concerned with self-enrichment? Why should that be? Any body can do what you are paid to produce. The fact being that original thought and inventiveness hardly if ever begin with you. Advisers, assistants private and others do your thinking for you. You are a facilitator, a conduit, passing the needs and wishes of society, which very rarely originate with ministers. They are told what to 'do and say' most of the time. Managers, on the other hand, very often have to live and function on their wits. Thus they are more creative, use more faculties and as such need to be better rewarded. There is also the probability that unseen rewards are attracted to ministers which the bulk of society are in the dark about. It would not surprise anyone if in the fullness of time some of these would come to light. In the event that such exists, and only a few besides the individual minister would know that. Your case would be very flawed! It is clear that you feel to be among the elite of this land and your attitude suggests same. These arguments are latently disguised to support that status. As in aristocracy of old, you are looking for the rewards to support that status! Another indication that your party has really and truly lost its way!*

ac. *Did you not feel that before you went about asking people to vote for you? Nobody forced you to run for the post! There are lots of other individuals, who could easily do a better job than singing stupid songs. Others who would willingly do wthat you are doing without making these efforts to line their own pockets further!*

ad. *Receiving pay increases are the norm if they are reasonable! People could accept that. It is when you make rules to award yourselves pensions for life, after serving only one term and award yourselves outrageous increases is when the public gets to be alarmed, concerned and justifiable so! It is exactly because they are intelligent, why they ask questions, when the acts of your Cabinet do not make a lot of sense to the rest of us!*

ae. *Is that what this is all about? Because when the relatively new parliamentarian totals his monthly returns from efforts expended, he gets more than you? Resulting with you guys taking it out of the public purse? Why does that make me feel that all that former display of concern for the people cannot ring true! Your greed has shown you for your true self. You really are just in the game for what you can get. Please remember this, the next time you feel the urge to bamboozle the masses with your shallow concerns for them.*

af. *Is that what we have in you guys now? "good committed and able"? There are a number of citizens who would question that. Lots of examples have already been mentioned as to why those attributes could be considered, not be applicable to your bunch. Do not kid yourself into believing that replacements for you guys would ever be hard to find and better ones too. If you don't believe me ask all those who stood against you in past elections, they would be less expensive than you lot in the long run and most probably, much better at it also.*

ag. *Clearly, the point of this particular article and topic is to influence the tri-men commission, charged with recommending parliamentarians remunerations. The article uses pathetic arguments in the cause of that aim and it worked because ministers did get a raise of between 34% to 35% increase. Quite a number of citizens and I count myself among them, said that such an increase was scandalous for a number of reasons: civil servants got 10% before the election as a bribe and pensioners got somewhere in the region of 3%; The writer failed to show effectiveness in many instances: failed the tourism industry by allowing the Florida based Cruise Federation to 'walk all over' the industry here; failed to show sufficient encouragement and patience to locals, hastily bringing in non-nationals with incentives that nationals do not receive and failed to unify tourism within the region, thereby effectively making the industry more vulnerable here. Barbados, who a short time before the award was suggested; had similar recommendation from its commission but the prime minister there on behalf of his ministers declined to take the offer because that country had concern for its people. The greedy ministers here unwisely failed to take a lesson from the Barbadians' politicians: ours, without regard for the people, nearly bit the commissioners' hands off, in their haste to line their pockets further. What a debacle and ugly display of greed!*

14 May 2005

Over the past ten years, the number of vehicles in St. Kitts has doubled and the number of licensed drivers has increased significantly. Over that same period, although we have built a considerable amount of new roads, we have not doubled it. (See comment 16a) So we have a real problem and it seems to be getting worse. The problem is bad enough during the week. But it gets worse on weekends, particularly holiday weekends when licensed drivers rent cars to get around and have their weekend fun. It's not just the additional vehicles on the road. That's only one aspect of the problem. What is scary is the carelessness, even recklessness which we are seeing out there. There is a stark contrast between people's driving while they are taking driving lessons and after they receive their licenses. In the former situation, they drive as if they are going to a funeral, while in the latter we drive as if we want to cause a funeral. It seems that upon getting our licenses many of us believe that the need for careful and responsible driving ends and it is now time to become road terrorists. For example, when was the first time you saw two vehicles tearing down the road at high speed, the one behind only a matter of a few feet away from the one in front? That is called tailgating and it is a dangerous practice. (See comment 16b) These might be two small private vehicles. It is even worse when they are two passenger buses whose drivers are so rushed that they would recklessly disregard the lives of their innocent passengers and themselves not to mention road users including pedestrians. When was the last time you found yourself driving along the island main road between villages or anywhere on the Frigate Bay Road or the Southeast peninsular road, minding your own business and being a careful driver, only to have the fear of death thrown into your heart by one or more vehicles rushing by at 60, 70 or 80 miles an hour, or faster, and putting life and property at great risk? And what about the loud music? Why is it some drivers have to try so hard to gain our attention by deafening and distracting the rest of us with thunderous, heart-jolting noise coming out of their cars' sound systems? (See comment 16c) Don't they know that they are only impressing a few? Don't they know that the attention which they are getting g is mostly negative and hostile? Don't they know or care that they are disturbing our peace and creating more anger, inconvenience and risk on the road? Don't they know that it is impossible for the human brain to properly concentrate on and control a moving automobile and still pay due care and attention to his responsibilities to the public and the users of the public road while he has a boom box blasting from his vehicle? (See comment 16d) And on top of all that doesn't he realize that he is being presumptuous and even rude to be 'entertaining' us with music or noise. Is that a macho thing with the vehicle being an extension of the man, and so the speed, the loud music and the engine noise tell us that there is a real man driving that vehicle? Real men don't need to do that kind of thing. So it's mostly little, insecure, attention-seeking boys occupying men's bodies, who do it. And don't talk about the motorbikes. Recently, a group of young men have been trying to deafen St. Kitts with these loud, fast bikes. Why? Does it get the chics? If so, what happens to them when the noise and the speed aren't there? And what kind of 'chics' can this nonsense be getting them? But this tailgating, the speeding and the noise are not the only nightmares we have. All too often when busses stop to pick up and discharge passengers the drivers do not pull over to the left. They just stop in the traffic, thereby blocking the flow of other vehicles and causing a great deal of inconvenience and anger. (See comment 16e) This type of disregard and disrespect is not what we should expect of men who use the road to make their living. They should know better. Then there is the matter of reserved parking spots. I believe that only doctors, certain Government officials and full fledged diplomats should be given such spots. Honorary consuls, businesses and others should not have them. (See comment 16f) I get particularly annoyed when I see objects placed outside Courts on Liverpool Row and outside the same Courts and Rams on the Bay Road. Those objects are put there to block other people from parking there. The police should remove the barrier and take legal action against the offenders. (See comment 16g) What about vehicles whose motors are left running, sometimes even turned off, in the middle of the road while these drivers run inside a building to make a message. And what about all of those vehicles parked on yellow lines and even on cross-walks? What are we going to do about them? And drivers who drive through cross-walks in total disregard of pedestrians, who have the right of way, trying to cross the street? People driving under the influence of alcohol and other mind-bending substances is also a matter of growing concern. Then there are so many situations in which people park their cars close to each other on narrow streets but on opposite sides of the street. When that happens, regular vehicles, but more critically, ambulances, police vehicles and fire trucks would have great difficulty getting through. Yes people just park up as if they don't know or care about others or the danger they are creating. It is time we become more careful and responsible on the road. Already too many lives have been lost and too much property damaged. I am callin on citizens and the police to do the right thing. To us drivers I say: don't drive for yourselves, drive for others. And to the police I say: issue tickets and prosecute offenders. After all, it's life we are talking about here. (See comment 16h) Until next time. Plenty peace.

Comments Sixteen:

a.   *What percentage is considered significant? From what I see, there are not many new roads as they go within their own right. Mainly, the new ones are by and large associated with project developments because without them, communications around these new communities would be stupid. This could well be another fantasy claim.*

b.   *See it happening every day, in both directions, between buses, at times more than two in speeding convoys, racing along the busy highway outside my door. Accidents occur quite rarely and it is surprising and thankfully that there aren't more. The road is the main artery between the various communities in this part of the country. What is even more surprising though: since the practice is known to you, the minister for that sort of thing; Why have has there been an absence of noticeable activities to curb or eradicate the practice? Especially among passenger carrying vehicles? Another area where your performance is sadly lacking!*

c.   *It is not your or my attention the loud music-playing drivers are trying to attract. Could be members of the opposite sex but it certainly is not you and me. Is that not the sort of thing that makes them 'macho'? in any event, when the vehicle is on the move, to the bystander, the sensation only lasts for an instant!*

d.   *I know what you are trying to do; however, I am not satisfied that you are right here. It is quite possible to have music as a background activity while some other primary function focuses the brain. For example, one can listen to music while reading or driving. The appreciated volume of the music will vary from one person to another. In some cases, right up to very high decibels.*

e.   *There are times when such behaviour is understandable and I have seen examples of such on occasions: when they are discharging school children who need to get to the other side of busy roads. They deliberately block vehicles which are behind and 'blind' from overtaking. Thereby, giving safe crossing corridors to the children getting off.*

f. *Even doctors should be restricted to one parking space outside their surgeries. I have seen one doctor on Church Street with two vehicles outside his place of work and on occasion when a government official dared to park in one of those spaces, the police was called to censor the parker in that yellow-lined space. How can one man drive two cars at the same time? Ridiculous!*

g. *Surely, businesses of the type named should have some 'leeway' when deliveries are expected? It makes sense that to have space immediately close to any storage area when large or indeed any delivery/loading has to be. Like everything else, these situations are abused from time to most of it. If the police were sensitive and smart enough to distinguish between legitimate transfer of bulk goods and casual parking convenience, then yes prosecute when abuse is the case.*

h. *And to you: the elite of society; the law makers; the spenders of our taxes. More could be spent on: making our roads safer; Widening all major arteries; repair so many roads that have or is in the process of turning to gravel, which has potential to damage vehicles; improve drainage of the numerous roads that collect water whenever there is significant rainfall. Instead of focusing on the obvious which has the advantage for you, in dissing ordinary folk; do your job and improve the main infrastructure which has the potential to improve road safety!*

21 May 2006

I dedicate this week's piece to my friend Shaka Buum who passed last week at the age of 48. I had not known him personally and closely for a very longtime, but from the moment our lives connected directly several years ago, a good vibe was created and maintained between us. (See comment 17a) For me he was a man of peace, a thinker, a creator, a social commentator, a musician, and a singer and songwriter with a wide variety of material. I loved his haunting, raspy voice, which seemed to come from the deepest recesses of his heart and soul, and I also loved his lyrics and melodies. I believe God had put him on the earth to make music. Shaka believed that too. And he lived his life true to that belief. (See comment 17b) Shaka Buum had a strong and positive influence on my life. He was very generous to me with the things that count most in life, namely, faith, truth, sincerity, compassion and good works. (See comment 17c) Almost every time we spoke I felt a wave of serenity and peace come over me, as well as a greater clarity about things which may have come up in our conversations. And we spoke about all manner of things. And as I reflect on him and the beauty of his life, and indeed on the very gift of life, I pray to God that we will spend more time looking at and for the beauty of each other. (See comment 17d) May the brother enjoy eternal joy in the bosom of the Master. And I ask his dear wife and family to accept on behalf of my son, Jesse (who was, like me, quite fond of Shaka Buum) myself and my constituents in central Basseterre, sincere condolences and assurances of our prayers and love. (See comment 17e) I think that it will also be important that a lot of his prodigious body of yet unpublished work which remains unreleased be well managed and respected manner so that we can all continue for years to come to be entertained and edified by his unique and captivating creativity and at the same time providing his family with an opportunity to benefit financially from his efforts. One of the lessons we need to learn from this man's life and death is that we must respect, honour and reward our people's talents. We in the Caribbean are talented in the arts. We create a lot. We produce a lot. But we benefit very little. Shaka Buum's death ought to be used as a wake up call for the community, to have us understand that with all of Bob Marley's fame and talent, he, his family and his country still did not reap their fair and just rewards for it. Other people controlled the business and robbed him and his people blind. And pirates and scavengers in his midst, parading as friends and brethren, sold him out. (See comment 17f) yes, Bob Marley's name will be etched indelibly across the pages of history and will remain until 'Kingdom come' as part of the Jamaican and Caribbean psyche and ethos. But that cannot change the fact that the Marley family, the Jamaican music industry and the Jamaican economy could have been inordinately better off if the moves had been made by Jamaicans, conscious and conscionable, to ensure that command and control of the creative, productive, managerial and marketing processes had been vested in the right hands. It is high time that we in the Caribbean understand that all of this musical and other artistic talent that we possess is not only to be used for fun. We also have to start playing for take too. (See comment 17g) And shaka Buum is not the only artiste in St. Kitts & Nevis with a prodigious body of good work. Just go back over the past 40n or so years and see. I have to compliment and encourage people like John Francis and Adrian Lam who, like others, are trying to establish this music thing as the industry that it ought to be. And I am heartened at the number of persons who have established studios. We must now really move with unswerving tenacity and vigour to breaking through with a few top-of-the-world artistes coming through on labels that are owned by locals in whole or in part, our intellectual assets, our creativity, our music and other artistic talent will be the main driving forces in our economic development in the future. And we must not limit ourselves to music. We have to get into short films, video productions, documentaries, full length films, post production, etc etc. (See comment 17h) I had tried to initiate the process when I wore other ministerial hats, but I don't think that the essential, initiative needs to come from the public sector. This thing is a business, and one with mind-boggling potential to bring massive and ongoing benefits to the people of this country. Look, if an American man can make a movie and put it on HBO and in our cinemas, why can't Caribbean people do the same? Some of the brightest minds in the arts and the production thereof in the USA, Canada, England and France are Caribbean People. (See comment 17i) this is the world of the World Trade Organization. They say we are now living in a global village in which political borders are evaporating. So just as Royal bank and Bank of Nova Scotia can open branches here, so can National Bank open branches in Brooklyn, Toronto and London, and just as American and European artistes, managers and producers can put their hands into our pockets and take our money, so can and should we do the same. All 'legit' and above board, these are the new rules of the game, and it is high time that we in these countries master the game rather than continue getting our tails cut just like the present West Indies cricket team. (See comment 17j) It's not only they who can create and sell. After all the experience of slavery, indenture and deprivation will have created a sufficiently high level of collective creativity and skill, back then simply to survive, to position these countries, now that we are relatively freer, to hold our own against everybody and everything they can throw at us. (See comment 17k) If we capitalize on education and ensure a sustained sense of discipline, dignity, pride, productivity and purposefulness as a people, the centuries old learned and deeply embedded survival and success skills, coupled with unquestionable high brain power, will guarantee success. These are some of the things Shaka Buum and I used to talk about wistfully and optimistically. You know, I was in New York last week. I had some very encouraging meetings with the Police Commissioner, the Fire Commissioner and the Deputy Corrections Commissioner. My objective in meeting with them was to establish institutional connectivity in an effort to assist in the development of our human resource, equipment, and so on, and also to establish a face to face relationship with these people. (See comment 17l) I also had the opportunity to meet with the editorial board of the famous Carib News, the top West Indian newspaper in the USA, owned by Dr. Carl Rodney and his dynamic wife Faye, who gathered around their boardroom table an array of Caribbean luminaries who showed me love and understanding and a great commitment to serve the cause of Caribbean people both here at home and in the Diaspora. I was also given an opportunity to deliver the feature address at a power breakfast put on by Dr. Roy Hastick, a Grenadian dynamo who head up the Caribbean American Chamber of Commerce & Industry (CACCI). Dr. Hastick is married to a Kittitian lady who has been a professor at Medgar Evers University for many years. (See comment 17m) At that breakfast were representatives of major New York City and State officials, including the State Governor. And all of these representatives were Caribbean people. At the same meeting was Mr. Edmund Sadio of Nevis who is a very successful business man in New York. **I tell you, we people up dey ain't mekkin' joke, you know!** And you know something that I hardly saw up there? Young men with their pants down over their bottoms and exposing their boxer shorts. So for those of us here who like to follow fashion, be advised that the fashion seems to be disappearing up there. I also met with a number of members of the New York City Council and was introduced along with the members of my delegation (which included high-level officers from the Police, the Defense Force, Fire & Rescue, the Prison, and my Ministry) to the Council sitting in public session. Councilwoman Ms. Yvette Clarke, a most brilliant, dynamic and popular New York politician Jamaican descent, proudly set up a flag of St. Kitts & Nevis on her desk at the Council Chamber as she introduced my delegation. We were received with a rousing New York round of applause by the Council members and the full public gallery. What was particularly heart-warming about our visit to the 52-member council was to see so many Caribbean people as members, and most of them under the age of 45. We also saw the same pattern when we attended a function at the Brooklyn Historical Society. The Vice President of the Brooklyn Borough Council is a young Jamaican lady. Then there are other Caribbean people running for District Court Judge posts, etc. Yes, Caribbean people making a master move up there in New York, and it is absolutely necessary that we down here understand and appreciate the critical importance of what they are doing and the enormous benefits that can and will accrue to us as a region if our folks up there are successful in taking a significant chunk of the political pie in the City and Borough Councils of that great city and other communities in America, Canada, England, etc. (See comment 17n) What we are seeing here is the beginning of what one hopes will be a paradigm shift in which the peoples of the world who have hitherto been marginalized can now get closer to the levers of big power and make the difference that the world absolutely needs if we are to survive as a planet and a civilization. Let's be brutally frank. Those who have controlled things for the past thousand years of so have made a mess of things. So its time to introduce a new culture. (See comment 17o) Not one which jingoistically oppresses, suppresses, excludes, demeans, deprives, cheats, depletes and subjugates. Rather, one which spreads the word of equal opportunity, equity, hope, inclusion, empowerment, enlightenment, peace, and respect for individual, cultural and governmental differences in the name of God and goodness. A culture of love, humaneness, tolerance and civility. (See comment 17p) I am convinced that mankind's only earthly hope will come from this new culture which I am seeing with pellucid clarity being developed in New York. It is now for us in the Caribbean to join hands with them, and, of course, with each other, so that instead of being regarded and dismissed as a set of disparate and inconsequential whisperers and complainers, we can raise a thundering, meaningful and well-intentioned voice in the debate and direction of mankind's future. These are things that Shaka Buum and many of our other conscious and caring artistes have spoken in verse and otherwise. May the force be with us. Bye bye, Shaka. See you on the other side. (See comment 17q)

Comments Seventeen:

a.   *By "maintained between us", do you mean that you were in regular communication with Shaka Buum? If so was it by telephone, letter, the internet or what?*

Have to say that I find it surprising that someone like yourself would have been a personal friend of an internationally famed superstar. Still, life is full of surprises!

b. *Why do I get the feeling that this is another of your inventive exercises? You are talking as if you two were old friends and I sensed that there was a hint of that when the article began but somehow I feel that your life's path and his were somehow, not in sync for the better part of your lives. For a start he was 48 and you were at that time somewhere in your early sixties at the time of his death. That puts you two in different generations, which is not exactly a setting for being of like minds or with a propensity to be friends. It really sounds to me as if you are pulling a 'fast one'!*

c. *When were Shaka's generosity with those things that matter most in life shared with you? As I recall, by the time you and I had a working relationship, none of those attributes were any part of your demeanour. You had: little or no faith with me; the truth did not show through at all as far as I was concerned; sincerity, compassion and good works were certainly very absent. Thus if you had them at some time in your life it must have been after us or they were conveniently forgotten by the time my existence emerged into your life-space!*

d. *"We will spend more time looking at and for the beauty of each other"! are you joshing? When was the last time you saw beauty in anyone but what you see in the mirror, looking back at you? Even if that happens? That phrase must have slipped out during a period of melancholy because it really does not strike me as natural at all. Perhaps, if you keep working at it, one day it might become a reality but forgive me if I do not hold my breath.*

e. *Were your constituents, fans of Shaka Buum also? If they were, how did you find out? Were they canvassed one at a time? The sources of your information are quite amazing.*

f. *Seems that there possibly could be a parallel somewere near here! If it is true that you and your fellow ministers are parading as saviours of the people and are also in the process of selling out this country in whatever form, then there is not much difference between you guys, the friends and brethrens of Shaka Buum!*

g. *I am glad to hear that kind of talk or writing because as I write, one of your government's institutions is in the process of engaging an international firm to analyze the Port Authority with a view to modernize it. Ironically, when I worked for that organization, as part of my commitment to the work, a number of mod-*

els for improvement and developmental ideas were presented freely, to the then board of directors. No response was ever returned. I don't mind wagering that my ideas then will not be much different from what the Port will now be paying vast sums for! Please tell your own government that this talent that we possess should be taken seriously. Look at the waste that could have been saved if my ideas were seriously considered. It would be something if your money could replace the talk!

h.   *What about writers? Especially those specializing in political criticisms about the antics of politicians locally! Should artists of that caliber be encouraged also?*

i.   *This is a statistic I don't know, have not heard about and coming from you, do not trust! Of course your 'some' could easily be two or less in each of the countries listed. The sum of the individual countries could be called 'some'. It would indeed be nice and encouraging if the claim was true. However, since such statements of that ilk are suspect, another source will have to be awaited.*

j.   *You do write an incredible lot of 'bull'! No Kittitian, Nevisian or indeed Caribbean person could simply expand or create branches in any developed country and for a host of reasons, not least are the myriad of entry restrictions to most countries outside any region. Differentials in costs, standards, logistics and other variables are all tilted against any such move. Since you think that you are capable of encouraging such innovative pioneering; why do not your government make the tax burden on companies with such plans easier, so that resources can be channeled to that sort of ambition? The odds are, that will never happen and such fanciful dreams have to be put down to your usual puncheon to fantasize.*

k.   *This does not feel right. The 'we' part before 'relatively freer' and the 'us' at the end of the: "throw at us". They don't sit right because you and your ancestors were not in the suffering that would evoke such emotions. It is the people of my persuasion, who did the suffering and were exploited by those of your kind. Thus, you may find it fashionable to be identified with us descendents of the down-trodden. As far as I am concerned though, you are not welcome. You see, really and truly, we are still being 'ripped-off', to some extent by these absurd articles but more materialistically, by the conspiracy which your Cabinet indulges in, against the people of this country, collectively in the main but the signs are that some individuals from that club are not too badly off, thank us very much.*

l.   *It was a 'joy ride' at our expense! At the time of writing, over one year after the event. No visible results are evident from where I am. In any case, why does any*

minister or other local official want to establish any kind of face-to-face relation-
ship with public officials from New York City? Does the minister not know that
we are not in the same league with these people? We live according to different
systems and have very little apart from a bastardized form of the spoken language,
in common. So what relevance or meaning could there be to the objective
defined? It was a waste of time and a waste of tax-payer's money!

m. *Hope she does not decide to come back here with the idea of helping her country*
of birth. If she does, you lot will make short shrift of her. Just like the experiences
of yours truly. Her reputation and aura will remain in tact as a long as her per-
formance is outside of this Federation. Pity you did not recommend that some of
these dynamos, whom you met, that they get hold of a copy of "Pitfalls of A
Returning Resident"?

n. *As per usual, you generalize in ways unacceptable. How on earth can you extrap-*
olate what you saw in New York to Canada, England and who knows what
other places your over active head is working in? Such generalization is logically
daft! The image of your hands itching at the expectation that Caribbean persons
who do well in their adopted countries will somehow send some of it your way in
time to come! That also could well be as a result of your membership of this gov-
ernment, who could easily be seen as a begging government. As such therefore, it is
easy to see why you would get so excited and maybe even rubbing you hands
together as you drool about future prospects. My advice to you is that you do not
count your chickens before they come home. Especially, knowing your attitude
towards those of our country people who come back home. My sincere hope is that
your localized, negative attitudes towards returning residents are not spread
around the Caribbean! In time no doubt, those who read the book will be suffi-
ciently warned! Still looks as if the applause and receptions that you reported still
adds up to a joy ride at the poor tax payer's expense! You can't fool all the people
all the time!

o. *Seems that you have returned to the land of 'cloud-cuckoo' once again. As long as*
this world is inhabited, it will always be dominated by the strong countries and
no amount of cosmetic dressing like those you got so excited about on your 'gad
about' in the 'big apple' is going to change the real dynamics. That philosophy is
very much reflected here in this federation. The fact of the matter is that you and
your cabinet colleagues are not exactly the best for the country, you probably are
aware of that but let any other group try to take the reins of power away and you
would all want to scratch their eyes out. Of course, what you are probably trying

to say is that the likes of 'Bush' and leaders of the larger countries should hand over the reins of the world to people like you? It's always the same with you petty hopefuls: what you have, you hold on to; but what someone else has, if it is shinier than yours; you want to get your hands on that! Your greed showing again.

p. *It might be an idea to put money where the mouth is: instead of spouting all of that philosophy on paper. You are a minister; get your government to adopt, honour and practice such principles. First though the need for clarity and transparency will have to be worked out. The truth will have to somehow find its way from you guys to the people and since that will have to be the norm! What will be the effect on your cabinet? It will have to go, since there will be no need for it. Then what will you do? When you begin to move in that direction, then we will know that you are not just blowing hot air to fill the columns of your article.*

q. *Much of the sentiment about the accompanying article are spread throughout my comments. However, there is a glimpse of frivolous traveling, for what appears to be no good reason. One cannot help the conclusion that for a small country such as ours, there ought really to be more care exercised in spending our money on jaunts. Can't help but remember an earlier article, where 'cheats' was a very frequently used word throughout the article. Matching that with this one, suggests that was a bullying tactic in an effort to accumulate scarce resources that were frittered away on this jaunt to the big apple. Such an attitude suggests one that is unconcerned and selfish. I suppose that there are those who would not be surprised at that revelation.*

28 May 2005

There is a chap who writes in The Democrat every week under the name 'Straight Talk' He walks around like Arnold Schwarzzenegger. But he is more, like daffy Duck. Schwarzzy has a friend who also writes in the Democrat under the name 'Watchdog'. His personality is more like a Rug Rat, but I suppose he thinks that 'Watchdog' is more macho. Go, Doggie! These two chaps hate me like hell! But all I have for them is peace. Doggie wrote an article some years ago that earned me $35,000.00 in a libel suit. Thanks be to God, and Allah be praised, because that money went to help a number of needy people in my constituency and elsewhere. One PAM woman got some help out of it to have a mammogram and other procedures to check out a suspicious lump in her breast. She is alive and apparently well today. Again, thanks be to God, and Allah be praised. So as you can see, I have been able to turn their hatred for me into good. (See comment 18a) Schwarzzy and Doggie are two cowards though. I'm talking about two big men, and they have big jobs in town. So I don't know why they would be so terrified of putting their names to their articles. And their employers are corporate giants which are heavily invested in PAM. No, that is not correct. They work for companies which own PAM. Oh yes, along with the Herberts. This 'ownership' of PAM by a certain section of our corporate community was clearly and dramatically illustrated in a comment made to me some years ago by one of its leading members, his stomach and bladder bursting with Carib, his brain pickled like a pig's snout, his tongue loose and reckless, and his heart bursting with arrogance. He said: "**PAM** and dem are a bunch of (bad word) but at least they are our (bad word)". That statement resonates through my head every time I see that guy. He and the cabal of corporate overlords of the country **hate** labour and they own PAM. This hatred of Labour and love ownership of PAM forms a deeply embedded composnent of the socio-economic-political dynamic that has characterized this country for the past hundred years of so since grassroots people started seriously organizing themselves and we saw the formation of the Musical Improvement Society, the Benevolent Society etc. Another of the overlords who used to say that Labour was better for the country but PAM was better for him, says nowadays that he will always be a PAM, but, lord have mercy,

"ah mekking money can't dun under Labour". He says he believes that under Labour he is making more money than even Damian Hobson, Michael Morton, and the Sprat Net fellows. He is one who enjoys saying that Labour is in government but PAM people are doing better than ever! These overlords and their companies would sit complicity in diabolical silence, perhaps even giving encouragement, while their spoiled brat Lindsay Grant threatens all kinds of violence and mayhem in this country. (See comment 18b) However, they would deafen you with their screams of self-righteous hypocritical indignation, directly or institutionally, if a Labour person only belched hard. They would make all kinds of calls for transparency, good governance from the public sector and talk about the national debt, but they would rob the treasury, and their own shareholders employees and customs without any blinking conscience.(See comment 18c) Maybe they don't know or don't care about Proverbs 1, Verse 19 which says: **"So are the ways of everyone who is greedy for gain; it takes away the life of its owners".** In other words, greedy people are consumed and destroyed by their own greed. (See comment 18d) Maybe they still haven't learned that the road to economic, social and political stability is paved with, and only with a sense of social conscience and compassion, justice and equity. Sometimes the transparency talk goes from the ridiculous to the sublime. For example the recent situation in which City Drug Store, operating as a private company was sold to TDC, a public company traded on the Eastern Caribbean Securities Exchange. The chairman and perhaps leading shareholder of City Drug Store is a person who is the immediate past chairman of TDC. I am not accusing anyone of wrongdoing in the transaction. What I am say though is that if such a transaction had occurred in the USA the Securities & Exchange Commission would have been all over it with a wire brush to ensure absolute transparency. Questions such as who negotiated the sale on behalf of the two parties, how the final price was arrived at, were the shareholders of TDC apprised before hand, etc, etc. But none of that took place. It makes you wonder if these people really believe that they have credibility among sensible people when they talk about good governance, transparency and all of that good stuff. (See comment 18e) And it isn't too late for the Eastern Caribbean Securities Exchange's general manager (or whatever his designation is) to call the parties together to ensure full disclosure, considering that the buyer in the transaction is a company whose shares are traded on the Exchange. (See comment 18f) I have written about this before, but none of them has taken me on. Perhaps people at the highest levels of the financial system will do so, in the interest of transparency and good governance, and also in the interest of credibility of all of the institutions involved. (See comment 18g) It is time the friend-friend thing be put aside in the interest of transparency, decency and credibility. Failing that, all of them should shut their traps. He corporate over-lords would cry out and say that the Labour government imposes too much tax on poor people, yet every time the same poor people get a little raise in pay, up go the prices in their stores. In fact, the poor people don't even need to get a raise of pay for prices to go up. (See comment 18h) And maybe they are right to some extent, because the Labour government should have long taken firm and uncom-promising steps to make sure that the big tax and customs duty cheaters pay what they owe and were brought to justice. Had that been done early and steadily, the national debt wouldn't be any way near where it is today. So we, the Labour Gov-ernment, have to take much of the blame for allowing these scamps to wax mor-alistic and ethical when we all know the reality top be different. You all know what I'm talking about. (See comment 18i) These are the same people who used to say that Marriott wasn't going to happen, and when they saw it happening they said its owners were building it with drug money. Yet they can't stay away from Vic De Zen's casino where they gulp down his free liquor, and suck up to him. And his presence here has made some of them millionaires, and other multi-millionaires. Where is their dignity? How can you accuse a man of having drug money, and yet suck up to him and look to grab up his money? (See comment 18j) They used to say that there would be no Scenic Railway, yet look who got work there from the start: three PAM activists. They claimed that La Vallee Golf Course was nothing but an election gimmick. Yet, they can't stay away from the place, looking to sell and scavenge. They used to refer to Port Zante as Port Panty. Now they are flocking to see how much money they can grab out of the hands and pockets of the international businessmen who have now invested in a big way at Port Zante. They ignored and mocked the place for ten long years, dis-regarding our encouragement to jump-start the place and get St. Kitts a higher profile as a destination for quality international shopping and other commercial activities. But as soon as we got these international players on board, the bawling and howling started. All kinds of chupidness 'bout we giving the Indians conces-sions that they can't get, and calling for level playing fields? (See comment 18k) However, now that they are being brought to order, they are bawling and scream-ing "murder"! And the funny thing about this, is that although there had been virtually no local investment at Port Zante for ten years, it didn't mean that some 'nice guys' weren't making money from the facility. Between you and me, some of them have been doing well out of Port Zante, smuggling in stuff from St. Maarten for their businesses, their homes and their friends. In the process they too have been robbing the Treasury. (See comment 18l) One of those 'nice guy' smugglers was heard gloating and drooling in his usual confused and drunken stupor last Saturday night about how the Antigua & Barbuda Prime Minister had socked it to the Douglas Government on the national debt, and calling upon "Lindsay Grant, our next PM, Lindsay, to fix up things here in this country, and we will surely get our hands on those sugar lands. Just wait and see". That's what the cretin is alleged to have said just last Saturday night when he was over there drinking off Vic De Zen's liquor. (See comment 18m) It is in this 'elite' company that Schwarzzy and Doggie find themselves, not by any means as principal players, but as major gophers who are comfortably ensconced in jobs that pay plenty for the little work they do. And incompetent as Schwarzzy and Softie are, and as busy as they are throughout the working day writing their articles, engaging in political conversations on the phone, sending off e-mails, and writing crap on the St. Kitts Internet Chat Room, their makko companies still find it easy to pay them salaries of over $12,000 a month, plus travel allowance, free company car, free gas, free gas, free this and free that, and allow them to use the company's phones and computers to carry out PAM propaganda. (See comment 18n) These two chaps are safe. And even if there was a 'falling out' between their companies and themselves, a sort of corporate-executive-musical-chairs arrangement would be worked out in order to ensure that, as members of the PAM elite-gopher class, Schwarzzy and Doggie will remain in bread, while the ordinary Joe and Mary have to fight for biscuit. Remember when, just a few years ago, one of the corporate giants laid off about 35 people and in that same year they shared over a million dollars in bonuses among the top four executive officers? So the worst that would happen to Schwarzzy and Doggie is that they would receive a gentle rap on the knuckles and probably get transferred from section of the cartel to another. So what are Schwarzzy and the Doggie so afraid of that they cannot put their names to their articles in the Democrat? (See comment 18o) After all, the 10th June survivor can't play with them the same way he can play with Mitch, because they are members of the PAM elite and they write in the Democrat, while all poor Mitch can lay claim to is that he has worked hard to develop the Company (and he has done a pretty good job at it), that he does not write in any newspaper, and that he is a friend of Denzil Douglas. Yet, Schwarzzy and Doggie are mortally afraid to put their names in the Democrat. For all of Schwarzzy's big chest and Doggie's big hair, they are really more like Daffy Duck and Rug Rat. So last week Schwarzzy writes that I took a bunch of Labour supporters to America on a joy ride. He said that "no one really understood the purpose of his (my) visit. Poor Schwarzzy. He went on to say that "because there is no transparency in St. Kitts speculators and rumour-mongers proclaimed that the Hon. Minister might have been negotiating the release from prison of a convicted drug trafficker". I have mentioned transparency already but perhaps Schwarzzy can say if there is transparency in a company in which retired executives are still getting full pay and all other perks that came when they were active. Do the shareholders know about that? (See comment 18p) I wonder if he finds transparency in a company which is guilty of cheating on its taxes with total contempt and without the slightest sign of contrition. Indeed, abusing and insulting government officials even while they are caught red-handed, pants down, and their hands deep into the public cookie jar! So in that moment of characteristic, vintage nincompoopery and self-definition, poor old Schwarzzy decided to dive into the cesspool of speculation and rumour-mongering, ending up inevitably with mess all over his face. Which would probably be an improvement to his face, but which still indecently exposes his asininity and that of the leadership and the mouthpiece of the party whose cause he so fervently seeks to promote. It doesn't exactly flatter his employers either. (See comment 18q) Funny, eh! He and Doggie are so proud of PAM, but not proud enough o put their names to their articles in PAM's newspaper week after week, after week. Go figure that one out! This convicted drug dealer to whom Schwarzzy referred. I wonder if he meant the PAM fellow in the US prison who helped set up the arrangements some years ago when PAM operatives started allowing the transshipment of cocaine from Columbia through St. Kitts on its way up to the USA and Canada? Or is it the one who helped set up the local gun trade here in the early 1980's, or the one whose name has been sometimes linked on the street with the assassination of police officer Stafford Grant also in the early 1980's? Or could it be the other PAM operative doing a life sentence in America who said that he had voted three times in three different constituencies for PAM in the 1989 general elections? Foolish Schwarzzy also castigated me for not carrying the Defense Force Commander and the Police Commissioner on the trip, notwithstanding his claim of their "perceived unworthiness to hold these offices". (See comment 18r) Wha' happen to Schwarzzy, eh? I suppose that Schwarzzy is in a hurry to insert Keithley Phillips as Defence Force Commander and to bring Mokko Stick out of retirement and make him Police Commissioner. I also understand they might be looking at bringing back the Morris fellow who is in the US Witness Protection Program to head up the Drug Squad. Then in one breath he says that he did not know the purpose of the trip, yet in the other, he wants to dictate who I should have taken with me. Poor fellow is confused. I knew it all along. I hope his new foreign lady friend can help him disentangle himself. (See comment 18s) I wonder when Michael is going on trips for TDC if it is the top officials who always go. Doesn't Schwarzzy get to go on trips too, so that he can get his $100.00 a day travel allowance too. Back to transparency and all that other good stuff, I wonder what the shareholders of TDC would have to say if they knew how much company time and other resources Schwarzzy uses up in the service of PAM. Maybe it's time for TDC's internal auditor, Shawn Richards, to step into Schwarzzy's department and check things out. Maybe it's time for the shareholders to start shaking the tree, and ask some tough questions. (See comment 18t) Schwarzzy said that we went on a joy ride. So here is what I've decided to do. I am making sure that the organizations, institutions and individuals with whom we visited in New York will get a copy of his article, so that they might develop insights or new insights towards PAM. He said that the trip cost over $100,000.00. Well, Shawn really has to go in there and audit Schwarzzy! Because if that's the best arithmetic that Schwarzzy can come up with, then TDC is headed for problems. Already Grant has declared his shares to be worth a dollar each, which would be enough to have plunged TDC into the abyss were it anyway near being true, and now his suck-up lieutenant Schwarzzy comes up with this new math. I tell you, this could be trouble for the big boys. Can you take Schwarzzy seriously? Of course not! And if you can't take Schwarzzy, who is a major member of the PAM elite-gopher class, seriously, how can sensible people take PAM seriously? (See comment 18u) The fool says that the country is poised for economic shock. We had 4% growth last year, we are managing our debt, we have a plan to reduce it and to re-organize our food production sector as we replace cane sugar production. In the process of a whole heap of empowerment of poor people will take place, (See comment 18v) which will again put more money into TDC's ppocke4t, and generate major economic activity generally. More and more homes are being built (which is fattening the coffers of TDC'S Building Materials Division and SNIC). FINCO is prospering. Cars are selling like hot bread, and all of the big companies that can't wait to see Labour out of office, are making more money than ever before. (See comment 18w) On top of that investors are flocking to our shores like flies, TDC itself is building a villa project, and looking to get involved in hotel at Frigate Bay, and the pappyshow says that we are in for an economic shock. His own company is exhibiting great confidence in the government and the country (not withstanding the fact that it has taken on an unmistakable and unapologetic PAM personality), (See comment 18x) yet poor Schwarzzy is expressing gloom and doom. Don't you see that Schwarzzy needs help? Don't you see that he is at odds with TDC? Don't you see that he is out of step with reality? Will the new lady friend fro overseas be able to help? I hope so, because Schwarzzy really needs help. I pray that God will guide him and help him out of his abysmal ignorance, confusion and wickedness. Only time will tell. (See comment 18y) Until next time, Plenty Peace.

Comments Eighteen:

a.   *Did you not use any of it to help with your mortgage?*

b.   *If what you say has any truth in it, then for your team, there ought to be a sense of 'de-ja-vous'! As there are recollections of similar tales during 93-94, when you guys were desperate for power. 'Little Chef' from the restaurant of the same name, after you guys failed to recognize and reward him properly was heard to testify, unofficially, how he used to leave crates of empty bottles out for the havocs indulged in then. Thus, your critique suggests that you are saying: do what I say; not what we once did when we wanted power.*

c.   *Are you saying that it is wrong to ask for transparency and good governance? As far as I can see there is nothing wrong with the people knowing what you guys are doing with our money. Seems to me that there is a perpetual lop-sidedness about your attitudes: when any negative forces are applied to your money collection mechanisms then you are 'up in arms', calling fictitious persons all sorts of names. However, when call is made to account for what you do with that money within your coffers, you sneer at those. There is nothing wrong with such calls!*

d.   *I can't believe that you are quoting a scripture on the theme of greed? Why only a few short weeks ago, you demonstrated that very same streak. Then, you went on about how deserving a pay increase would be to you and your colleagues; yet, here you are in this article using Proverbs 1, Verse 19 to warn greedy people about losing their lives through greed. Are you not in the same set of people being warned so cataclysmically?*

e.   *Seems you are fantasizing a fuss about what appears to be nothing! As far as I am concerned, a sale took place. To my simple logic, that required an agreement between two parties, one selling and the other buying. If there was agreement in all dimensions of the transaction, I see no problem! If there was any dissatisfaction with any aspect of the sale, someone, somewhere would have protested and as far as can be recalled, none of that took place. Is this another example of your greed-jealous driven hysteria at work?*

f.   *Seems to me that your level best is being employed to stir up unpleasantness for TDC. The obvious facts are: TDC executive is elected by their shareholders each year to run that company according to collective decision process. Expansion and other policies are arrived at by methods peculiar to that body. The Eastern Caribbean Securities Exchange Commission has no control over how the company does business! Maybe, if there were complaints form shareholders on either side of the transaction, then maybe. It is perhaps instructive that no heed was paid to your advice because it was probably seen for what it was.*

g. *People who live in glass houses should not throw stones. You belong to a cabinet which operates in secrecy. Whatever you collectively do, good or bad and the public only gets to know whatever version you chose to reveal. The private sector is open to their members unlike you. Therefore, attributes such as transparency and good governance are the business of its members; the same can not be said for your organization. Thus, it would be a good idea to pick 'the beam out of the appropriate eye. Perhaps the reason why no one took you on over the matter you wrote of before is that your real motives were recognized!*

h. *There is a general feel that government is more prone to lead price increases than any other cause, including private led increases and do not forget that increase on imported goods is not strictly speaking, the fault of local private enterprise! Government increases utilities more frequently, including adding fuel surcharge to electricity bills. That has a multiple effect: there is the direct increase due to household bills; the secondary all-round effect due to suppliers of goods and services having to raise their prices caused by fuel surcharges biting into their operational costs. Thus, when private enterprise put their prices up, there is only one effect but when government does it; the resulting rises are multi-dimensional!*

i. *To some extent, we, all of us are scamps in one sense or another. You cabinet members are scamps collectively, in the sense that you rig the law to suit yourselves. Thus even though, in the legal sense, the benefits you take for yourselves are made legal, the rest of us know that they are not fair and exploit the people who put you there to govern, the same people who you are supposed to look after are sucked almost without them knowing what you are doing to them. That is scamp-ish! When you huddle together in your secretive cabinet and conspire against citizens because of vindictive or spiteful reasons, that is worse than being scamps. What do you call those involved in shielding a high government official who was reportedly intercepted at a regional airport carrying a briefcase filled with money, reputedly as a courier, who had to be rescued by a government minister and to this day no charges were brought against the roving courier. Indeed, for him, it looks like business as usual! That is scamp-ish-ness in the extreme!*

j.   *One cannot win all the time. They also said that nothing would materialize from the 'Stevic' boast. The building at the airport roundabout was predicted to be a waste of time when Conaree village was robbed of its sports field and they were right. It is in the nature of politicians to 'suck-up' to somebody or other! Thus, it is as wide as it is broad. To talk about 'where is his, hers or anyone's dignity' is to forget or fail to appreciate what dignity is. Oftentimes, I have asked many a person: where is your dignity as a country when your beloved Marriott can rough ride over the citizens of this country and their sensitivities, while you lot make excuses for the flimsy lines of stories they feed you, which you and your 'hangers-ons' swallow whatever lines you are fed! Thus, anybody's dignity has to be relevant to them/you. The universal standard of dignity has long been lost here!*

k.   *If what they are saying is true, how could it be stupid-ness? There certainly is talk that those who you brought here to trade at Port Zante gets advantages that our people do not. If that is so, then such biased treatment has got to be wrong!*

l.   *Why is it that such smug vibes are vibrated from your writing when there are remarks about someone robbing the Treasury? Is that smugness derived from the consideration that you are not in positions to share in activities that are classified as 'Treasury robbing'? Then again, that is not necessary in your cases? Not since the ability to circumvent your needs by making rules to suit those of serving ministers? What was the courier doing, who was reputedly apprehended in the Bahamas with a brief case, packed with US currency? He was on your side of the political divide, was he not? If any of that report was true and you should know for he is supposed to be one of yours. Would that be considered as robbing the Treasury? If it was true, how is it that no arrests were made? Is it perhaps, that your commentary venom is reserved for non-labour supporters?*

m.   *If there is anything in that report, then whoever it is, hoping to get his or their hands on sugar-lands will most certainly be very disappointed. Since by the time PAM gets into power, the bulk of the sugar-lands would have been passed to mainly non-Kittitians, some would say, at less than market values! No wonder you appear to be so up-beat, because you know that they can live in hopeless-hopes!*

n.   *Where do you write 'from your desk' articles? Are they written at your desk at work? Do you not use the Government phone and computer to conduct party-political work? I do not believe that the answer to any of the above is no. I have seen your use of government paid personnel to perform personal domestic services*

*on your behalf and during election time. No one, not even you, is without blem-
ish in the regard of misappropriating employer resources.*

o. *The guess would be they are afraid of the same reason why you have not called
them by their real names. Not since this article began. Indeed, I do not ever recall
you naming those two in any of your previous articles! That therefore, begs the
question: What are you afraid of?*

p. *Perhaps their rules permit them to behave that way. In much the same manner
in which your cabinet changed the rules to allow full pensions after being in office
for only term, other groups have rules peculiar to them also. It would be a reasonable conclusion to predict that their companies would be more transparent than
government. Alas, they only have to satisfy their shareholders; whereas you, ought
to answer to the whole country but you don't. Thus on the scale of right and
wrong, your government is well off to the left!*

q. *That personal reference to that person's face was really uncalled for. How could
mess all over anyone's face be an improvement? The irony is that in my view, he
is better looking and has a better build than you. Logic would demand to know
that if he is better looking than you and mess would improve his face. The question has to be: what would mess do to faces of those who is not as good looking as
he is?*

r. *That begs the question: were any of you who made the trip worthy of the offices
held? It is that you like to say that the people voted for you. Trouble with that
statement is that the people voted for Labour which was wrapped around you at
the time. At the time of writing would the same people vote for you again?*

s. *If it is that he has a lady friend, foreign or otherwise, at least she is a woman!
Have you got one? Have you got anybody apart from a son? Perhaps if you had
somebody to straighten you out, such drivel would not flow from your desk?*

t. *The citizens and residents of this country are effectively shareholders in your government. Me-thinks that they have more grounds to shake your tree and ask some
tough questions of you about all sorts of subjects, ranging from missing funds to
government high civil officials carrying loads of money through a regional airport. However, it would not matter if they did ask questions because you guys and
your newspaper mouthpiece do not give straight answers, indeed, one would be
lucky if they got relevant answers at all. However, because in general people are
like sheep and would blindly follow you lot, forgetting those poor civil behaviour*

spasms, when they occur, forgetting them by the time election returns to being current. Therefore, it is not only shareholders of large companies who should be shaking trees. The people of this country have a more urgent need to do exactly that!

u.   *Why stop there? That question could be further extended even more generally: how can sensible people take any politician seriously? Especially those elected to run government? They fail to take those who elected them seriously. They rip off the country they are supposed to be running on behalf of the people by shunting the cream of resources to themselves. They make themselves the elite of the land and pretend to be doing so for the good of the masses, when there is no relevance or relationship there anymore. Politicians of these days have become so dishonest, that it is difficult to trust any of them anymore.*

v.   *When? It has now been nearly one year since the Sugar Industry has been perma-nently closed! When will empowerment of those who were thrown out of that industry happen? Words like empowerment are frequently used; they are just words without substance because no empowerment can be seen anywhere. It may be that such was in the plan but something went wrong. I wonder if all that money apprehended on its way to 'who knows where' by the Bahamians, had anything to do with the reason why that plan for those poor people were never empowered? If it was there in the first place?*

w.   *What ever happened to the philosophy that prevailed: The country is for all of us! You promoted PAM persons over Labour individuals who helped you get into power. We are the government of all the people for the whole country, you used to say! Now you are running down pammites because they make money under a Labour administration as if it was your divine intervention that prescribed 'manner from heaven'. People live by their wits and business persons are no dif-ferent. It is not necessarily true that their performance successes are related to your being in government; some would say that it is in spite of that!*

x.   *Personality is of the person; a business cannot have a personality, since it is not a person. A business can have character and as such, the word characteristic would be a better fit. TDC's activities need not necessarily reflect confidence in govern-ment, it could function on the projection that regardless of government they will progress. All they need to do is whatever obstacles they encounter, pass them on to the customers and if they are not Kittitians, then so much the better! The analysis ought to consider who buys TDC's homes? Resulting in the fact that in spite of you TDC is blossoming!*

y. *Indeed, only time will tell! That cliché` is true for a host of circumstances, including what your government is doing to this country and the irony is that the people who support that so called Labour Party of yours are not perceptive enough to understand what you are doing to the country! They associate the word 'labour' with the old time ideals, even though most of them were not around at the time. They only heard about what the stalwarts of those days did. They are not astute enough to appreciate that in this day and age, these times do not have need for the kind of injection that was necessary when the masses were exploited. Today, the exploitation is performed by wolves in sheep's clothing. That is, individuals pretending to have Labour attributes but are really 'get rich quick merchants', creaming off the best and richest resources of the country, riding whatever natural development is taking place by pretending that they are the architects when what has really happened is that they just happened to be in the right place at the right time! It is just as well that there is still plenty of land left to dispose of. For it seems that is where the money is. There perhaps lies the source of and potential for exploitation. It is said that some politicians are boasting that they will never be poor again. It could be that the basis for such boasts lie in the yet to be disposed of available land mass! God help future generations!*

Summary

It may be that Astaphan thought that a new method of swamping the populace with ideas, via his captive newspaper would be a 'sure way' of pinning readers to whatever he had to say. Still On Dwyer's Desk (SODD) is still my way of telling him: what is good for the 'goose' can work just as well for others with ideas. It can never be right to be held captive by a secular medium, whose function it should be to enlighten but has tended towards indoctrination and conspiracy against neutral readers who seek bona-fide information. In an atmosphere where no newspaper can be trusted to talk to its readers honestly and frankly; readers perpetually have to form their own conclusions about reported events. Even when the two prominent mediums report on the same event, one is left wondering which is closest to the truth.

SODD has not commented on all the points that could have been tackled. Reason being that there is a repetitive quality in places and a high portion of overlapping ideas, spread out over time' others are so infantile that to respond to them would have been insulting the readers' intelligence. Where similar points are responded to, reflects levels of frustration and anger with Dwyer's conceit, ambiguity and hypocrisy in what he tries to put across. Also there was not much point in commenting on the obvious or even on those rare occasions when some form of agreement could be.

Throughout the work, the word 'Labour' is used without mercy. In most cases, mean-ings are intended to portray a sort of club, relying heavily on its historic value and fooling people into believing that there is commonality between the rulers and the ruled. This author recognizes the 'con' of that word's contradiction. Those shielding behind the word have either forgotten what it meant or never did know. They are now the aristocrats of society, extracting from the masses scarce resources, not much different from foregone administrators of colonial days. Though fewer in number their greed is just as fierce and loyalty to the masses is dodgy at best!

The overwhelming hope is that in the future, Dwyer will give more thought to what-ever subject he plans to pontificate about because if he does not; would that not be more material to comment on?

978-0-595-41482-6
0-595-41482-6